D1497697

deadly logic

Philip Green

A Publication of
the Social Science Program
in National Security of the Mershon Center

Ohio State University Press

deadly logic

The theory of nuclear deterrence

The excerpt from Hanson Baldwin's "The Treaty and Power," *New York Times*, August 15, 1963, © 1963 by The New York Times Company. Reprinted by permission.

The excerpts from *Hostage America: Human Aspects of a Nuclear Attack and a Program of Prevention*, by Robert A. Dentler and Phillips Cutright, are reprinted by permission of the Beacon Press, copyright © 1963 by Robert A. Dentler and Phillips Cutright.

The excerpts from *The War-Peace Establishment*, by Arthur Herzog. Copyright © 1963, 1965 by Arthur Herzog. Reprinted by permission of Harper & Row, Publishers.

The excerpts from Sidney Hook's "Western Values and Total War" are reprinted from *Commentary*, by permission; copyright © 1961 by the American Jewish Committee.

The excerpts from *On Thermonuclear War*, by Herman Kahn, are copyright © 1960 by the Princeton University Press. Reprinted by permission of the publisher.

The excerpts from *Thinking about the Unthinkable*, by Herman Kahn, are reprinted by permission of the publisher, Horizon Press, Copyright 1962.

Excerpts reprinted by permission of the publisher from Thomas C. Schelling, *The Strategy of Conflict*, Cambridge, Mass.: Harvard University Press, Copyright, 1960, by the President and Fellows of Harvard College.

The excerpts from *Deterrence and Defense: Toward a Theory of National Security*, by Glenn Snyder, are copyright © by the Princeton University Press. Reprinted by permission of the publisher.

Excerpts from "Armaments Policies for the Sixties" by John Polanyi are reprinted with permission from the December 1961 issue of the *Bulletin of the Atomic Scientists*. Copyright 1961 by the Educational Foundation for Nuclear Science, Inc.

To my parents

MY SOLE REGRET regarding Professor Green's *Deadly Logic* is that it could not have appeared earlier. Social scientists have waited a long time for this evaluation of deterrence concepts, and, hopefully, the literature of deterrence will never be the same again. On the other hand, social scientific contributions to the analysis of national security formulations will henceforth rest on firmer foundations. And all writers on military policy will receive encouragement to consider most carefully the moral and psychological implications of their subject.

This is, in short, a broad and complicated work. While it must necessarily cite chapters and verses *in extenso*, its purpose, as the reader will readily recognize, is neither negative criticism nor *ad hominem* argument. What concerns Professor Green has troubled a few others, who have not had patience, training, or skill to explicate their worries so systematically. After World War II there appeared a coterie of writers who suggested that the utility of nuclear arsenals could be definitively determined. Analysts of the ranges of options made available by existing systems, they also simultaneously became, even if implicitly, advocates of particular policies.

Nothing unique or troublesome so far. But let us be reminded of some basic points elaborated by Professor Green. The comparative utility of various weapons systems could be asserted only on the basis of theoretical postulates: with insignificant and confusing exceptions relating to technical effects, empirical evidence was fortunately lacking. The systems themselves evolved so rapidly that analysts, for all they were policy advocates, peered backward from a series of *stati quo* constantly being eroded. The demand for deterrence studies was so prodigious and so unanalytical that errors, discontinuities, discrepancies among so-called theorists, as well as within the writings of individuals themselves, went substantially unchallenged. Presumptions of rationality were arbitrarily made and often unacknowledged regarding the behavior of the primary opponent, as well as regarding American policy-makers, and those who did seek to build concepts of irrationality, imperfect communication, and information into their constructs necessarily weakened the base of their conclusions as they narrowed their horizons. The exclusion of ethical implications dug a chasm between statesmen and the society they supposedly were charged with serving, and, inevitably, reconstruction of viable bases for international comity was rendered more lastingly difficult. Major practitioners of the art of deterrence-theorizing acquired a substantial vested interest in the booming market. Although they were far from agreement with one another, they knew a good thing when they saw it and, again with exceptions strengthening the generality, criticized one another only mutedly in the open market place for ideas. Private, "in-club" critiques served only to advance the common cause. Last and importantly, the grub-stake claim was recurrently advanced that military conceptualizers were in the very forefront of social science analysis, rigorously applying new techniques and refining those techniques in the process.

We may be in a new era, equally poisonous for social science study and research—the era of counterinsurgency theorizing. If some of the deleterious effects are avoided, it will be because of the example set by Professor Green's exegesis. Detailed it must necessarily be, yet the over-all design remains with the reader. Constructive it is also, both in pointing the way for others and in illuminating the present possibilities and limitations of social science for the comprehension of national security policy. For the Mershon Social Science Program in National Security *Deadly Logic: The Theory of Nuclear Deterrence* undergirds such recent studies as William P. Snyder's *The Politics of British Defense Policy*; Walter Goldstein's *The Dilemma of British Defense*; John S. Ambler's *The French Army in Politics*; Edward A. Kolodziej's *The Uncommon Defense and Congress*; and *The Western Alliance,* the published version of a series of lectures on NATO.

EDGAR S. FURNISS, JR.
Director, Mershon Social Science
Program in National Security

THE SUBJECT OF THIS STUDY is rather narrow; its implications are, I think, far-ranging. The inspiration for an
inquiry into the methodology of deterrence theory was,
initially, a feeling of strangeness induced by a lengthy
study of the literature of nuclear deterrence. That feeling
may be described as follows. Almost all the works one
encountered in this field seemed invested with a tre-
mendously authoritative air, an air that one associated
with scholarly work in the most well-established and
systematically researched disciplines (or subdisciplines).
Yet clearly the study of nuclear deterrence policy was not
in any meaningful sense a discipline; and somehow all
this authority produced policy proposals and arguments
that one felt absolutely no urge to agree with. Some were
at best questionable: e.g., the assertion that there was a
"delicate balance of terror" at a time when one could
perceive no visible reason to feel delicately balanced.
Others seemed absurd: e.g., the casual assumption that
the "rational" response to a nuclear strike on one's cities
is a counterstrike on the attacker's cities. Still others
seemed absurd given one's own preconceptions: such as
the development of complicated contingency plans requiring more and different levels of nuclear armament,
plans that seemed designed to further accelerate an

already dangerous arms race; and the concomitant denigration of the idea of disarmament, which so clearly seemed to be the only eventual solution to the problems of the nuclear era. Finally, one did not know what to make of the assertion that nuclear war could be survived and was therefore "thinkable" when it was so obviously (in Herman Kahn's odd locution) "unthinkable."

Evidently, either the preconceptions were wrong or the air of authority must be spurious. Actually, the investigation I undertook to see which was the case did not produce such an either-or result. Although I still hold to the prodisarmament, antinuclear armament bias with which I started this study, it has become obvious to me that some of the arguments for a deterrence posture are very strong. Given the realities of world politics, it is perfectly understandable that many find nuclear deterrence to be the best of the practical policies available to us now, although I would still demur because of moral qualms and lack of faith in the ability of national leadership on all sides to handle the complex problems of a nuclear world.

However, the strong arguments I am speaking of are all variants of the view that between great powers deterrence is virtually automatic; they thus amount to not much more than a wildly hopeful prophecy that nuclear weapons are too horrible ever to be used, and that therefore it is relatively safe to retain a stockpile of them. These are precisely *not* the arguments that have been made by the writers discussed in the following pages. On the contrary, they have developed a completely different, more intellectually elaborate kind of argument for a nuclear deterrence policy. And the conclusion I reached after studying their work was that (one's own preconceptions aside) their air of authority was and is completely spurious. If the discussion of deterrence consisted solely of academic deterrence theory, then it would be of little or no value as a guide to policy. What follows is an attempt to explain why this is so. Such a study is especially needed because of the peculiar interplay that has developed between the reputation of social science in general and the theory of nuclear deterrence in particular.

The growth of the academic literature of military strategy has been one of the major intellectual phenomena of the cold war era in the United States. This literature has had a twofold effect on the various social science disciplines. The first effect is quantitative: a great amount of work is being done on problems that were once almost completely outside the ken of social scientists. The change is so striking that the incoming head of the American Political Science Association in 1961 was led to predict that national security analysis would become one of the important "fields" in political science and in the social sciences generally;[1] this prediction has long since come true.

Second, there is a qualitative effect: social science appears to have finally become a key element at some levels of national policy-making, as the following quotations, one from a popularizing journalist, one from a well-known "lay" writer, and one from an expert, indicate:

> Collectively (Herman Kahn, Albert Wohlstetter, Henry Kissinger and Thomas Schelling) are the vanguard and foremost representatives of a new element in the counsels of American government: the Academic Strategists.

The two principal sources of this new theory are the simulated situations of the traditional "war games" and the transposition of the mathematical theory of games into the military-political matching of wits and threats involved in deterrence theory. The final product . . . [requires] knowledge and sophistication drawn from a number of exacting disciplines. . . . As a result, the traditional military strategists have been replaced by a new breed of men—intellectuals like . . . Herman Kahn, Thomas B. Schelling, Henry Kissinger, Donald Brennan, Oskar Morgenstern, Albert Wohlstetter, Glenn H. Snyder.

Whatever the explanation, academics *have* moved into the military policy field, and have brought to it a degree of subtlety, sophistication, and intellectual rigor that was long overdue.[2]

In addition to statements such as these, book reviews, publisher's blurbs, testimonials by "experts" to each other, and even deferential remarks by major military figures, all testify to the impact these new theorists have had.[3]

Thus the intellectual reputability of the idea of nuclear deterrence is very largely a reflection of the reputability of the social science literature in which it has been put forth; and a certain increase in the public reputability of social science may have accrued because of the activities of the deterrence theorists. This condition has come about largely because of our society's great respect for the claims of science and expertise; if those claims are false, then both social science and the democratic process are being undermined.

The deterrence theorists' claim to the mantle of scientific expertise is thus the subject of this book. Because of the way in which these theorists have presented their arguments, my discussion deals largely with certain techniques in social science, such as systems analysis, game theory, and simulation, and is therefore methodological in its approach. However, the concern with methodology is less restricted than it may seem. There is no such thing, after all, as "*the* method" of, say, systems analysis or game theory. There are as many methods for putting systems analysis and game theory to use as there are purposes in the minds of the users, and questions of methodology arise only when one asks whether a given technique and a given purpose have been correctly matched to each other. Thus those techniques in the abstract are not the real subject of my discussion. For other purposes they might indeed be fruitful, but we shall here be concerned with only one of the uses to which they have been put: the justification of various policies of nuclear deterrence. The validity of the supposed connection, in this instance, between public policy and social science is therefore our ultimate concern; inferentially, perhaps, the idea of nuclear deterrence itself is also called into question.

PHILIP GREEN

THIS BOOK was completed on a grant from the Mershon Center for Education in National Security, at Ohio State University. I am very grateful to Edgar S. Furniss, Jr., Director of the Mershon Social Science Program, and to his assistant, Mrs. Anne Trupp, for the aid they have given me, in so many different ways, in shepherding the manuscript through to publication.

Professor Furniss also read the manuscript in several drafts, as did Harold Sprout of Princeton University, and Charles H. Green; the comments and criticisms of all three were absolutely invaluable to me. In addition, I have benefitted from the advice of Richard A. Falk of Princeton, Walter Goldstein of Brooklyn College and Mershon, Edward A. Kolodziej of the University of Virginia and Mershon, and Charles H. Withrow of the Ohio State University Press. Finally, I should especially thank Robert Paul Wolff of Columbia University, who kindly permitted me to read and draw material from his unpublished manscript on deterrence theory; and George

Kent of Mershon, from whom I learned virtually every-thing I know about game theory. What I failed to learn, or to learn correctly, is entirely my own responsibility and not his.

I have been working on this study for several years. In all that time the greatest help I have had has been the advice, support, and constant encouragement of my wife, Dorothy Green.

PHILIP GREEN

deadly logic

1

THE GREAT CONTRIBUTION of the academic literature of deterrence theory has been to spell out, as Joseph Kraft puts it, "A coherent body of doctrine: a theory of war and peace in the nuclear age." [1] This doctrine, or theory, is known familiarly as the idea of (nuclear) deterrence.

To deter, as Thomas Schelling has written, is somehow to persuade another whom one defines as a "potential enemy" to abandon a certain path of activity by making it appear to him to be in his own self-interest to do so; [2] "deterrence" is the process of persuasion. There is nothing novel in the idea that a strategy of deterrence can avoid war; the thought is expressed perfectly, for instance, in Theodore Roosevelt's aphorism about carrying a big stick. Deterrence in the nuclear age might be thought offhand to be novel, in that one's ultimate deterring threat is made not against a potential attacking force but against the very body of the nation that is to be deterred; but as Glenn Snyder points out, it would certainly be incorrect to argue that the latter threat has never before been present in situations of potential belligerency, at least in some limited sense. [3] Thus from one perspective there is no "essential" difference between nuclear deterrence and other forms of deterrence, and those who prefer to think that only differences in kind are really consequential might ask why writings about *nuclear* deterrence should be separated out for any special critical treatment.

There are two reasons, I think, that such a treatment is appropriate. In the first place, it seems to be the case that the "mere" difference of degree between nuclear deterrence and other historical forms of deterrence appears to most people today to be so great as in fact to be virtually a difference in kind. It is true that national destruction has always been a possibility: Carthage, after all, was destroyed; and Hitler could conceivably, though only with great difficulty, have made one gaping Lidice out of Czechoslovakia. But though the perception of threat may have been just as strong on the part of the potential victims then as it is on the part of potential victims now, we still know that there is an "objective" difference. Our destruction would be astonishingly easier and quicker; from the decision to undertake it to its accomplishment might conceivably be the work of no more than a few days or even hours or minutes. We need only ask ourselves whether we would rather be the victims of a full-scale nuclear assault or a full-scale attack by an invading army to see the force of this distinction.

More important, the threat of destruction in all previous times that one can think of was the threat of a stronger party against a weaker, usually a helpless one. In none of the historical examples of total devastation that are usually given was the deterrent threat of national destruction a mutual or dual threat.[4] Today two nations well stocked with long-range, nuclear-armed weapons can each conceivably say to the other: "If you attack me, I will be able immediately to destroy you, whatever you do to me in your initial attack." Before, the most fearsome threat that could be uttered between nations of relatively equal strength was: *"After* the war is over and *if* I have won it, I intend to wipe you out." The difference between these two threats suggests what may justifiably be considered a unique feature of the era of nuclear deterrence.

Second, the concept of nuclear deterrence deserves to be treated as a unique phenomenon because that is the manner in which it has been represented to the interested public by those who have made it well-known. The astonishing outburst of intellectual energy that has been put into the study of national security issues, and which shows no signs of abating before the cold war itself does, has almost entirely revolved around the single question of what particular national strategies are best justified by the "novel" ability to make "ultimate" nuclear threats.[5] Regardless of whether our situation is unique, it has been treated as such in the relevant literature; thus that literature presents a substantially unitary body of thought, which may be dealt with critically on its own terms. On the other hand, as is so often the case, it is easier to know who deterrence theorists are, than to know what deterrence theory is. Therefore, a definition is obviously necessary here.

We may begin with the process of definition by exclusion. Roughly speaking, deterrence theorists (or advocates of a deterrence strategy) are those who reject both a disarmament strategy and a win-the-war nuclear strategy, vis-à-vis the Soviet Union (or perhaps in the future, Communist China). The implied triad of positions may be defined more precisely (though still loosely) by isolating one central question on which they disagree. Those who propose a strategy of disarmament, in one form or another, feel that nuclear armaments can neither keep the peace nor preserve national values effectively, and that therefore we must rid ourselves of them in one way or another. Those who favor a win-the-war strategy feel that the kind of "peace" that advocates of disarmament propose is incompatible with the preservation of important national values, in that the absence of overt conflict favors the expansion of Communism. In their strategic thinking they are thus either relatively indifferent to the question of whether the United States would have to initiate a nuclear war, or they insist that the Soviet Union would "back down" in the face of a serious nuclear threat from the United States.

Deterrence theorists, in contrast, seem to be united in emphasizing two concerns. First, they fear that "peace" through disarmament would lead either to a greater likelihood of nuclear war than now exists (because a disarmed world would be more unstable than an armed one) or to national "defeat" through successful Communist "cheating."[6] Second, they feel that an aggressive win-the-war nuclear strategy poses too great a threat of national destruction in the long run. Deterrence is thus proposed as an alternative national strategy that may be expected to optimize whatever possibilities exist for both keeping the peace *and* preserving national values at the same time. We should not disarm, but we should arm only to "defend" ourselves rather than necessarily to fight.*

---

* This formulation is perhaps unfair to those who favor a win-the-war strategy, in that the chief component of their thinking consists of the notion that we have already been "attacked." However, for purposes of definition it seems best to ignore the argument of ideologues like Strausz-Hupé and James Burnham that the traditional definitions of "aggression" and "provocation" have

Arms control may be proposed, but it is the *retention* of arms that is really emphasized.[7]

This definition of deterrence theory thus being really a residual one, we can expect some fuzziness at its edges. J. David Singer, for example, proposes one version of nuclear deterrence as a short-run policy and complete multilateral disarmament as a long-run policy.[8] Is he an advocate of deterrence, or disarmament, or both? Since he seems to propose his version of deterrence only as an alternative to other, competing versions of deterrence, and to think that the arguments in favor of it are ultimately inferior to the arguments in favor of disarmament, I find it proper to consider him a disarmament theorist of a somewhat "conservative" sort, rather than a deterrence theorist; but a different interpretation of his position could be reasonably advanced.† Similarly, it is sometimes hard to differentiate Herman Kahn's proposed first-strike strategy (what he calls "type II

---

been hopelessly outdated by the advent of "international Communism," and to adhere to those definitions—always remembering that contrary definitions do exist and can be justified.

† On this point, Robert Levine has offered some helpful distinctions. Within the bounds of his own special (and quite useful) vocabulary, in which deterrence theorists are called " 'analytic' middle marginalists," "forward strategists" like Strausz-Hupé are "anti-Communist marginalists," and advocates of negotiated disarmament are "anti-war marginalists," Levine makes much the same distinctions as I have made here. "Marginalist," as he uses it, is a term implying that one is willing to work within the limits posed by current practical political possibilities. To the three categories I have noted already, Levine adds descriptions of "anti-war systemists" and "anti-Communist systemists." By "systemists" he means those who are radically disaffected from the existing system—e.g., unilateralists on the left and Birchites on the right.[9]

deterrence") from the "forward strategy" of Robert Strausz-Hupé and his associates.[10] But on inspection, one sees that whereas for Strausz-Hupé the mere existence of the Soviet Union has already (or should already have) provoked us beyond endurance, for Kahn the traditional definitions of "aggression" and "provocation" still roughly hold good, and his stance is thus the distinctively defensive one that we associate with the idea of deterrence.[11]

Having carved out a general area within which all those who call themselves deterrence theorists may roughly be seen to fall, we may now go on to describe the specific ideas and doctrines that are central to the concept of deterring both war and Communist advancement by maintaining a nuclear arsenal of strategic (i.e., long-range) weapons.

The hope of all deterrence theorists is that the maintenance of such an arsenal will, if certain precautions be taken, either do away with the prospect of nuclear war entirely or at least mitigate the consequences of it (or of any other kind of war) if it does occur at some less-than-all-out level of violence. This possibility is seen to exist because, given the destructive force of nuclear weapons wedded to the long-range, high-speed capabilities of post-bomber delivery systems, it is obviously self-defeating to initiate a nuclear attack on another nuclear-armed power unless that attack is certain of success. In order that such an attack not be assured of "success," certain conditions are prerequisite.

1. Some portion of one's own nuclear striking force must be capable both of surviving an enemy's first strike and carrying through an assigned retaliatory mission.[12] This is the aspect of force deployment generally referred

to as "invulnerability," but the term is misleading—first, because no weapon has yet been shown to be absolutely invulnerable to attack; and second, because there are other ways than invulnerability of securing a retaliatory force (such as sheer weight of numbers).[13] In any event, the main point is that such a force, however described, must exist.

2. The "survivable" retaliatory force must be capable of not only retaliating, but of retaliating with a certain effect.[14] The required effect can only be stated tautologically: there must be enough of a probability that enough of the attacker's society will be destroyed in a retaliatory strike to make him feel that a first strike by him presents too great a risk of eventual self-destruction. This sounds like an empirical proposition that can be investigated by the arm of government known as "intelligence," but the appearance is misleading. Our knowledge of the two quantitative relationships involved in the statement above must obviously always be vague. The closest we can come to an empirical statement in this regard is to say: "a pretty good chance" that enough of one's forces will survive to do "a great deal" of retaliatory damage to the other's society ought to present potential attackers with a deadly enough risk so as to make them hesitate to incur retaliation under most circumstances.

It has been proposed, in an attempt to mitigate the apparent harshness of deterrence theory, that the United States should have the capability for making a limited nuclear strike, rather than an all-out annihilatory one, in response to a nuclear attack on itself if deterrence fails. This proposal has become known as the "no-cities" or "damage-limiting" doctrine, and has been espoused on occasion by Secretary of Defense McNamara.[15] However, no deterrence theorist proposes that the United States *unilaterally* renounce the ability to make an all-out second strike if need be, for then it could no longer deter a massive first strike.

3. Mere retaliatory capability is not enough, however. In addition, a retaliatory force must also not be "trigger-happy." That is, a nuclear power must feel so secure in its retaliatory capability that it can afford to "ride out" potentially destabilizing events in the international system, such as nuclear accidents and apparent (but not actual) attacks, without feeling that prudence requires a massive strike. Put differently, both sides to a conflict must under all circumstances feel that they can afford to make a massive (countercity, annihilating, all-out) strike *second.*[16]

4. In a world in which superpowers possess such forces, and other forces of various kinds as well, why does A not simply decide to make an all-out first strike against B, destroying B's society *in toto*? Such a strike is considered to be "irrational," on the grounds that if A really has a sufficiently threatening survivable retaliatory force, nothing B can do against A's society (as opposed to A's weapons) can prevent A from doing "unacceptable" damage to B's own society in a counterstrike. This is the principle, to use a term made famous by Thomas Schelling and others, of the "exchange of hostages." Each side is capable of making a major retaliatory strike under the worst of circumstances; therefore, each side's population—each side's very existence, perhaps—is at stake. To see the force of this condition, we may imagine what would happen if the United States succeeded in erecting an impenetrable

dome around itself. Only moral inhibitions and a sense of international public relations could prevent the United States, if it so desired, from utterly destroying, say, Soviet society and then picking off the futile remaining Soviet weapons: deterrence would have failed.

5. In the above four paragraphs I have stated the requisite conditions of nuclear deterrence. However, there is no deterrence theorist who thinks that mere possession of the ability to make an ultimate threat—of annihilation—would be a satisfactory situation. On the contrary, it is generally agreed that the ultimate threat is credible[17] only against extremely serious "provocations." Therefore, any variant of deterrence theory must have as one component, perhaps its chief component, a doctrine for response to *limited* provocations. It is with regard to the question, what responses are appropriate for what provocations, that deterrence theorists begin to divide into schools. Various proposals may be distinguished: (1) Conventional limited war capability for meeting all provocations short of all-out attack. (2) Conventional capability plus tactical nuclear capability for meeting all such provocations.[18] (3) Either of the first two capabilities plus a "limited nuclear reprisal" capability (i.e., you bomb one of my missile bases, I'll bomb one of yours; you attack a position I can't hold, I'll bomb one of your cities after warning, etc.).[19] To this is usually added the "damage-limiting" capability referred to above, since there is a logical relationship between the intention to use nuclear weapons if need be and the need to prepare for escalation afterward. And in any event, the "damage-limiting" capability should not be considered analytically separable, for a counterforce second-

strike or some kind of "controlled counterforce war" is in essence a very large, but still "limited," nuclear reprisal.[20] (4) Any of the first three capabilities (but for the same reasons as above most logically the third) plus some kind of counterforce *first*-strike capability, ranging from the capability for attacking single weapon sites or carriers to the capability for attacking all an opponent's forces in a massive blow.[21]

The last two strategies described, which involve the strategic use of nuclear weapons in a more or less limited war, are comprehended by Herman Kahn in the phrase, type II deterrence; the ultimate deterrent—that is, a force deployed to make a strike second on an opponent's cities—he calls type I deterrence. On the whole, the first two strategic doctrines listed above, which depend only on type I deterrence to deter all-out war, have fallen into disfavor among academic deterrence theorists and are adhered to only by those who still find it reasonable to think of deterrence as automatic or semiautomatic. Thus I have devoted special attention to the theorizing of Herman Kahn, with whose work the proposals for limited nuclear and (potential) first-strike strategies are intimately associated. One point must be kept clear though. Kahn's specific proposal for a credible (or "not-incredible") first-strike capability is endorsed by few other deterrence theorists, who mostly seem to favor some variant of (3) above. On the other hand, that latter capability also requires some civil defense to be credible. Therefore, the reader should keep in mind that although comments about the problems of a credible first-strike capability do not apply to any theorist who has not endorsed Kahn's proposals, comments about the reliability of the civil-defense study that is discussed in the next chapter do apply, *ceteris paribus,* to all those who favor limited nuclear reprisal and damage-limiting capabilities. Generally speaking, however, this variant of type II deterrence, or any other, should be understood as the subject of my discussion only when so specified. Otherwise, when specific reference is not made to type II deterrence postures, my comments should be read as addressed to the notion of type I (also called passive) deterrence, which is the original and most basic conception of nuclear deterrence, and ultimately stands behind all other strategic or limited nuclear postures.

2 Systems Analysis and National Policy

I. The Importance of Herman Kahn

THERE is obviously nothing new in the study of the subject matter we are concerned with here. Clearly, then, the chief reason for the aura of authority I have noted is the impression, fostered by deterrence theorists, that the work on which they have based their conclusions is somehow more "scientific" and rigorous, and less impressionistic and casual, than the kind of work that has previously been associated with the study of national security policy. In succeeding chapters I shall be analyzing various techniques that deterrence theorists have used to create this impression. To begin with, though, it seems best to consider the uses and merits, in arguing about deterrence policy, of what has come to be called "systems analysis" (or, as Wohlstetter puts it, the analysis of "conflict systems").[1] For systems analysis, in the guise of a study of the prospects for civil defense, forms the core of Herman Kahn's massive strategic compendium, *On Thermonuclear War*. And since that book is without doubt the most significant single contribution to arms policy discussion during the nuclear era, close study of its accomplishment is repaid by a fundamental insight into the uses to which systems analysis has been put, and to which it can be put.

The importance of *On Thermonuclear War* cannot be overestimated. Since the appearance of this book, proponents of both armament and disarmament strategies have had to cope with Kahn's unassailable demonstration that policy-planners cannot simply choose between end-of-the-world nuclear annihilation and total nuclear "peace," but must be prepared to deal somehow with the possibility of a whole series of in-between states of nuclear war. All sides to the arms debate have benefited from this demonstration. Professional and academic military planners have been pushed to new levels of sophistication in their development of strategic alternatives, as have the opponents of nuclear armaments in their counterarguments. The advocates of a nuclear strategy have been given material to show how difficult must be the achievement of a stable state of nuclear disarmament; their opponents, on the other hand, have been given material to show how equally difficult must be the achievement of a stable state of nuclear armaments. All students of this complex subject, clearly, must be grateful to Kahn for grappling so well with this difficult new material.[2]

At the same time, however, *On Thermonuclear War* is significant as much more than a "compleat strategysts" guide to the arms race. For the most noteworthy of the creative efforts at strategic thinking contained in that work has been Kahn's attempt to infuse deterrence doctrine with the stuff of science: an attempt that has apparently impressed many authoritative members of the executive branch of the United States government as being successful.[3] Since we are investigating the connection between the uses of social science and the development of deterrence theory, I shall concentrate on this aspect of Kahn's work, though it bears remarking here—and repeating later—that Kahn's prescriptive concepts, as distinct from his purely analytical ones (a distinction hard to make in any event), are tightly bound up with his claims to scientific rigor.

What is the nature of these claims? In the course of his two major works on nuclear war, Kahn makes repeated reference to computered studies at the RAND Corporation, which use the tools of mathematics to give answers to the question of survival, and illustrate the benefits of "Systems Analysis" and "Operations Research" [4] for the study of military affairs. These references to systems analysis and operations research are supported by tables, graphs, and other simplified models for illustration, the whole often taking on the appearance of the report of a laboratory experiment.

The question that immediately comes to mind is whether Kahn has used these methods properly, given the nature of his subject. Has he made out a case, first, that they are truly tools for scientific work, and, second, that they are helpful in the policy discussions that are so markedly a feature of both *On Thermonuclear War* and *Thinking about the Unthinkable*?

In attempting to answer this question, one must offer a necessary caveat. What is called systems analysis obviously offers some important benefits in the formulation of military strategy. A recent collection of essays written under the auspices of RAND, *Analysis for Military Decisions,* makes these benefits clear.[5] For example, summarized there is one of the earliest examples of systems analyses: out of the systematic study by a RAND team of factors in the selection of overseas bases for the Strategic Air Command emerged the first clear definition, in a concrete setting, of the operational demands of a *second*-strike strategy, and of the way in which these demands differ from those implied by a *first*-strike strategy.[6] Other real and paper examples of both the monetary savings and the strategic (and tactical) clarity and control that can be generated by the use of rigorous analytical methods are adverted to throughout these essays, as well as in Hitch and McKean's *Economics of Defense in the Nuclear Age*.[7]

However, there is a common ground between all the various examples of systems analysis referred to in these essays that does not exist between any of them and Herman Kahn's (or RAND's) civil-defense study. To put the case most broadly: the value of a given method of work is determined by asking the opinion of those who have hired it done. Several ways of accomplishing a stated objective are proposed. If the employer is satisfied that the best option has been conclusively demonstrated (or if only obvious bias or stupidity is keeping him from being satisfied), and if over time his satisfaction is justified,[8] then the method of study that indicated the selection of that option is justified (except perhaps to philosophers).

In the case of all the various studies of comparative cost effectiveness of competing weapon systems that are referred to by systems analysts—even in the case of the bases study—the relevant employer is the Department of Defense or some branch of the armed services. But when certain kinds of broad policy questions are being asked, the employer who asks them is not the Department of Defense but the public; and the answers being sought are not technical estimates of cost-effectiveness but complex and indissolubly *political* judgments (see below, pp. 259–60.)* It is important to keep in mind that we are making a distinction not merely between two types of subject matter—"strategic" vs. "tactical," or "broad" vs. "narrow" questions—but also and more fundamentally between two different clients for the product of a given study. The DOD, the Air Force, etc., commission research in order to help them fulfil their missions. But what is good for the Air Force is not necessarily good for the country. As to the latter, in democratic theory "the people," or their representatives, are the final judges, and political recommendations must be designed to help them make their ultimate choice among competing policies. What we want to know, therefore, is how helpful for this purpose are rigorous scientific procedures for arriving at technical answers to technical questions? We shall see that a close look at Kahn's work, keeping this distinction always in mind, suggests a decisive conclusion.

II. The Method of Systems Analysis

It must be said at first that no matter how much one reads on the subject one simply cannot find out what "systems analysis" is. The various attempts at definition one encounters are not very instructive:

> [S]ystems analysis might be defined as inquiry to aid a decision maker choose [*sic*] a course of action by system-

*Although we may not be absolutely clear about the precise line of demarcation between the technical and the political, "It is common, indeed usual, to be uncertain of a boundary but quite certain of what lies well to the east or west of it." [9]

atically investigating his proper objectives, comparing quantitatively where possible the costs, effectiveness, and risks associated with the alternative policies or strategies for achieving them, *and formulating additional alternatives if those examined are found wanting.* Systems analysis represents an approach to, or way of looking at, complex problems of choice under uncertainty, such as those associated with national security. . . . It offers a means of discovering how to design or to make effective use over time of a technologically complex structure in which the different components may have apparently conflicting objectives; that is, an approach to choosing a strategy that yields the best balance among risks, effectiveness, and costs. Its purpose is to place each element in its proper context so that in the end the system as a whole may achieve its aims with a minimal expenditure of resources.

The systems analyst must take a systems approach; that is, he must attempt to look at the problems as a whole.

[I]n complex problems of military force composition or development, we are dealing with a field so broad that no one can be called expert. A typical systems analysis depends critically on numerous technological factors in several fields. . . . No one is an expert in more than one or two of the subfields; no one is an expert in the field as a whole and the interrelations. So, no one's unsupported intuitions in such a field can be trusted.

Systems analyses should be looked upon not as the antithesis of judgment but as a framework which permits the judgment of experts in numerous subfields to be utilized— to yield results which transcend any individual judgment.

At its best, operations research or systems studies in national defense should be conceived as the quantitative method of science applied to the refractory problems described.

Insofar as possible, a systems analyst should try to use the methods of science and to establish the same traditions. He should be objective and quantitative; all his calculations, assumptions, data, and judgments should be made explicit and subject to duplication, checking, criticism, and disagreement.[10]

What I mean by conflict systems design and analysis . . . is the *explicit* outline and study of alternative systems of interdependent parts where the comparative performance of a system is affected not only by the machines and the men who are elements in the system but also by the opposing behavior of men and machines outside the system. In particular, I mean the design of systems on the basis of an explicit analysis of the effects of opposing strategies.

Systems analysis is the comparison of . . . enlarged systems of interrelated elements. . . .[11]

Evidently systems analysis has something to do with looking at a problem as a whole, looking at it over time, being quantitative where possible, being realistic about potential conflict, and drawing on a wide range of technical expertise. The guiding principle seems to be to start with a simple model for a "system" of goals and capabilities and then to make it progressively more realistic by adding, step by step, such constraining factors as cost, competing objectives and their costs, an opponent's capabilities, degradation or otherwise of all these elements over time, chance, etc.* In other words, as far as I can gather, one analyzes a system by trying to see the real-world context of its operations, rather than by simply imagining its ideal performance without further sophistication of analysis.

*Any techniques that will help explicate the implications of the model are used for this purpose; *viz.*, "scenarios," war-gaming, formal game theory, computer programs, etc.

The use of this method, it should be added, is supposedly necessitated by the fact that the old-fashioned way of analyzing the workings of military systems is no longer feasible because of the progressive technological revolutions of the nuclear era. As Klaus Knorr remarks in the "Foreword" to *On Thermonuclear War,* "The problems of defense have become inordinately complex, and their solution is not susceptible to the rules of thumb, often called principles, which the military derived from past experience." [12] That is, the study of experience, which no one really has, is to be replaced by the study of hypothetical but relevant models of systems, using all the techniques here mentioned.

Unfortunately, all this seems very much like saying that "systems analysis" is "thorough analysis" or "good analysis." Apparently there are no generalizable principles of the science of systems analysis that can help us understand what is particularly thorough or good about it, why it is being used, what it adds to some other method of study, etc. Thus if we want to test its adequacy for the study of what I have called broad policy questions, we can only do this by looking at systems analysis in action: to be specific, by studying Kahn's description and use of his *RAND Report R-322-RC, A Report on a Study of Non-Military Defense,*[13] which has been incorporated (with some flamboyance) into *On Thermonuclear War.* When we do this we are also studying the workings of Kahn's strategic logic qua logic, for the two elements of his thought are so intertwined that to analyze one is really to analyze the other. Kahn's grand strategy of what he calls "multistable deterrence," based on the possession by the United States of both a second-strike and a "credible first strike" nuclear force, is necessarily dependent on his proposal for the development of a credible civil-defense posture.[14] This is so because, as he frequently asserts, one cannot plausibly threaten to start a nuclear war unless one is prepared to "ride out" the likely retaliation. Thus all of Kahn's complex strategic theorizing hinges on the answer to the pivotal question: would the kind of civil-defense system he proposes have enough of a chance to work to make the proposed strategy seem acceptable? Kahn's answer to this question is conveyed in his report of the civil-defense study. As we shall see, to call the logic of the latter into question is thus to call into question not only the relevance of systems analysis but also the substantive logic upon which the most important school of deterrence theory has created its view of the arms race.

III.   The Civil-Defense Study: Data and Assumptions

For understanding what has actually been accomplished by Kahn's civil-defense analysis, we should be interested in answers to, among others, the following questions:

1. What kinds of "hard" data are available for studying the outlines of possible nuclear and deterrence crises?

2. Where do the assumptions upon which the analysis is based come from? How compelling are they? If alternative assumptions are neglected, why are they neglected?

3. Is the analysis which produces whatever conclusions are reached compellingly rigorous or merely personal? If the latter, what reasons are there for preferring it to other ways of looking at the same subject-matter?

4. How has the problem for study been formulated? Are there alternative, equally good, or better ways of formulating it?

In discussing Kahn's development of data in his analysis, to begin with, we need not repeat the various figures and other evidences of "fact" that he adduces. Where necessary, these will be brought out in the discussion of the interior logic of the civil-defense study. Here I rather wish primarily to distinguish the types of materials that Kahn presents as data from those that he presents as assumptions.

When one does this, one finds that Kahn's empirical material—his handle, so to speak, on the real world—consists of the following: (1) A numerical statement of "permissible peacetime standards" for exposure to radioactivity, and calculations, based on those figures, of expected genetic damage under assumed conditions of radioactivity resulting from nuclear war. (2) Statements about the expected effects of nuclear attack: that is, the fallout to be expected from different levels of attack, in the short and long run. (3) An estimate of the life-expectancy shortening effects of radioactivity. (4) The expected incidence of bone cancer due to the fallout of Stronium-90, and the possibility of the human organism's tolerating that incidence. (5) Charts and tables quantitatively descriptive of certain aspects of the American economy during the 1950's.

With the exception of the last-named item (which I shall consider later), all of Kahn's descriptive data fall in the general area of facts about the effects of radioactive fallout. It would seem on first thought that this is a rather limited amount of empirical information on which to base such a study. Of course it is quite possible for systematic scientific work to suggest important conclusions on the basis of very little accurate data. This result can come about if the hypothetical assumptions with which the researcher manipulates his data are powerful assumptions: that is, are either derived from a prior body of "verified" theory or simply turn out to have been reasonable on an intuitive basis. Since Kahn refers to no body of theory, we must be interested in the apparent reasonableness of his assumptions. No doubt, as John Polanyi remarks, those who find Kahn's conclusions convincing will tend to feel the same about his assumptions; but in any case it is worth knowing what those assumptions are, and measuring them against whatever other knowledge or theory may be available in the area of his interest.[15]

Essentially the assumptions are of two kinds. The first kind is strategic: statements of the level of attack that we ought reasonably to expect (or the worst we ought reasonably to expect). Thus Kahn, in *On Thermonuclear War,* postulates two possible attacks, an early (light) and a late (heavy) attack. In the early attack 500 bombs are dropped on 150 targets (including 50 cities) ; in the late attack 2000 bombs are dropped on 400 targets.[16] (Although Kahn varies his assumptions so frequently that one can never be sure quite what they are at a given moment, it appears that the most fearful test he envisages for his civil-defense system—the total destruction of America's 53 largest metropolitan areas—is meant to be, roughly speaking, a possible result of the late attack.) Implicit in these suggested figures is also an unstated assumption about the size of nuclear arsenals up to about 1970 (the projected period for the late attack), the strength of bomb (or missile) warheads, and the amount of megatonnage that we can expect to be delivered per target point.*

In addition, throughout Kahn's discussion of civil defense there is a general, though unstated, assumption: that of rationality in decision-making. This notion is perhaps at the core of all his strategic thinking, even though he often explicitly disowns it (in common with many other deterrence theorists, as we shall see). The idea that opponents in a cold (and hot) war may hopefully be expected to act "rationally" is central to all the strategic concepts—limited nuclear reprisals, limited strategic war, controlled counterforce war, limited general war, and postattack blackmail—which Kahn and his colleagues have developed to illustrate the idea that a nuclear war can be *fought* with some chance of "success," rather than merely being deterred on the one hand or being the occasion for a spasm of destruction on the

*Robert Paul Wolff, using information supplied by Kahn in personal conversation, has calculated that "the average bomb in the light attack works out to five megatons, and the average megatonnage per target point to roughly seventeen megatons." [17] Additional information is necessary because Kahn has supplied, in his Table 8, "Two Possible Attacks on US," only data about the fission yield of the bombs, for purposes of calculating genetic effects. Repeating Wolff's calculations for the late attack, we find that Kahn has postulated approximately 16⅔ megatons per bomb, and 83 megatons per target point. According to Wolff, Kahn says that the fission yield/total yield ratio is ⅗. Thus 20,000 MT fission yield gives 33,333 MT total yield. Table 8 shows a late attack involving 400 target points and 2000 bombs; the calculation is simple. For the early attack, the corresponding figures are 1500 MT, 2500 MT, 150 target points, 500 bombs. Throughout, "warheads" would be a better word, of course.

other. (In sum, these are all the strategies which together make up Kahn's proposal for developing a credible first-strike capability, a capability itself dependent on the successful development of the civil-defense capability that is at the heart of his discussion.)

This is not to say that Kahn asserts warring opponents will always or even usually be rational. Rather he assumes that there is enough of a chance of their being rational to make strategic planning for such a contingency a more realistic option than planning based on a different assumption. The crucial point is that whenever he is confronted with the necessity of making predictions based on either expected rationality or expected irrationality (whatever that might be), he invariably prefers the former. He assumes on behalf of any and all participants in a nuclear war that that strategy which minimizes damage to one's self will be preferred; that one's enemies will be expected to have the same preference; and that the result of these dual analyses of preferences will be that each side will actually choose the mutually preferred strategy.

There is one apparent exception to Kahn's assumption of rationality. Presumably, the 50- and 150-city attacks are what he thinks of as irrational city-busting attacks—outside chances that might come about if we adopt one of his first-strike strategies, and which must therefore be investigated to discover if we can survive even the worst.[18] But there are two points about this "exception" that diminish its importance. First, the assumption that these are the worst attacks at all likely to befall us is itself based on an assumption of rationality, since worse could befall us if our enemies were so moved. (See, for example, my remarks on firestorms and "doomsday machines," below, pp 67–68.) Second, whenever Kahn talks about probabilities rather than mere possibilities, the assumption of rationality colors his judgment. This is true with regard to such questions as whether a given assumption is "optimistic" or "pessimistic"; or whether a given likelihood is worth worrying about or not (e.g., what will be happening during the period immediately following a nuclear war that must be spent in fallout shelters, about which Kahn says, " . . . a war is likely to continue for a few days after the first strike and then terminate . . . probably by negotiation. . . . ").* More important, it is true of all his discussions of casualties, as we shall see when considering those. It is only the assumption of rationality that enables Kahn to suggest, for example, that "counterforce plus avoidance" and "straight counterforce," the two types of nuclear attack most directly designed to keep casualties down, are the attacks most likely to occur.[20] It is only this assumption that explains his apparent preference for the 2-20 million range when he is estimating casualties, among all the other possibilities he develops. (See below, page 43.) Most important of all, an assumption of rationality is implicit in the idea that the kind of massive civil-defense program Kahn ultimately proposes is a feasible one. All he says in this regard is that the economy can "afford"

---

*In his most recent full-length work, however, Kahn writes that "*Antirecuperation attacks* are also possible. There are many reasons why a country might wish to be able to deliver such an attack."[19] As we shall see, it is a constant habit of Kahn's to impeach his own assumptions—and what better authority? one might ask.

it—a statement that as he himself points out is quite meaningless, since the economy can "afford" anything the people want badly enough.[21] The real question is, on what grounds do the people (or their representatives) decide what they "want," and this question is never discussed. Thus the effect of his treatment of this issue is to deny the relevance of politically determined fiscal restraints, as well as all other kinds of psychological and cultural restraint, against the adoption of any course of behavior that a "rational" analyst has proved will "pay off."

The second kind of assumption that Kahn makes concerns the ability of American society to recuperate from the effects of nuclear war, economically and socially. These are assumptions, in other words, which have to do with (1) the effect of devastating crisis on human personality and social organization; and (2) the effect of massive destruction on an organized economy. In this context, Kahn rarely makes his assumptions sufficiently explicit; the only way in which one can clearly see what he has in mind is to cull from his presentation the relevant passages and put them together to form some kind of whole.

On the first problem, Kahn has little to say; the following passages appear to indicate his views:

> The fifth optimistic element in our calculation was the assumption that people would be willing to work at reconstructing the country and would have a productivity at this task about equal to that of their prewar work. To many this seems like a rather bold assumption. . . . Nations have taken equivalent shocks even without special preparations and have survived with their prewar virtues intact. In past years these

shocks were spread over many years; the one we are considering would take place in only a few days. But . . . from the viewpoint of character stability it is better to take this kind of shock in a short time rather than in a long one. It is my belief that if the government has made at least moderate prewar preparations, so that most people whose lives have been saved will give some credit to the government's foresight, then people will probably rally round. . . . It would not surprise me if the overwhelming majority of the survivors devoted themselves with a somewhat fanatic intensity to the task of rebuilding what was destroyed. . . .*

One of our most important assumptions was that it would be possible to adopt "workable" postwar health and safety standards—workable in many senses: that people would be willing to accept them from both the political and individual point of view; that they would not be so high as to result in any large economic costs or so low that the medical problems get inordinate. . . . Doing this may be very difficult because it may make the people setting up the standards look somewhat callous. . . .22

Earlier, Kahn has also appended a more or less parenthetical—and well-known—passage that seems to imply a great deal about his view of the relationship between human nature, social organization, and catastrophe, not to mention his sensiblity as a social commentator in general:

Now just imagine yourself in the postwar situation. Everybody will have been subjected to extremes of anxiety, unfamiliar environment, strange foods, minimum toilet facilities, inadequate shelters [sic], and the like. Under these conditions

*Here Kahn adds, "of course, if there is a fantastic disparity between the government's preparations and the problems to be solved, then none of this would hold. . . ." "Fantastic" is a word that we usually use to refer to events or things the existence of which seems absolutely incompatible with the physical world we know; one cannot tell if this is the meaning which Kahn wishes to give the word here.

some high percentage of the population is going to become nauseated, and nausea is very catching. If one man vomits, everybody vomits. Almost everyone is likely to think he has received too much radiation. Morale may be so affected that many survivors may refuse to participate in constructive activities, but would content themselves with sitting down and waiting to die—some may even become violent and destructive.

However, the situation would be quite different if radiation meters were distributed. Assume now that a man gets sick from a cause other than radiation. Not believing this, his morale begins to drop. You look at his meter and say, "You have received only ten roentgens, why are you vomiting? Pull yourself together and get to work." [23]*

Concerning economic organization, Kahn is somewhat more explicit. He begins by positing a distinction between the urban part of the nation that will be largely destroyed in the late attack, and the relatively undamaged non-urban remainder of the nation; these he calls respectively the A country and the B country. His argument then consists almost entirely of the assertion that, despite the contrary beliefs of "many laymen, professional economists, and war planners," the B country could prosper—re-create or rather maintain an undestroyed, livable economy— even though the A country had been destroyed, together with its "one-third of the population," "half the wealth," and "slightly more than half of (the) manufacturing capacity" of the United States. The key steps in his argu-

*The example is puzzling in that Kahn, as we shall see, has earlier imagined a nuclear attack from which the average survivor receives *250* roentgens—a circumstance in which vomiting, among other things, might seem somewhat more reasonable than is indicated here by Kahn. However, there are so many other puzzling things about the example that it is hardly worthwhile quibbling over such points.

ment, which may be taken to denote his theory of economic activity, are as follows: (1) The United States can "about double its GNP every fifteen or twenty years," so the level of destruction being considered would merely set us back "a decade or two" and destroy many luxuries" rather than being a "total economic catastrophe." (2) The calculation sounds "naïve" if we think of highly integrated modern economies as organisms, but the "organism analogy" is false, at least for purposes of "long-term recuperation": actually the economy is more "flexible than a salamander," and "no matter how much destruction is done," the survivors, if there are any, "will put *something* together." Thus even if a critical part of the economy is destroyed, one can use the remaining parts, as one could not with an organism, in the reconstruction effort. (3) Specifically the A and B countries are in the relationship of "a mother country and a vigorous, wealthy, and diversified colony." Thus the B country can "survive without the A country and even rebuild the A country" in about 10 years; in fact its problems will be easier than those faced by the U.S.S.R. "in constructing the Soviet Union of 1955 from its 1945 base." Here, with the remark that "We tend to exaggerate . . . the impact of losing valuable people, equipment or resources," Kahn's theory of economic development comes to an end. No sources of any kind are cited in support of the two key points in the last paragraph (or any other, for that matter).[24]

Kahn then proceeds, as he might put it, to quantify the problem. First, he lists the total "tangible wealth" of the United States in a table (17) and estimates that "at current rates of investment" this represents a generation's worth of economic activity: indeed we would be in even better shape than that statement indicates because "we are likely to work harder and consume less" and (again) "much of the destroyed wealth will be a luxury." He follows this remark with an example: "[If] half of our residential space is destroyed, then, even if everyone survives, these survivors will be better housed than the average (very productive) Soviet citizen." The only part of our assets both "in danger of being destroyed" and "critically needed in the immediate postwar period," is "producers' durables and manufacturing structures," and "business inventories." These remarks appear to sum up Kahn's thinking about the sociology of economic organization.[25]

Next, in Table 18, we are shown that the B country contains "more than one-fourth of our capacity in almost all industries," which during reconstruction would undoubtedly operate "at more than their theoretical capacity." The table doesn't take into account possible bottlenecks, but these might be avoided by "advance preparations" such as stockpiling; and anyhow, "entrepreneurs and engineers are very capable at 'making do' when necessary." In Table 19, finally, Kahn gives the value of 'capital goods used in industry" and estimates "the minimum that should survive." He adds that our problem is to have in the short-run postwar period "a manufacturing industry that at current prices would be worth something like 100 billion dollars," and concludes that "if we can do this, protect a few items, and use the things that will automatically survive, such as people, land, transportation facilities, rural areas with their power stations, utilities, non-manufacturing industries, and so on, *there is every expectation that we will have an economy able to restore most of the prewar gross national product relatively rapidly. . . .* " [26]

Kahn next notes "seven optimistic elements" contained in his analysis, although he believes that on balance "the calculations are more likely to be pessimistic than optimistic." These elements are, first, "that we will be permitted to reconstruct"; second, that society will, concurrent with the war's "end," start to function again at the level of basic necessities such as clearing up debris, restoring "minimum communications," restablishing credits and markets, providing basic transportation and utilities, etc.;* third, that economic activities particularly will "be started rapidly, even though society can live for a time on inventory and stocks";† fourth, "that there be no specific crippling bottleneck problems";‡ fifth and sixth, that peacetime work habits survive at the same time that people are willing to accept "workable" postwar health and safety standards (see the paragraphs quoted on pp. 29–30 above) ; and finally, that there be no "catastrophic" side-effects of the war, such as

---

*It is in this context that the remarks about vomiting occur. They are one instance of the generalized statement that "some forethought would certainly facilitate recovery." [27]

†Kahn adds, " . . . there should be between two and four years' food supply in the country; this means that there is no need for getting agriculture started full-swing immediately. . . . While the other essentials . . . all seem to survive in sufficient supply to get things started, some inventories would be in much more critical supply; unless we started to produce them soon, parts of the economic system might falter or even grind to a stop." Therefore, "Preparations must be made now to facilitate effective use of . . . untouched resources." This will require "the establishment of markets, and the furnishing of labor forces, credits, and management."

‡Here Kahn notes, "If further study should show that there are important specific bottlenecks, we ought to stockpile the scarce items or protect the capability for making them."

unexpected "effects of lingering radioactivity," "unsuspected ecological consequences," disastrous fire storms, etc.[28]

IV. The Civil-Defense Study: Analysis of Recuperation

At this point, then, I have either described or reproduced the most important of the materials out of which a systems analysis is supposed to produce a compelling prediction about the workings of civil defense in nuclear war. A discussion of the way that analysis is conducted should lead us to an evaluation specifically of the RAND study and generally of this type of "scientific" approach to questions of national strategy.

The question that Kahn sees as crucial to the problem of civil defense is this one: will the survivors of a nuclear war envy the dead? This question, obviously, would seem to imply a host of value judgments of the loosest sort: one can answer it any way one wishes. Kahn, however apparently wishes to show that his rigorous approach to these questions can create at least a partially objective framework within which to consider such problems.

Thus let us consider the first element in the question about survivors, the logically prior question, will enough people survive to make the war seem to have been worthwhile in some sense, when compared with other alternatives? How can an answer to this question in any sense be made "objective"? Kahn's approach is to attempt to make a concrete quantified statement of national values. This goal he has reached by conducting an informal survey, in which he has asked people to state how many deaths they could "accept" in a nuclear war and still think survival had been worthwhile—assuming some other vital interest, such as national integrity, had been preserved. According to Kahn, Americans' "estimates of an acceptable price generally fall between 10 and 60 million, clustering toward the upper number."[29] Unfortunately, the statement is based on an error in logic, an error that seems indicative of this approach.

The question Kahn asks his informants, to be precise, is " . . . what price would we be willing to pay . . . for punishing . . . the Soviets for [an] aggression . . . ?"[30] Now what is misleading about this question is that there is no such thing as the "price" of a war until after the war has been fought, at which point one does not get to indicate one's preferences. One does not estimate how many will die with certainty—unless one knows with certainty how many will die. If one is unsure about the exact number of dead in a future war, then one can only talk about the *expected price* of the war. The expected price or average price, is obtained by taking all the possible prices that one judges a war may have, estimating the probability that each of these prices will be the one that eventuates (all the probability estimates put together would add up to one, of course), multiplying each price by its estimated probability, and adding up the results.

What does this correction of Kahn's question do to his results—that is, what claim can he make about his findings? He cannot claim that "people" are willing to pay an *expected price* of 60 million dead. For if that figure represents the average price of a war, some prospective prices will probably be very much higher—180 million conceivably, in some probability distributions. Indeed, any expected price of 60 million dead probably includes in its calculation the possibility that all or most of us will be wiped out—and since Kahn has not asked people how much of this risk they are willing to put up with, his question can have no meaning if so interpreted.

Of course, one can interpret Kahn's question as intending to elicit the *top* price that people are willing to take any real chance on. However, Kahn himself admits time and again that much higher prices than 60 million in war dead may possibly have to be paid if deterrence fails, so he can hardly be intending to relate his strategic proposals to that American value estimate. In sum, it is impossible to assign any usable meaning to Kahn's question relative to his strategic proposals; it is equally impossible to imagine any way of asking the question that would have enabled respondents to give answers usable in a rigorous analysis. We cannot meaningfully quantify public values.

Withal, the resulting "statistic" forms the keystone of Kahn's assault on competing strategies of deterrence and disarmament, since he bases his justification of a "credible first-strike capability," and the civil-defense effort that logically follows, on the willingness of Americans to stand up to disasters within this range. Thus from the beginning we see that the systems analysis and the resulting strategic logic are based on a kind of number-mongering that consists of an attempt to quantify the unquantifiable, to make objective the subjective, and to invoke the terminology of probabilistic reasoning where no discoverable probabilities exist.

Kahn next proceeds to discuss the physical effects of nuclear war on human life and its environment and reaches the conclusion that a doubling of the normal peacetime rate of genetic defects is the worst result we should expect from a nuclear war.[31] This conclusion is the heart of his work; it is therefore surprising to discover in his development of this point a number of errors of omission and commission. These are too numerous to discuss exhaustively, and I shall mention only those which seem to be explicable on the same grounds as the one that I have just discussed.

Kahn estimates* the genetic consequences of a nuclear war in which the average survivor received a dose of 250 roentgens of radioactive material. (He gives no reason for selecting this figure, other than to say on p. 46 that he can "easily imagine" such a war.) However, when he calculates the genetic effect of excesses over the "permissible" doses resulting from a possible nuclear war in which the average survivor received 250 roentgens, his figures are based on a straight-line extrapolation of National Academy of Science estimates about the effects of 10 roentgens. We must take his word for it both that this is the proper way to extrapolate and that the NAS figures are accurate or at least not overly optimistic for levels of radioactivity that have never been reached *en masse*.

Similarly, though he postulates various nuclear attacks, and then discusses the effects of fallout from them, he nowhere offers any information about the relationship between megatonnage, fallout, and long-run fallout. We must therefore again take his word for it that the radioactivity he discusses will result from the attacks he discusses. Even if one makes this act of faith, the important

---

*The estimate is based on an extrapolation from Table 6 of *On Thermonuclear War*, p. 44. Kahn has an aversion to ordinary methods of documentation, so one never knows from where he got his figures; he also ignores the existence of antithetical interpretations of the data.

point remains that since he fails to be precise about the *quantities* he is discussing, the reader not conversant with the technical facts about fallout is unable to consider the effects of an attack other than those Kahn has postulated. Furthermore, with regard to the nuclear attacks that Kahn postulates a new problem arises: at the point where he describes in his Tables 9 and 11 the radioactive environment three months and one hundred years after an attack he fails to establish or even mention the method of calculation for deriving levels of radioactivity at a given time from a given level of attack. (And in his discussion of the effects of Strontium-90, his manipulation of data without citation of sources is so impenetrable that one simply cannot make even the faintest effort at checking his statements.) [32] Finally, we must note the rather odd passage in which occurs Kahn's only estimate of the life-expectancy shortening effects of radioactivity:

> . . . [W]e assume that on the average every roentgen would shorten life expectancy at birth by three and one-half days. While this number is only one-half to one-tenth as large as some of the numbers mentioned at the 1957 Congressional Hearings on fallout, it is actually large for the circumstances we are considering. Current data and theory suggest a figure closer to one or two days per roentgen for small chronic doses continued through the life of the exposed individual. (However, if the dose is more concentrated, as it would be in the immediate postattack exposure situation as opposed to the long-term postwar environment, the loss in life expectancy at birth might be about three times greater or about five to ten days per roentgen.) [33]

Thus, the verifiable empirical content relevant to this step in Kahn's reasoning is certainly very limited, and one is drawn to the conclusion that this fact is inherent in the nature of a "systems analysis" of such a subject.

For if the subject of analysis is as hypothetical as in the present instance, it is unlikely that there will be very much available information that is not largely suppositious. Furthermore, Kahn concludes this part of his discussion as follows:

> A final remark on the genetic problem. Only survivors can have children. It would be difficult to have a war in which the average survivor got much more than 1,000 roentgens before the age of thirty. (Giving [sic] this amount of radiation rapidly will kill a person.) Unless the enemy has deliberately adopted self-defeating tactics (for example, deliberately degraded his wartime capability by using "cobalt" bombs in places and at times he should be using militarily more efficient bombs), the long-term radiation should also be much less than this, particularly if even modest precautions were taken.[34]

This circular reasoning is a major feature—perhaps *the* major feature—of Kahn's discussion from there on. It is quite true that a doubling of the genetic defect rate might be bearable in some sense. One of the main reasons it might be bearable is that there would be so few people left around to worry about it.

What Kahn has done in effect is to separate the question, "Will the survivors envy the dead?" from the question, "How many dead can we tolerate?" But the two questions are not separable. In answering the second, we certainly want to know how the survivors will live. More to the point, in answering the first we want to know how many survivors there will be. This Kahn, as we shall see, never tells us precisely. His exercise in genetic logic thus becomes academic, as it has no social context. It should also be pointed out that when Kahn asked people how many dead they could tolerate, he apparently asked them no questions about genetic effects of nuclear war. Again, the supposedly rigorous method appears to offer no help in the necessary but terribly difficult task of somehow amalgamating the separate questions.

Taking these aspects of Kahn's argument into consideration—the dubious worth of his sourceless data; his misleading way of phrasing the question about tolerable death limits; and his separation of the discussion of war casualties from the discussion of genetic defects—it is obviously important to ask just what casualty estimates Kahn *does* develop, either in the course of the RAND study or elsewhere.

In *RAND R-322-RC*, and in *On Thermonuclear War*, Kahn gives three rough estimates. Given various degrees of fallout and other protection, casualties could range, in an early attack against SAC and the 50 largest urban areas, from 5 to 90 million; in a later attack against SAC and 157 urban areas, from 3 to 160 million.[35] The upper figures refer to an attack with no civil-defense measures; since Kahn is arguing for the benefits of civil defense, we should in fairness ignore those figures. The range is then from 3 to "over 85" million casualties; the progression, in terms of states of preparedness, is from 70 per cent strategic evacuation* plus minimum fallout protection, through a complete civil-defense program without strategic evacuation, to a minimum fallout protection

---

*"Strategic evacuation" refers to the large-scale national evacuation of cities, undertaken not as a hurried response to attack warning, but as a deliberate move in a round of threats and counterthreats, signalling a willingness to undergo a counter-city attack.

program alone. (With regard to the 150 city attack, protection of Strategic Air Command is also a key variable, since a hardened SAC would draw fire away from cities, presumably.) Kahn himself sums up the argument based on these figures in this way:

> With a complete civil-defense program, adequate warning, and a relatively limited Soviet strike (limited because of the unpremeditated character of the war or because the Soviet strike was blunted by the U.S. attack), U.S. casualties would probably be in the 3 to 10 million range.[36]

Kahn, however, provides no grounds for assigning probabilities to the various alternative occurrences that can increase or decrease these casualty figures. This would be a very difficult probability set to establish, but the supposedly major virtue of systems analysis is that it entails the making of just such estimates. Be that as it may, we are not told how this analysis was made. Thus if we ask, how likely is the institution of a "complete" civil-defense program (including strategic evacuation)? adequate warning? a "relatively limited Soviet strike?"— we get no answer.* It is worth noting that if one assigns a probability of .8 to each of these three required contingencies—a probability which offhand seems quite exces-

---

*Kahn does not explain how a strike limited because of "the unpremeditated character of the war" *and* "strategic evacuation" could occur at the same time (see the definition of the latter in the note on p. 41). Since the concept of strategic evacuation is consonant with what we have seen is one of Kahn's major premises— the assumption of rationality—and the notion of "the unpremeditated character of the war" is not, this seems to be a clear case of the author's ignoring the logic of his own argument.

sive—the probability of casualties falling within Kahn's range is only 50 per cent; with a probability of .7, it is only 34 per cent. Furthermore, for any probability of casualities, Kahn apparently assigns a "range" factor of 2 or 3 (e.g., 3 to 10 million) ; and we have no way of knowing whether someone else might not assign a much higher—or lower—factor.

Once again, in other words, close inspection of Kahn's figures has cast a different light on his "calculations," making them seem arbitrary. And one's willingness to concede credibility to them is further weakened when one notices that but a few pages back, Kahn has said:

> Our study of nonmilitary defense indicated that there are many circumstances in which feasible combinations of military and nonmilitary measures might make the difference between our facing casualties in the 2-20 million range rather than in the 50-100 million range.[37]

It is not a reassuring fact about the rigor of systems analysis that its practitioner (practitioners, actually, since the original study was a group effort) finds no essential difference between a range of 3 to 10 million and one of 2 to 20 million.

However, this is only the beginning of one's difficulties with Kahn's casualty figures. In *Thinking about the Unthinkable*, Kahn offers a different set of figures. Here he postulates five possible types of attack, on a descending scale of casualty expectations: (1) countervalue; (2) counterforce + countervalue; (3) straight counterforce (narrow military considerations only) ; (4) counterforce + "bonus" (population and property) ; (5) counterforce + active "avoidance." The postulated casualty ranges are

43

(1) 50 to 100 million or more, depending upon the state of civil-defense preparations; (2) unstated; (3) 1 to 20 million or 5 to 30 million, increasing by a factor of as much as five by the middle or late sixties; (4) 5 to 100 million or 10 to 150 million; and (5) "less than five million so long as the attacker is careful, no weapons go disastrously astray, and we have a modest civil-defense capability." Kahn then continues: "In an actual war, which of these five types of attacks might we most reasonably expect? I have no idea."[38]

Since Kahn's civil-defense + first-strike capability strategy makes it quite possible that the U.S.S.R. will be "the side which strikes second," the prices we must expect to pay in war dead range upward to about total destruction. If Kahn himself were programming the war, we would still have to expect up to 20 *or 100 million dead* even with a "vigorous" civil-defense program previously instituted: and always assuming that the war stops after a straight counterforce exchange. Since Kahn offers no guarantees that it will do so, or reasons to believe in the worth of such a guarantee if offered, one hardly knows what to make of these later estimates. I can only suggest that they are quite inconsistent with the "3 to 10 million dead" estimate of *On Thermonuclear War.**

If we now return to *On Thermonuclear War* to make our own correlation between casualties in, and genetic results of, a nuclear war, we continue to encounter the

---

*Nor are either set of estimates quite consistent with Kahn's latest discovery, that civil defense "could save the lives of 30-50 million people."[39] Out of how many, he does not say; one wonders whether this would leave more or less than the all-important 60 million dead.

same type of difficulty. Kahn's summary of the genetic problem begins with a rough—very rough—quantitative description of an early and late attack.[40] He then goes on to describe the postwar environment 100 years later.[41] Most of the nation would not be "uninhabitable"—though some of it, of course, would be. (Kahn hardly ever makes clear *which* attack he is talking about at a given point.) Radioactivity levels would still be higher than they ought to be, but they would be "bearable," though there would be a considerable life-expectancy shortening effect from lingering radiation. The following passages are worth quoting extensively, in order to convey not only the flavor but the "quantitative" nature of the analysis.

> If we assume a three and one-half day decrease in life expectancy per roentgen* then 100r would mean the loss of a year and 1000r the loss of ten years. Ten years happens to be the amount that has been added to an American *adult's* life expectancy since 1900. . . . Since it is difficult to have exposures by fallout that would give a person 1000r without killing him, ten years is about the greatest decrease in life expectancy that could be expected in survivors as a result of long-term chronic exposure.
> . . . [A]n average life-shortening of from five to ten years for, say, a small per cent of the population is not, compared to probable casualties, a catastrophic additional burden.
> . . . [D]uring the initial recuperation period . . . [t]he *straightforward* factor by which we exceed the NAS standards is now really horrifying. . . . However . . . [a] reduction in the neighborhood of 100 might be comprised of a factor for decontamination ranging from 1 to 100, a factor of about 3 to 5 for weathering, terrain and deviation from theoretical decay rate . . . and a factor of 2 to 30 to be

---

*See above, p. 39. Kahn offers no particular reason for choosing any one of the estimates over any other.

obtained by limiting exposure to the unshielded environment.
. . . *

If we assume that we have made at least modest preparations before the war, the over-all factor of 100 is probably
conservative for the long-term exposure due to the small
attack. . . . We do not know whether such a factor would
be conservative for those who have to spend appreciable
time in large, open spaces such as farms. . . . Not only is
shielding . . . more difficult but experiments . . . indicate
that it may be more difficult to decontaminate open land than
was previously thought, but these data remain to be verified.

If these same factors can be applied to the heavy attack,
the postwar environment resulting from such an attack would
be bearable. . . . [42]

To these passages Kahn appends an inconclusive discussion of the problems of Strontium-90 and Carbon-14
fallout. At one point he announces that "a mere 13
megatons (MT) of fission products spread uniformly"
over the nation's agricultural land would "make the
food unfit for human consumption." However, we can
"increase the requirements for contamination by a factor
of 50 to 100" if we take into account "the inefficiencies
of distributing fission products by exploding bombs" and
the probable effects of "weathering and decay." At this
requirements level, as we might call it, a 1000 MT attack
*"could suspend agriculture in the United States for 50
years or so."*

---

*Here Kahn adds parenthetically, "The rest of the time we
would have to live in protected areas. This would not mean that
we would have to give up our homes and factories, though we
might have to give up some of their aesthetic appearance and
convenience. For example, sandbags might be placed around some
houses for the first year or two." It is not clear whether Kahn
means to imply that the *only* inconvenience of having to live in
"protected areas" would be "aesthetic."

Since Kahn's late and early attacks envisage 20,000 and 2,500 MT of fission products respectively (see the note on p. 26 above), this would seem to be a frightening prospect. However, this problem too is alleviated "if we are willing to envisage relaxing the peacetime standards to the point that the incidence of cancer begins to change life expectancy by a significant amount"; given the decontamination "factor of 75" (i.e., 50 to 100) and the fact that the fallout of fission products will not be uniformly concentrated on arable land, the land will then become "usable," and agricultural life will be able to proceed.[43] Kahn's summary of this presentation is as follows:

> What we have shown is that *if* we can get through the first three months of the war and postwar period, and *if* we can do the necessary decontamination and provide the necessary protection for most of the working and living hours, we can probably live with the lingering effects of radioactivity. The two *ifs* can scarcely be ignored, however.[44]*

Among the dubious calculations in this discussion three have a crucial effect on the argument:

1. Kahn's calculations about the shortening of life expectancy appear to be arbitrary. If one took the "numbers mentioned at the 1957 Congressional Hearings on fallout," [45] which he rejects for no verifiable reason, the range of life-expectancy shortening from 100r to 1000r would be, not 1 to 10 years, but 2 to 100 years. If one

---

*Actually, Kahn follows this conclusion with the treatment of the problem of Strontium-90, which he says makes even that conclusion tentative. What conclusions one can reach when Sr-90 has been taken into account, he does not say.

takes the 5 to 10 day figure, which again is rejected for unspecified reasons, the range would be 1½ to 27 years. (Nowhere in these pages does Kahn correlate his various tables with the "easily" imaginable attack discussed earlier, in which the average survivor received 250 roentgens.)

2. The over-all "conservative" factor of reduction "in the neighborhood of 100" seems to be made up out of whole cloth. Actually, the reduction factor, using Kahn's own estimates, ranges from *6* to *15,000*.[46] No reason is given for preferring any figure within that range to any other—or, as I have noted, the range itself (which is more a continent than a neighborhood, one would think). In general, Kahn's "factors of reduction" wherever one finds them appear to be drawn, in R. P. Wolff's phrase, "from the same secret cache of figures in which (he) found the original radiation levels." [47]

3. Even more important, though Table 11 describes the "radioactive environment three months later," and Table 9 the "radioactive environment 100 years later," no quantitative analysis is proffered concerning the effects of these environments on the human organism. At the most critical point of his analysis, we have only Kahn's word for it that these environments will be "bearable." It is odd that Kahn, who with other deterrence theorists is always criticizing those not exposed to the benefits of systems analysis for their use of fuzzy adjectives such as "intolerable," "annihilatory," etc.,[48] can do no better than "bearable" himself, and that he fails to reveal any concrete speculations (let alone data) as to what this "bearable" environment will actually look like. Still one can understand his problem: he has

neither more nor less data available to him than do his antagonists.

At this point, on rechecking Kahn's own summary of his argument, one finds that he also has virtually no information about either of the two "if's" he mentions. Looking first at the question of three-months survival, we encounter two problems. Will the immediate post-attack period be free of further nuclear destruction and thus contamination? Can the shattered population of a shattered nation survive three months in fallout shelters in good fettle? The first question is dealt with by Kahn only in passing, and by assumption: " . . . [W]e have assumed that we are in charge of our own destinies—that we will be permitted to reconstruct. . . ." [49] The basis for this assumption is apparently the anterior strategic assumption, which I have noted above, that " . . . *a war is likely to continue a few days after the first strike and then terminate* (probably by negotiation). . . . " [50]* What we have here is the reification of one version of a nuclear attack, so that we fall into the trap of discussing not survival in nuclear war but survival in Kahn's nuclear war. How much damage would be done to Kahn's theorizing if one made the *contrary* assumption: that the war would go on, sporadically or otherwise, after the initial exchange of strikes; that nuclear war, in other words, would not bring about peace on the spot? Unless one can think of a better way to read the future, it does not seem that a "science" of strategy has very much to offer on these questions—

---

*What exactly will happen in those "few days" Kahn again does not say. One would imagine that with the right weapons we could demolish the planet in that time.

and what is important about Kahn's flawed approach is that it is difficult to imagine what a better one would look like.

As for the second question, Kahn's treatment of shelter survival is on a par with his treatment of the "postwar" period; except for a discussion of non-contaminable foods that could be stocked in shelters, and methods of preparing them, he has little to offer but words of good cheer. Toward the end of the same part of *On Thermonuclear War*, however, one's eye is caught by this remark: "We explored unconventional and sometimes extreme (though we feel practical) solutions. (Some of the programs we explored envisaged people living hundreds of feet underground for as long as three months. . . .)" [51] Does this mean that only an "extreme" program would bring the indicated number of survivors safely through the three month period? One cannot tell. How many persons could be expected to survive in good shape three months or more in limited-facility, limited-supply underground hideouts, under conditions of extreme fear, frustration, panic, and lack of traditional social controls, is a question which, though basic, remains unanswered.[52] It is clear that systems analysis has not made this "if" into any less of an "if."

Kahn's treatment of the second "if," the problem of decontamination and protection, is equally unsatisfactory, being extremely cursory, as these remarks indicate:

> If we are suitably prepared before the attack, we will be able to decontaminate the more valuable areas. We might put enough effort into the decontamination to clean up a significant portion of the country by factors varying between 2 and 100 in the first two postwar years. . . . When we put these corrections into the calculations, even the heavy attack does not seem so frightening at the 100-year point.[53]

To this Kahn later adds the famous passage on vomiting, quoted above, which appears to sum up his thinking on the physical problems of decontamination. But that passage is purely hortatory. Furthermore, since the example of a worker who has received "10 roentgens" does not seem to jibe too well with the picture of a war in which "the average survivor" receives 250 roentgens, it becomes clear that his assumptions do not exhaust the possibilities of the situation, even in his own mind: apparently they can be not merely varied, but varied at will.

At this point, having been provided with a host of unanalyzed "if's" rather than with either a concretely qualitative description of the situation or a quantitative estimate of the probabilities involved, we can turn to the next and final step in Kahn's study. This is his consideration of the possibilities for social and economic recuperation when the shelters have emptied after the necessary waiting period.[54]

As Robert Dentler and Phillips Cutright, two critics of this study have written: "This economic analysis is perhaps a classic in view of the chain of *if-type* assumptions that must be made before the conclusive estimate of recovery is reached."[55] Once more, therefore, the rigor of Kahn's method in the abstract seems irrelevant when we get down to details. Let us consider, for example, Tables 18 and 19, which Kahn relies on so greatly. In these tables, Kahn has established undestroyed capacity and values merely by subtracting from the current total of capacity and values the amount currently contained in the 53 largest urban areas. Then (in Figures 1 and 2)[56] he describes a recovery rate that consists of a straight-line projection of economic growth from the supposedly remaining industrial base, assuming a rate of growth comparable to rates of growth traditionally achieved by the United States in peace time. (No particular argument is offered on behalf of this assumption.) Thus one seems expected to reject completely the "organism" analogy, and accept completely the salamander or self-regeneration analogy. This may explain why few professional economists agree with Kahn, since empirical economic analysis seems in many cases to be based on a concept resembling the "organism" analogy.[57]

Again we are dependent on an assumption to which we can see no reason to give credence. If the "organism" analogy carries any weight at all, then Kahn's conclusion of Table 19—"Estimated United States Capital Surviving Destruction of 53 SMA"—becomes quite implausible. Dollar values of "capital" or anything else have little meaning in the abstract. They represent the value of a thing's or person's contribution to a specific economy, that is to say, to the organization of economic activity in a specific social system. Take away the defining elements of the social system and of the subsystem for allocating goods and services, and assigned values in that system lose their meaning. For the kind of catastrophe Kahn envisages it is quite possible that the idea of money itself might drop away or take on a completely different significance.

The Hungarian and German inflations after World War I are cases in point; and the latter may be seen without too great a stretch of the imagination as having been a contributing factor in the development of a new social system—a system which there is no apparent reason to prefer to what might result if the United

States "surrendered" to the Soviet Union. Since Kahn does not attempt to prove anything by this particular table, his argument could stand without it. But the argument depends on Kahn's estimate of the likelihood of various economic events, and it is therefore important to see how he conceives of economic phenomena. One's impression that his assumptions in this area are wholly arbitary is reinforced.

As for Table 18, its relevance to the argument is beyond question. Without doubt, we want to know how much productive capacity exists, undestroyed, outside the large cities for the purpose of analyzing his study. This table, in fact, may be said to represent the totality of the "data" upon which the study of recuperation is based. But the table cannot possibly bear the burden of significance which has been rested on it. At the very least, one would want to have instead even the most elementary representation of a national input-output analysis, in order to make an educated guess about the likely real nature of certain capacities in the postwar situation Kahn describes. For example, what will be the net result for recuperation of the following collocation of "capacities": * most of our crude oil, 36 per cent of refining capacity, 23 per cent of transportation equipment, X per cent of pipeline mileage (it does not seem to occur to Kahn that this might be a crucial category), and finally 23 per cent of primary metal industry? Could the level of manufacture suggested in that last figure be

---

*The very notion of treating "capacities" in this manner is dubious, but I shall not belabor this point, since it is but another instance of the damage to economic reasoning caused by Kahn's rejection of the "organism" concept.

maintained? If not, how would such items as 23 per cent of electrical machinery, 29 per cent of rubber products, etc., be affected? (All these figures are taken from Table 18, and represent B country capacities.) In the absence of any consideration of such problems, Kahn's analysis is unconvincing.

The climax of this kind of pseudo-quantification is Kahn's Table 3, and Figures 1 and 2, which purport to show rates of recuperation after a nuclear war. These once again demonstrate the same tendentious treatment of arbitrary assumptions. I have said earlier that these "figures" merely show straight-line projections of GNP growth, from B country productive base. Here Kahn seems to have confused the terms "recuperate" and "grow." Thus, it is possible for a society to *recuperate* from a disaster—i.e., re-create the conditions of existence —but not *grow*. It is quite possible for a social system to stagnate, or even decline economically—not just for a few years, but for centuries, until barbarism is reached. Growth does not occur inevitably but only when conditions for it are present. And a certain capital and resource base is but one of many such conditions.[58] Thus, to say that the United States would still be a "wealthy" society after a nuclear war is to say very little; to say that "actually, a country like the United States can about double its GNP every fifteen or twenty years. . . ." is in context to say nothing. For the United States after a nuclear war, whatever it will be like, will quite probably not be like the United States before a nuclear war—it will be at least a different kind of society, and it might not be amiss to refer to it as a different society altogether. To halve the GNP at one stroke, for instance, might very well leave, not a society with a "standard of living" still higher than that of the Russians, but rather a society in utter collapse. Kahn's remarks thus show a misunderstanding of the problem with which he is dealing. As for Table 3 (p. 20), which seems to be intended as a partial prefiguration of the conclusions about recuperation, it reads as follows:

TRAGIC BUT DISTINGUISHABLE POSTWAR STATES

Dead	Economic Recuperation
2,000,000	1 year
5,000,000	2 years
10,000,000	5 years
20,000,000	10 years
40,000,000	20 years
80,000,000	50 years
160,000,000	100 years

Will the survivors envy the dead?

This table is repeated on p. 34, preceded by the sentence, "Here again is a summary of the situation"; again on p. 551, in recapitulation, it is referred to as though it represented a definitive finding. Thus Kahn puts an immense burden on a table that, even more than his other attempts at quantification of the recuperation problem, is all arbitrary assertion and no calculation. Indeed, the table seems to be divorced even from Kahn's own notions of reality. He nowhere offers any reason to believe that a particular number of dead is associated with any particular rate of recovery. He has simply made up some "numbers" to illustrate the point that if "we can cut the number of dead from 40 to 20 million, we have done something vastly worth doing." [59] Furthermore, the interior logic of the table is deceptive. That is, the table purports, without any demonstration, to show that the two series both increase geometrically (roughly), and this "correlation" gives the appearance of demonstrating an unproved relationship between the two variables. This is the substitution of a semantic device for true calculation; it is significant that at no point in his explanation of the civil-defense study does Kahn make any further effort to demonstrate this supposed relationship. There is no avoiding the conclusion that it does not exist except in that realm of imagination that seems so prominent a feature of systems analysis of the strategic future.

The passages from which I have quoted also contain much exhortation to actions that must be undertaken beforehand if recovery is to be feasible. It is not always clear what kind of assessment of the future is behind these exhortations. One cannot really tell whether Kahn expects an attack as devastating as the one he investigates or if he is merely conceding such devastation in order to be able to say, "Look, even this we can survive and recover from." But there are two reasons to assume that Kahn is serious about his 53 city attack.

First, the over-all strategy he advocates—development of a not incredible first-strike capability, and use of it if need be—has as an essential component our willingness to consider threatening and thus fighting an all-out nuclear war. (Indeed this is the precise point involved in Kahn's advocacy of strategic evacuation if a threat fails.) [60] In any event, this is certainly the way Kahn's reasoning is interpreted by his colleagues, many of whom seem to have been influenced away from simple notions of pure second-strike deterrence by his arguments, as is indicated in the following passage from Morton Halperin's definitive *Limited War in the Nuclear Age*:

> Herman Kahn . . . and others have proposed that the United States aim for a "not-incredible," first-strike capability, that is, a capability which might be used in very dire circumstances, not because one has a high probability of coming off scot-free, but because one emerges with something like two to twenty million casualties.* This might be acceptable in retaliation for certain drastic Soviet provocations. However massive retaliation could also rely simply on the threat to unleash a general war with great destruction for both sides should the Soviet Union or China attack a local area.[62]

Second and most important, Kahn claims to have proved something by his analysis. At the end of the section on recuperation there occurs the following paragraph:

> How much confidence did our researchers have in these recuperation calculations? In the sense of having taken account of *all* factors, not too much. While in the study we looked at more aspects of the problem than are discussed here, we have already suggested that our study was not complete enough to be a full treatment of this complicated problem.

*Halperin's discussion here shows the tendentious nature of Kahn's flexible casualty estimates if other theorists take them seriously. And note Wohlstetter's comment, in his "The Delicate Balance of Terror," that "an economically feasible shelter program in the United States might make the difference between 50,000,000 survivors and 120,000,000 survivors." Of course Wohlstetter is more cautious than Halperin: anything "might" happen.[61]

Yet we believe that it shows rather convincingly that if thermonuclear war damage is limited to something like the A metropolitan areas or the equivalent and the levels of radioactivity are about as indicated, then all the usual reasons for being skeptical of our ability to recuperate are probably wrong. We may not be able to recuperate even with preparations, but we cannot today put our finger on why this should be so and I, for one, believe that with sufficient study we will be able to make a very convincing case for recuperation, if we survive the war, and, more important, that with sufficient preparation we actually will be able to survive and recuperate if deterrence fails.[63]

It is therefore a test of the rigor and adequacy of the argument to see whether this claim stands up under investigation. Interestingly enough, nowhere in the public record, including available RAND memorandums, is there any indication of a more "complete" treatment of the problem that Kahn reports on here. On first reading *On Thermonuclear War,* one speculates that perhaps Kahn has simply wished to avoid boring the general public with such esoterica, and has reserved complex subanalyses for more technical and less generally available forums. For this speculation R. P. Wolff has written the following accurate epitaph:

Of course, there are . . . constant allusions to unnamed associates who, if the text is to be believed, have carried out elaborate investigations. "In our study we assumed," says Kahn . . . conjuring up the image of a team of experts feeding endless streams of data into computers and applying the latest techniques of economic analysis to the outputs. The only RAND report on the subject which is ever cited is . . . R-322-RC. . . . Although it is not mentioned explicitly in Chapter II it would seem to be the study on which the chapter is based. When we turn to R-322-RC, we discover that it is shorter than Chapter II, and contains even less in the way of concrete data. It is also, if anything, less adequately documented.[64]*

If, then, taking Kahn's choice of a problem seriously and assuming that his report of it in *On Thermonuclear War* is definitive, we turn back to his analysis, we come upon this surprising piece of information, which follows almost immediately the passages summarized on p. 58 above.

But perhaps what is most important of all, we did not look at the interaction among the effects we did study.

In spite of the many uncertainties of our study we do have a great deal of confidence in some partial conclusions—such as, that a nation like the United States or the Soviet Union could handle each of the problems of radioactivity, physical destruction, or likely levels of casualties, if they occurred *by themselves.*

We also believe that if the destruction of the 50 or so major metropolitan areas in either country were all that happened so that the ensuing reconstruction program was not complicated by social disorganization, loss of personnel, radioactivity, and so forth . . . the United States would (not) have any critical difficulty in rebuilding the equivalent of the destroyed metropolitan areas in the time we have estimated, or even less. . . .

But if all these things happened together, and all the other effects were added at the same time, one cannot help but have some doubts.[65]

*Wolff is apparently unfamiliar with RAND Research Memorandum RM-2206-RD, "Some Specific Suggestions for Achieving Early Non-Military Defense Capabilities and Initiating Long-Range Programs," by Herman Kahn, January, 1958. This memorandum contains an appendix, titled "a brief summary of the back-up material [*sic*]," which is even more objectionable than *On Thermonuclear War* and R-322-RC, in that not just Kahn but 16 other experts manage to discuss their "back-up material" with the same casual disregard for citation of sources that Kahn evinces.

This passage is the final fruit of Kahn's earlier step in divorcing his various calculations from one another: of his attempt, to repeat, to quantify the unquantifiable. Where no firm knowledge exists that would make possible some assumptions of constant behavior—when one is working, that is, with the presently limited knowledge that social scientists have—one simply cannot aggregate in any meaningfully rigorous way the virtually entire universe of potential behaviors that is relevant to predictions of the human future. Analysis of prospective behavior then becomes pseudo-analysis. In stating that his work is of this nature Kahn here seems almost to deny any credence to his own study.

At this point, I refer to the study not only of the specific question of recuperation, but of the more crucial question, Will the survivors envy the dead?—the answer to which is the basis for Kahn's whole theory of nuclear deterrence. By his own estimate, there will be anywhere up to "over 85" million casualties to begin with, a severely restricting postwar environment due to lingering radioactivity, and a badly damaged economy. Let us consider the specific aspects of Kahn's analysis, some of them of great importance, which become questionable once his own admission is taken into account.

1. Decontamination is presumably a function of available personnel. Therefore the achieved "factor" of decontamination will vary with the casualty rate, at least in the immediate postwar period. Kahn pays no attention to this difficulty.

2. Kahn asserts that an average life-shortening effect of say five to ten years "is not, compared to probable casualties, a catastrophic additional burden." But *if* casualties were high and the population consequently

reduced in the short and middle run; *and if* the incidence of the genetic consequences of radiation—defective births, early mortalities, decreased fertility[66]—were fairly high in the long run as well; *then* the demographic consequences might very well be "catastrophic." Furthermore, what happens to this question of the "burden" of life-shortening when we add the additional problem—separately considered by Kahn—that the incidence of cancer from Sr-90 might create? That too, if we "relax" peacetime standards, might begin to change average life-expectancy by a significant amount. Surely the effects of this "relaxation" should be put in their proper context.

3. Table 18, in the section on recuperation, includes as part of the B country's productive capacity approximately 95 per cent of the nation's agriculture. That is to say, the B country's chief resource is land. How valuable will this resource be after exposure to short-term and long-term radiation, the accumulation of Sr-90, "searing firestorms," etc.?

4. The maintenance of arable land and the production of food is a society's first line of survival. (Or, if the society is short of arable land, it must be able to produce other goods that can be traded for food products.) While Kahn has much to say about the need to build up food stocks before a nuclear war, he acknowledges that this is only a stopgap measure. How easy will it be in the light of all aspects of nuclear disaster to maintain the agricultural sector? How much energy will have to be diverted from other activities? Kahn admits that land decontamination may be a feat "more difficult" than was previously thought; but he does not see any significance in this difficulty.

5. With regard to all recovery activities, the nature of the remaining labor force will be of paramount importance. Kahn's vague descriptions of the amounts of labor necessary to perform all the tasks of recovery takes little account of the various problems that may arise. For example, I find it somewhat startling that Kahn can consider losing one-third of the population but not correlate this loss with the economic needs he discusses. And to say, as he does, that "we tend to exaggerate . . . the impact of losing valuable people," and that "entrepreneurs and engineers are very capable at 'making do' when necessary," hardly qualifies as a discussion of the problems of labor force composition that would arise.[67] Furthermore, prolonged exposure to hard radiation will presumably cause both health and diet (i.e., the available food supply) to deteriorate.[68] The result may well be a labor force less and less capable of doing hard work, and forced to devote much of the work it does to merely keeping itself going. In earlier sections of this study, Kahn continually talks about "lowering peacetime standards"—for exposure to radiation, induction of Sr-90, diet, etc. In his section on recovery, he ignores the possibility that lowering all these standards also might mean a considerable lowering of peacetime standards of work. And to frame this problem in terms of the maintenance of "bourgeois" work habits seems remarkably insensitive.[69]

6. In general, every activity carried on in a postwar situation will have a high opportunity cost. There will be many crucial tasks for aiding the progress of recovery and recuperation, and to concentrate resources on any one or any few of them, to the extent seemingly de-

manded, may be to hinder others seriously. Kahn writes as though each economic and social activity will present an isolated problem to which we can devote enough resources to "solve" it. The presumption is implausible. Specifically, how much social energy will be available for the tasks of industrial recovery? Among the more or less absolutely required postnuclear war activities will be burying the dead; caring for the wounded; cleaning up; decontaminating the physical environment, especially open land; supplying food to the survivors; protecting living areas;[70] limiting the exposure of survivors to the "unshielded environment"; preserving morale; and perhaps preserving society, or at least, organizing the survivors for survival.

With all this work going on, according to Kahn, we are still going to find so much time to rebuild the economy that within a year (see Figure 1) normal economic growth rates will be resumed. The problems that are not considered if one cannot correlate all the possible interactions are both obvious and decisive; they make 100 years a more reasonable estimate than one year.

For example, out of the man-hours of work the society will be capable of providing, many will be required for the basic tasks of rehabilitation mentioned above and for decontamination and protection; where the necessary equipment will come from (e.g., sandbags for putting around houses) and how much of a drain on the economy providing, transporting, and installing it will entail, is not considered. Furthermore, much of the B country's productive capacity may be in "unshielded" areas. If exposure to those areas must be limited, the B country can hardly be expected to resume operations at a reasonable level of production. Moreover, if economic recovery is delayed, industrial plant must be at least maintained. Will there be a conflict between other needs and the need for industrial plant maintenance, and if so, which will be allowed to suffer?

More generally, labor will have to be distributed, and sanctions provided. This in itself may be a major task. The same may be true of morale-building activities designed to do no more than the basic task of maintaining society as a functioning entity. How much time and manpower, in short, will be available for the work of economic recovery, under anything approaching conditions of efficient utilization? Any answer to this question must be so dependent on the exact extent of the disaster that it simply cannot be given on the basis of Kahn's discussion. All we can say is that, seen in this light, the problem of recovery takes on an aspect of grimness that is absent from Kahn's account; and that, given some of the casualty and radiation figures, which he himself postulates, it may easily turn out to be an insoluble problem.

7. According to Kahn, the "bourgeois" work ethic would survive. If we accept this assumption for the moment, is there any reason to assume further that the instrumental goal of that "ethic" will be economic recovery? Offhand, it seems at least as likely that the best social energy will be devoted to sheer survival and morale-building. Depending on the extent of the disaster, it is quite possible to imagine a situation of great dedication to work and very little economic recovery, the ultimate result being economic disaster even in the presence of the productive capacity that Kahn postulates as still existing.

In any event there clearly is no reason to make the initial assumption. Kahn avoids consideration of a difficult problem by assertion, his assertion being that if the Russians could handle "disaster" in World War II, so will we be able to in World War III.[71] That what they did was not in the remotest fashion comparable with what we would have to do, given the war's limited impact on their economy,* the time given them for adjustment to loss of life and social disruption, the morale-building effect of success in the war, etc., does not prevent him from making this analogy. Recognizing its falsity, we must ask: What is the relationship between social and work morale on the one hand and the extent of damage on the other? Is there some level of disaster at which morale begins to decrease—and if so, what are the "laws" of its decrease? Can discipline and authority survive when there is no potential cadre organizing recovery which has not itself been numbed by catastrophe? Might not dedication itself—as ordinarily motivated in our society by the spirit of competition and the denial of scarcity—become a casualty of shock?[72]

What is finally unconvincing in Kahn's answers to these questions is his easy assumption—which goes far beyond a mere statement about the survival of the "bourgeois" work ethic—that "the moral fiber of a civilization," as Hans Morgenthau puts it, "has an unlimited capacity to recover from shock." [73] Nothing we know, as Morgenthau adds, gives reason for believing this. Our industrial civilization is extremely intricate and complex, and also has shown every indication of being relatively fragile; its ability to survive major dis-

*For example, the Germans barely touched Russian industry in their advance.

ruption without "a critical loss in equilibrium" is surely doubtful.[74] To say this—and to ask all the questions we have asked—is to put in much sharper focus than it is put by Kahn's approach the question, Is the catastrophe of nuclear war worth going through for any conceivable purpose?

V. The Civil-Defense Study: Strategic Assumptions and Analysis

All that we have said so far has concerned only Kahn's manipulation of assumptions about economy and society. We must also raise some questions that are suggested by the interplay between his other, *strategic* assumptions and the analysis of the survival and recuperation problems. I have already noted his assumption that a nuclear war would not be a protracted, progressively more devastating affair. This is but one instance of Kahn's general habit of making extremely tendentious assumptions—a habit that seems to be required because a slight variation of even one of his assumptions might knock the props out from under the whole affair.

To be specific, it is impossible to ignore the consistency with which Kahn adopts a different attitude toward contingencies that will make civil defense workable and those that will make it unworkable. For example, he appears to have made gratuitous assumptions about other determinants of the "devastation level" of an attack. Thus his conclusion that the United States will be able to deal with the effects of lingering radioactivity seems to be based on the notion that fallout-minimizing (or non-fallout-maximizing) bombs would be exploded at fallout-minimizing high altitudes. As Dentler and Cutright say, "all these considerations are open choices for the attacker, not for the agents of recuperation." [75]

Again, drugs that will protect against radioactivity, improved decontamination techniques, ways of overcoming bottlenecks and keeping up the economy's momentum, active air defenses, and other hypothetically helpful inventions, are talked about as though they are already here or on the verge of breaking into existence. More important, where the number of deaths from a "straight counterforce" attack is estimated, Kahn turns out to have made the assumption that "no weapons go astray"; and for purposes of calculating the amount of radiation that will linger on after an attack, he has assumed high-altitude bursts, no use of cobalt bombs, etc. [76] On the other hand, the possibility of "searing" firestorms and other unpredictable catastrophes is mentioned in passing and then ignored. In *Thinking about the Unthinkable*, Kahn writes:

Of all the technical issues raised by the Administration's civil defense program, none has given rise to more palpable nonsense than the question of firestorm. Those who predict metropolitan area-wide firstorms are in all probability wrong, and are certainly speaking without evidence or thought. The only serious estimates concerning firestorms restrict such phenomena to the heavily built up downtown areas and especially dense forests.

The attack may not be nearly so destructive for other reasons. The usual calculation, which simply extrapolates how much thermal energy is produced from a ground burst weapon, and then makes a simple geometric calculation assuming perfect transmission, is undoubtedly wrong. A high altitude burst does not produce much thermal radiation, but soft X-rays which in turn may heat up the atmosphere—which in turn may radiate heat onto the earth. The whole process is not well understood and undoubtedly a good deal less efficient than the naive calculation would indicate. None of the above implies that fire is not a very serious problem. Rather I mean to point out that many present "estimates" of death toll and damage caused by large thermonuclear weapons due to fire and firestorm are exaggerated.[77]

There are only three real points here. The first—"the only serious estimates"—apparently refers to the work of researchers who accept Kahn's assumptions. The second—"high altitude bursts"—is one of those assumptions. It does not occur to Kahn to ask why, if ground bursts from large-sized weapons could "burn up" the countryside, an angry enemy might not decide to do just that in a "countervalue plus counterforce" attack. The third point—"many present estimates"—is meaningless; will they still be "exaggerated" say three years from now? One wonders if as much "palpable nonsense" has been written about the firestorm problem as about so-called radioactivity-combating drugs.[78]

So too, a good bit more than half of Kahn's "analysis" of the problem of economic recuperation consists of exhortations to the nation to prepare now for the disasters that may come—and that will be irretrievable disasters if prior preparations have not been made. The potential cost of these preparations is immense and, if history is any guide, will surely be much greater than present estimates suggest.[79] And yet this huge preparatory war effort promises nothing more than that the problem Kahn envisages *may* be *barely* soluble if nothing goes wrong and nothing disastrously unexpected happens. No estimate is advanced of the likelihood that these preparations will be sufficient for the task Kahn assigns them; no probability is assigned to the prospect that nuclear war will be worse than Kahn imagines. He merely says tautologically that

> It is the thesis of this lecture that if proper preparations have been made, it would be possible for us or the Soviets to cope with all the effects of a thermonuclear war, in the sense of saving most people and restoring something close to the prewar standard of living in a relatively short time.[80]

To see the effects of Kahn's loading of the dice, one should note the example he gives, relative to the question of unpredictability, that the chemistry of Sr-90 seemed to predict a much more menacing effect on the human body than actually turned out to be the case.[81] It does not occur to him that the next serious misstep in prediction might not have so happy an ending. A case in point concerns his notion of "Doomsday Machines." Kahn devotes a good bit of space in *On Thermonuclear War* to a discussion of these hazardous instruments, which "within ten years" could be built by either side—though they probably won't be.[82] * In his discussion of civil defense, however, he does not question whether such a prospect might affect one's ideas about the value of a civil-defense arms race. He also does not inquire whether large scale civil-defense programs, the development of credible first-strike postures, etc., might influence the opposing sides in the arms race to try to build such

---

*It is the thesis of the recent movie, "Dr. Strangelove," and the novel from which it was taken, Peter Bryant's *Red Alert* (New York: Ace Books, 1958), that such machines *will* be built. Both the book and the movie rest their argument on logic which is clearly borrowed from Herman Kahn, among others—the logic, that is, of "keeping up" in the arms race.

machines where previously they might not have made the attempt. Nor does he consider the possibility that biological or chemical warfare might become significant elements in the great powers' deterrence or even first-strike capabilities, as nations "dig in" and the arms race progresses. What would the deployment of such weapons do to Kahn's 100 billion dollar-plus civil-defense program? Kahn's usual approach in cases of doubt such as these is to say that more "research" and "investigation" are called for.[83] Suppose the results of that research are not helpful?

Most important of all, Kahn makes dubious assumptions concerning the size and nature of a potential future attack, and these assumptions are problematical precisely because of some of the difficulties inherent in his method of analysis. It is not necessary to do anything but quote Kahn himself to discover some of these difficulties. The early attack calls for 500 bombs, and the late attack for 2000, to be delivered on American targets. A few hundred pages later, however, Kahn remarks that "Give or take a factor of 5, there are quite likely to be about 50,000 ready missiles in the world in 1973, each with its own button." [84] If I have correctly understood this particular one of Kahn's mysterious "factors," he is saying that by 1973 there will be anywhere between 10,000 and 250,000 armed missiles in the world: not to mention, presumably, the "bombs" that were being dropped in his early and late attacks. If this is an example of the way Kahn "calculates," then we cannot take his "model" attacks, early *or* late, very seriously without reminding ourselves that the number of "bombs" involved may be varied by, say, a "factor" of 5 "either way." (One is tempted to ask, Why not 10?)

With regard to the size of warheads and the expected megatonnage per target point, how useful are the apparent estimates of 16⅔ megatons per bomb and 83 megatons per target point (see above, p. 26) as implicit assumptions about the nature of a nuclear attack in "the middle or late sixties," the period for which the late attack is calculated? A tentative answer to this question is suggested by the following remarks, written by Hanson Baldwin in 1963:

> . . . [T]he Russians have what most observers believe is a considerable advantage in "very large-yield [sic] weapons," weapons with an explosive power of 50 to 100 megatons. . . . The Secretary [of Defense, Robert McNamara] made by implication what was probably the first official admission that the Soviet Union may soon have in operation a missile powerful enough to carry a 100-megaton warhead. . . . The Secretary's "pessimistic" estimate that one "very-large-yield [sic] Soviet missile" might destroy "an average of less than two" hardened and dispersed Minuteman sites was also a revelation of how our estimates and our technology have already been altered as a result of the development of 50- and 100-megaton weapons. . . . [85]

And if we project a little further into the future, "Pentagon estimates calculate that the Russian delivery system will be able to handle some 60,000 megatons by the early 1970's"—or *150* megatons per target for 400 target points.[86]

In the light of technological developments, then, Kahn's speculations about the expected force of a late attack are apparently dependent on Soviet unwillingness—if it indeed exists—to make full use of their capabilities. Kahn and other deterrence theorists, however, have not always been consistent in taking such a view of the future, for they were among the prime creators of the theory of the "missile gap." Indeed, Albert Wohlstetter's entire notion of the "delicate balance of terror" is really another influential example of systems analysis built up with deductive brilliance from one incorrect premise: that the Soviets would most likely destabilize the arms race by building as many missiles as they possibly could.

This theory of the delicate missile balance, moreover, led to the only genuine prediction produced by the systems analysts that has so far had a chance to be tested. As Kahn and Klaus Knorr put it:

> I suspect the Russians will asymmetrically buy a capability to win and terminate wars, while we will try to depend on some form of a Minimum Type I Deterrent [*sic*] plus inadequate Limited War [*sic*] forces.[87]

> What has shocked a large proportion of the informed public . . . is the appearance of the "missile gap." . . . From now on until sometime in the mid-1960's, the Western military posture will probably become weaker on the all-out war level than it has been. . . . [T]he United States it would seem, has . . . lost the "absolute deterrence" which permits the threat of massive reprisal to be widely used. . . . [88]

The prediction, of course, was false, as was the whole notion of the missile gap and consequently of the "delicate" balance. By 1962 another expert in national security studies was writing with equal authority that

> . . . not only [is] there no "missile gap" but in fact the US strategic force [will] at least through 1967, be so superior to the Soviet force as to be capable of absorbing a nuclear attack and still destroying most of the Soviets' remaining striking power.[89]

What is interesting about this episode in intellectual history is not merely the revelation of how varying just one assumption can bring crashing down the entire logical structure of a "systems analysis." In addition, what is revealed here is that the kinds of predictions— or recommendations—that a systems analysis of policy problems produces can themselves bring about a substantial reordering of the system that was supposedly being analyzed. For Kahn's prediction was wrong about American as well as Soviet behavior. The reason it was wrong about American behavior is that it (and Wohlstetter's and Knorr's and others' writings) influenced Americans to *change* their behavior. Furthermore, if the Soviets had responded to our new behavior the way we responded to our imaginary version of their behavior, the arms race would have been destabilized all over again—as it still may be if they solve their internal economic difficulties and get tired of playing second fiddle to us in military strength.

In other words, since the extent of their participation in the arms race depends partially on the extent of our own, acceptance of Kahn's proposals (or Wohlstetter's) by the American government could make the calculation on which they are based obsolete. This kind of blind alley, which might be called the "self-negating prophecy," is one toward which social science often tends, because it is dealing with conscious actors who are aware that they are being analyzed. A dynamic theory of social behavior, such as Marx attempted (but failed) to create, may someday overcome this particular problem. Systems analysis, incorporating apparently no theories of behavior at all but merely the personal predilections of the analysts, will not. Of course systems analysts are not alone in this dilemma. But clearly they have offered no special improvement over traditional modes of analysis.

There are also problems that are raised by what I earlier called Kahn's assumption of rationality. One of these concerns the prospect that we shall do all the things that he says we have to do to make civil defense truly efficacious: conduct all the necessary research, invent all the promised inventions, spend all the required money, etc. As Dean John Bennett of Union Theological Seminary has written:

> The kind of synchronized preparation for such a variety of unfamiliar threats and deficiencies . . . that is required here would call for a more prescient and efficient government at all levels than has ever been known in this country. It would call for a change in the lives of all citizens long before the projected disaster which it is difficult to imagine . . . it would also have to overcome a moral revulsion. . . . [90]

It seems probable that the political difficulties that would arise could not be handled without appealing to the most calculating, rationalizing elements in American political life. This is true, even if one concludes that the nuclear arms race is itself highly irrational, or that civil defense is. That is, even if a civil-defense program were adopted in a fit of national hysteria, it would still take concerted instrumentally rational behavior over a long period to implement it.

The other problems involved in the assumption or rationality concern the likelihood that wars will be fought "rationally," or that it is at least useful to hope they will be. I shall not discuss here whether this assumption is an appropriate one to make—that is the subject of Chapter V of this book. Nor shall I engage in a substantive discussion of Kahn's strategic insights.[91] In any event, the discussion of the case for civil defense is implicitly a commentary on any strategy of which a civil-defense effort is a major part. What can relevantly be mentioned here, though, is that even if Kahn is partially correct in his assumption of rationality, it still remains true that he never makes any clear estimate of the probability of rational behavior that must be assumed in order to assign to a specific level of civil-defense effort an at least vaguely specified probability of being efficacious. Without such an estimate, systems "analysis" seems to contain, necessarily, a low level of analysis indeed.

VI. Data, Assumption, and Analysis: Summary

If we attempt, then, a summary answer to the questions I asked earlier, the results are not promising. To begin with, Kahn's data are not only unsatisfactorily accounted for, but they appear to be inevitably so given the kind of study he has undertaken—an analysis of the hypothetical strategic future.* Because of this,

---

*Wohlstetter has written, "Of course we have no wartime operational data drawn from World War III, and hope we never will. On the other hand, there are plenty of relevant data, some of it in better form now than then. Voluminous data has been derived from peacetime operations and logistics, tests of existing equipment and components in future equipment, theoretical analyses of equipment design, state of the arts studies, and intelligence of enemy operations."[92] The reader can judge for himself the relevance of most of these kinds of "data" to "cardinal" choices, as Wohlstetter (after C. P. Snow) calls them; as for "intelligence of enemy operations," see my comments on the attitudes of deterrence theorists toward the "enemy" throughout this book—especially below, pp. 244–46.

and because the study is in any event so completely speculative, it is often difficult to tell, as we have seen, whether
there is any truly logical connection between Kahn's data
and premises, and the extrapolations he makes from
them. The premises themselves are at best exceedingly
questionable, as the assumption of (partial) rationality
or the idiosyncratic view of the economy; at worst they
are grounded either in arbitrariness or sheer fantasy, as
the various "factors" of decontamination. And no reasons
are given in *any* of the reports of the civil-defense study
for choosing the assumptions that were chosen.

Of course science always proceeds by the making of
assumptions: but not by the making of tendentious assumptions; not by the making of argumentative assumptions for which no justification is offered, and which have
not been fully debated in the relevant scientific community; and not by the assuming away of the most important and dynamic questions in the field of inquiry being investigated. Worst of all, we have seen that when merely
one or two of these many arbitrary assumptions are
varied somewhat, the whole tissue of the conclusions begins to fall apart, and it becomes possible for Kahn, for-
getting what assumptions he has made in the past, to
write a few years later that in an all-out nuclear war the
Russians, "unless their strike had been extraordinarily
successful . . . would be likely simply to disappear as a
nation—or at least to be set back 25 to 100 years in industrial and material wealth."[93] Flexibility is a virtue in
policy studies, but it ought to have its limits.

This last comment raises another point: namely, that
the systems "analysis" really contains very little true
analysis at all. For most of Kahn's "calculations" are not
really calculations but merely assigned values. Thus, for

example, in the study of economic recuperation, the figures concerning the B country's resources and their putative postwar value do not in fact *support* the assumption about the B country's "survivability," but merely *illustrate* it; similarly Table 3 illustrates rather than supports the argument that there is a relationship between number of dead and time required for recuperation (see above, p. 55). To rest the proof of a proposition on an illustration of how it *could* be true is circular, and thus almost all Kahn's work on recuperation is a circular development of his own assumptions. And although he does make calculations based on his genetic data, the calculations and the data are both useless except in the context of Kahn's assumptions about the shape and size of a future nuclear war.

How much value, after all, can an empirical study have when it is almost all utterly deductive? The result in this case can only be a neat illustration of one possible result of a nuclear war—probability unspecified. As a representation of what would be *likely* to happen, however, the study does not compel belief, for no true investigation of the world has gone into it: and nothing will come out of nothing.

VII. Problem Formulation and the Claims of Science

To this sort of critcism, as I have indicated earlier, Kahn, Knorr, Wohlstetter, and others have already made the obvious rejoinder, and one which is accepted by many critics. What else, they ask, is to be done? Here is a situation that demands analysis, a novel situation in the face of which all past experience with military operations fades into insignificance. A method of analysis is proposed. For all its drawbacks, what other approach can the critic advocate?

This question suggests the last two critical comments that must be made about Kahn's civil-defense study and about systems analysis in national security policy. The first is that his claims about its value are on their face greatly overstated. In the abstract, it may be quite reasonable to assert that systems analysis is the best method available for doing this type of work, and to attribute many (though hardly all) of the methodological failures I have noted to the historical condition of the time rather than to the analytic discipline. But concretely, if painful historical necessity severely limits the uses of a method in a particular context, so also does it severely limit the extent to which conclusions can legitimately be derived from the operation of that method. With this thought in mind, we may turn again to two contrasting passages that I have earlier quoted from Kahn, in which the operative phrases are: (1) "one cannot help but have some doubts"; and (2) "with sufficient preparation we actually will be able to survive and recuperate if deterrence fails." (See above, pp. 58–59.) If one has "doubts" due to a failure to analyze the most crucial aspect of the study—interaction among the various effects of a nuclear attack—then how can the second statement possibly be justified?

Moreover, in both *On Thermonuclear War* and *Thinking about the Unthinkable,* Kahn has made in almost identical terms the following claim:

> *Despite a widespread belief to the contrary, objective studies indicate that even though the amount of human tragedy would be greatly increased in the postwar world, the increase would not preclude normal and happy lives for the majority of survivors and their descendants.*[94]

Here one finally does not know how to deal with Kahn and his systems analysis at all. The language of this statement is indistinguishable from the kind of copy that advertising men write about toothpaste and soap powder. Nothing has ever been "shown," either in this study or any other, about the kinds of lives survivors of a nuclear war will lead. The only thing that can possibly be claimed to have been shown—and I have suggested some reasons for not taking even this claim seriously—is that by dint of great effort and imagination possible situations can be thought of and described in which such a statement *might* be true. That is, Kahn has imagined one big —even awe-inspiring—scenario, in which "survival" takes place. But what about all the scenarios he has not imagined?

As for Kahn's claim to the mantle of "objectivity," it is impossible to tell what he means by the word. "Objective studies" can refer to studies in which the assumptions have been followed out fearlessly and consistently to their logical conclusions. Except as a test of the integrity of the researchers, this kind of objectivity is unimportant for practical purposes unless one agrees with the choice of assumptions. In any event, Kahn's assumptions do not seem to have been followed out consistently, by his own accounting.

"Objective studies" can also refer to studies in which the researchers were bias-free, or emotionally detached from the problem they were studying. If this is the meaning Kahn has in mind, then he has every right to make such an assertion but no particular right to expect any given person to believe it, except on the basis of interior evidence, which in this case seems to be lacking. In addition, where the assumptions of a study necessarily

imply a host of political valuations, the best way of in-
suring or at least suggesting objectivity would be for
different groups of persons to supply the assumptions on
the one hand and do the research on the other.

Finally, "objective studies" can refer, simply, to studies
with the conclusions of which no other responsible researcher can possibly disagree. I shall not attempt to
make any arbitrary assumptions about whether the
RAND study of non-military defense is such; rather, I
shall refer the reader to pages 20 through 25 of Dentler
and Cutright's *Hostage America*. These pages summarize
the findings presented to the Joint Congressional Committee on Atomic Energy by two employees of the
Weapon Systems Evaluation Division of the Institute for
Defense Analyses, Hugh Everett III and George E. Pugh,
who, starting from assumptions about nuclear war similar to Kahn's reach almost diametrically opposite conclusions on the questions of survival and recuperation.
The disparity in the results obtained suggests, I think,
that the phrase 'objective studies" in this context is but
another way of saying "prophecies."

It *is* possible to find passages in *On Thermanuclear
War* that make, not the exaggerated claims I have quoted,
but the much lesser and more temperate claim that at
least civil defense, and consequently a first-strike capability, has been shown to have enough of a chance of being
valuable to deserve being given some action priority.
However, there is a serious problem even with this
limited claim. The *reductio ad absurdum* of Kahn's
method is to say, as Wohlstetter has said (see n. 102 below), that some civil defense will save some lives and
more civil defense may well save more lives, in the event
of a nuclear war. That is quite true, and I doubt whether

a person could be found who would disagree, but precisely for that reason we do not need systems analysis, or any analysis at all, to justify such a statement. If that were all Kahn had to offer, his work—his exemplary report of a systems analysis—would stand as a monument of wasted effort. (At times, indeed, Kahn does talk as though *any* effort saving *any* amount of lives were *ipso facto* justified, no matter what its ramifications, but I cannot believe that he would erect so complex an edifice of work on the foundation of a statement so absurd.)

Rather, ignoring Kahn's rhetorical exaggerations, we should read him as making the "moderate" claim that the potential benefits of civil defense are *significant enough* to justify adopting a national strategic posture—such as planning for controlled counterforce war or under certain circumstances for a counterforce first strike—based partially or wholly on the expectation that those benefits will be realized. And it is precisely such a claim that cannot be justified, even if one gives Kahn the benefit of every doubt concerning his data, his method, and the logic of his conclusions. This is because he has not set his study in an analytic framework appropriate to its content, and thus has vitiated its entire worth. To answer the most important of all the questions I asked at the beginning, his formulation of the problem is not acceptable as the most relevant formulation—and this too, I think we shall see, is inherent in the systems approach as applied to this kind of study.

What do we mean, after all, when we say that the benefits of a strategic system such as the civil-defense program Kahn proposes are significant, or justify the system's being given an "action" priority, etc.? We can only mean that the goal to be achieved is worthwhile, and that the potential cost of adopting and utilizing a system that is designed for that goal is less than the potential cost of alternative approaches to the same end.

The goal of Kahn's strategy is something we might roughly call "preservation of national values." For Kahn, this achievement, which mostly means deterring Communist "provocations," [95] is best accomplished by adopting a military strategy that deliberately takes a chance on catastrophe; the risk is less fearful than it appears because there is also a "good" chance of reducing the disaster of that catastrophe by adopting the substrategy of civil defense. Thus he offers a "calculated risk" (assuming one is willing to grant his work the quality of "calculation"). The simplest way of expressing this analysis of ends and means is to say that Kahn's proposed strategy for achieving his (presumably our) goals has an expected cost. [96] That figure, if we could express it as a figure, would be obtained by multiplying the expected price (above, p. 36) of nuclear war—for nuclear war is the limiting instance of Kahn's strategy—by the probability of its occurring. Since the goal sought is practically incommensurable, the expected cost is presumably worth paying, as long as it does not add up to the annihilation of America (or Western) civilization.

But may there not be better, potentially *less costly* ways of preserving national values? I can think of at least five possible alternatives:

1. A "finite" deterrence system—no first-strike capability, no major civil defense—in which, to use Kahn's terminology, the buttons are "connected" and ready to be pushed in the event deterrence fails.[97]

2. A finite minimum deterrence system in which the buttons are *un*connected: in other words, bluff, amount-

ing perhaps to surrender if it is called. (See my remarks on this posture in Chapter VII below.)

3. A finite or minimum deterrence system in which the buttons are connected, but we have studiously refused to make up our minds what we are going to do if an opponent pulls an appropriate trigger. Here we combine a chance of bluff/surrender with a chance of massive mutual destruction, and rely on the resulting uncertainty to deter potential opponents, leaving the decision up to fate in the event deterrence fails.

4. Negotiated disarmament of any and all kinds.

5. Unilateral disarmament/surrender.

These strategies fall into two groups. Strategy 1 can be compared directly with Kahn's strategy. The variables are (a) the likelihood of nuclear war and (b) the damage that will occur if it comes. If the former is much lower than in Kahn's strategy, then the expected cost of the strategy might turn out to be less. Strategies 2, 3, 4, and 5 demand a slightly different comparison. Here the limiting circumstance (c) is not just the occurrence of nuclear war, but also, and presumably rather more likely, some kind of "conquest" or "intimidation." As for the damage that will be occasioned by failure, that damage may thus well be of a different kind—not physical annihilation but political "defeat." Somehow, therefore, a scale has to be created on which one can make a valuational comparison of the two kinds of "damage."

Certain grounds for comparative analysis immediately suggest themselves; I shall mention only some of the more obvious ones.

1. Does Kahn's first-strike strategy make nuclear war more likely than would a finite deterrence strategy, as has been claimed? [98]

2. Would the institution of a massive civil-defense program be a provocative act making nuclear war more likely?

3. Assuming disarmament could be negotiated only by the United States' making concessions to the U.S.S.R. on time-phasing, inspection, etc., how likely would these concessions make (a) a nuclear war on, or (b) a warless defeat of, the United States?

4. How does the cost of "warless" defeat compare with the cost of nuclear war, in terms of the preservation of national values?

5. How great a value is involved in our not killing Russians? innocent bystanders? Or simply, how great a value is involved in refusing to use nuclear weapons, and how can it be compared with other values?

Two comments need to be made about this alternative and, I think, obviously preferable way of formulating the problem. First, Kahn has not made the slightest attempt to deal with any of these questions: to determine, that is, what is the *relative cost* of his proposed system. This fact sometimes makes his work look much less like analysis than propaganda, and led one critic, Norman Podhoretz, to write, "What I would like to see is a similarly hardheaded and coldly objective description of surrender, with the same object of determining how long it might take to 'recuperate' from Communist domination."[99]

Kahn himself apparently finds justification for this neglect in the fact that other analysts have neglected his area of concern; presumably someone ought to point out to them that they have failed to consider an alternative strategy with alternative costs. But Kahn has not done this. Actually, he writes as though he were proposing not an alternative to, but a necessary ingredient of, every other strategy; he insists that *his* strategy is both *good* and *better*.[100] And he does this in large part, not by analyzing other strategies, but by ignoring the true bases for comparison between them and his strategy.

For example, in *Thinking about the Unthinkable* Kahn treats the opposition of finite deterrists to civil defense by approvingly quoting an article which mocks the idea that "insurance" can be provocative. Thus he avoids confronting, or even admitting the existence of, his opponents' arguments—for their main argument is that civil defense is not merely "insurance," but also may be a threat. "Fire insurance," e.g., is not a means of deterring fire, or of limiting fire damage, but is rather, like Kahn's "War Damage Equalization Corporation" scheme, a means of assuring compensation *after* a fire—if one hasn't burned to death. "War insurance" would have no more in common with Kahn's strategic policies, including civil defense, than fire insurance properly conceived would have in common with the policy of building one's house completely out of asbestos, and from a hidden storm-cellar firing rockets off at any suspected firebug who happened to wander into the vicinity.[101]*

Much more crucial for the nature of the arms debate is Kahn's statement that "There seems to be little point in discussing the view that finds a solution in a totally disarmed world." [103] Why not write exactly the same sentence, only substituting "armed" or "dug-in" for "dis-

---

*Wohlstetter too derides opponents of "insurance," though not as caustically as Kahn. Wohlstetter is apparently speaking with regard only to small increments of civil defense, which should presumably, if defense is at all threatening, be less so than a full-scale crash program. But see my comments above, pp. 80–81.[102]

armed"? Assuming a disarmed world would be unstable
(or maybe not even disarmed because of the cheating
problem) why should such a situation necessarily be
worse than the one Kahn postulates?

The answer appears to be that Kahn, like most deterrence theorists, is possessed of a philosophical bias that
determines his judgments about what is "reasonable" to
discuss, and a political bias that determines the nature of
his predictions about, specifically, future Soviet behavior.
On the first point, he lectures Americans (in his latest
book) on their "unwillingness to initiate the use of
moderate levels of force for limited objectives":

> The common American attitude toward force is somewhat
> naive. Force is a permanent element in human society, used
> by good, bad, and indifferent nations and people. It has been
> used rationally as well as irrationally, wisely as well as
> foolishly, moderately as well as extravagantly, virtuously
> as well as maliciously. Even if we unreasonably or even
> immorally institute the use of force, coercion, violence, and
> threats, it is entirely possible to go on to use these things in
> a reasonable fashion.[104]

This bias, whether it is a reasonable one, makes genuine analysis difficult to engage in if one is comparing
systems that emphasize force with those that do not.
More to the point, however, is that in the case of deterrence theorists the emphasis on force is accompanied by
an anti-Communist bias of the most simplistic American
variety. This anti-Communism leads Kahn and others to
predict that the Soviet Union will, even if unprovoked, be
likely to take advantage of every opportunity to damage
the United States, even to the point of destroying it
completely. [105] Perhaps it is reasonable to believe that if
an opponent will always make the most devastating pos-

sible use of his capabilities, then the United States would be worse off if it had never prepared for such an event. But to reason that an "opponent" *will* behave in this manner is to ignore or dismiss the political universe that bounds the "system" that is supposedly being analyzed. Furthermore, this kind of bias even interferes with the logic of the analyst's own argument. For example, Kahn is inconsistent in his preference for treating of Soviet capabilities rather than intentions. [106] He does this, after all, when he is arguing against disarmament or "finite" deterrence but not when he is arguing *for* civil defense. The "enemy," I have pointed out, could always develop the capability to render even a super civil-defense program worthless, as Kahn himself admits. Why is this not as likely—and costly—an eventuality as that a disarmament system will be evaded?

Again, Kahn's highly praised "scenarios" and reports of "war games" [107] supposedly demonstrate that: (a) deterrence is extremely fragile; (b) therefore we must be well prepared for all sorts of wars. It would seem that preparing to disarm is just as clearly indicated by these findings—depending again on the specific political stance one adopts. [108] In fact, one might go so far as to make a more general point. If experience is indeed no longer a good guide in military affairs, that is as much an argument for choosing to disarm as it is for using admittedly limited analytical techniques to discriminate between alternative military strategies that remain both dangerous and unpredictable in their effects. The chief argument upon which Kahn relies—the paucity of our experience with nuclear war—does not of necessity lead to his particular conclusion.

Thus the result of Kahn's view of the Soviet Union and of international politics is that he is led to equate military security with security generally, the implication being that "they only understand force." Disarmament is seen as uniquely risky, not because it would be unstable —Kahn does not even attempt to make out a case that nuclear deterrence is stable—but because it is "not armament." This is to say that the risks of armament are *ipso facto* acceptable, and those of not-armament *ipso facto* unacceptable, because of the nature of the Soviet Union.

The sentence I have quoted from *On Thermonuclear War*, on page 85 above, therefore, should really read, "There seems to be little point in discussing the view that sees Soviet ambitions as potentially limited, and the Soviets as capable of being appealed to on grounds other than sheer force." If there is room for debate on that issue, Kahn—and in this he is no different from other deterrence theorists—does not contribute anything to that debate, nor attempt to distinguish between competing views with respect to the amount of scholarship or insight on which they are based. I should think that this amounts to a refusal to deal with one of the questions that arms policy discussion ought to be chiefly about. This refusal, which is implicitly made by most of Kahn's colleagues, has led one commentator to write:

> It has seemed to some of those who have listened to RAND experts at innumerable symposiums on arms control, disarmament and peace that, almost invariably, their attitude toward new schemes and proposals is negative, and that they exercise a conservative force on change. Those in the war-peace establishment who feel that deep change is needed regret that RAND cannot be pressured into service.[109]

My second, and more fundamental point about Kahn's formulation of the civil-defense problem is this: all these evasions of key questions appear, like so many of his other difficulties, to be inherent in the method of study that he used. Even had Kahn's analysis been truly rigorous it could not have produced anything more than arbitrary rigor, since the systems approach offers no criteria for discriminating among either the assumptions or values that one chooses. In fact, since Kahn has not been genuinely rigorous, not even that much has been accomplished. Is Kahn's lack of rigor idiosyncratic, or is it built into the very idea of applying "scientific method" to this kind of strategic problem?

On the basis of Kahn's example, it seems reasonable to conclude that where so great a part of the area of investigation ("political-military-strategic alternatives")[110] consists of political and other evaluative considerations, or is so far removed from practical human experience as to be insusceptible of "hard" analysis that does not import the hidden judgments and guesses of the analyst, those who hope to find any especially believable answers to the intellectual problems of our age in the results of systems analysis are whistling in the dark.

Although one hesitates to adopt the seemingly anti-intellectual stance of condemning the scientific approach to any kind of empirical material, one is here compelled to do so. Podhoretz' demand for studies of surrender that are as objective as studies of nuclear war must finally be taken as ironical. It is not merely that the idea of systems analysis offers no particular hope of dealing rigorously with the great policy questions inherent in deterrence studies; rather, one suspects that in this context the method of rigorous analysis may be inferior to informed and informal speculation. This is the case because the latter, more traditional approach to the study of policy emphasizes clear-headed, systematic thinking primarily about moral and political assumptions. Systems analysis, on the other hand, entails the focussing of attention on what is supposedly commensurable and calculable: which is precisely what is of secondary importance compared with the political and moral questions.

What good does it do to call in a team of experts if they share the same, mutually reinforcing bias, and trained incapacity to think seriously about fundamental issues? What good is expertness at quantification if there is nothing really to quantify? What help is clever model-building when one is only piling abstraction on abstraction? How useful is it to insist on one's knowledgeability in studying entire "systems," when the relevant "system" is actually an entire political and moral universe? No doubt thinking about politics cannot be as systematic or rigorous as thinking about the Circular Error Probable of a missile salvo—but as long as that is true, so much the worse for rigor.

VIII. Systems Analysis and National Policy: Conclusion

The above discussion, of course, should not be taken as asserting the general uselessness of systems analysis. Such an assertion would be egregious: any method is useful if it produces answers we feel we can use.

What is at stake here, rather, is the claim that our expectations ought to be higher when we are dealing with a systems analysis than with other forms of study: that is, the claim to be doing work that is peculiarly scientific. We have noted Kahn's reiterated references to having performed "scientific" studies. Those references are incorrect. Science is not merely a "method," as it is continually being referred to in the systems analysis text, *Analysis for Military Decisions*. It is rather the mating of a method and a subject that are relevant to each other. The method described by various systems analysts may indeed be relevant to the subject of, say, whether to build jet interceptors or jet bombers, or how to compare active air defense with other methods of defense or deterrence. [111] But as Charles J. Hitch, himself an economist who has engaged in the economic analysis of military operations, and who is presently Comptroller of the Department of Defense, has remarked, "the proportion of the relevant reality which we can represent by any such model or models in studying, say, a major foreign-policy decision, appears to be almost trivial." [112]

Thus we must reject the argument of Wohlstetter, the most sophisticated polemicist on behalf of systems analysis, that those who employ "the method of science" in "the analysis of political-military-strategic alternatives" are *ipso facto* more important as spokesmen on matters of strategy than those who do not:

In the letter that Bertrand Russell sent in 1955 to heads of state enclosing a call for what later became the Pugwash Conferences, he began: "I enclose a statement, signed by some of the most eminent scientific authorities on nuclear warfare." The signers were indeed without exception eminent scientists, but among the ten physicists, chemists and a mathematical logician who were included, not one to my knowledge had done any empirical study of military operations likely in a nuclear war.[113]

Indeed Russell's statement is hyperbole, but no more so than is the counterclaim of Wohlstetter and Kahn. The "method of science" has not been shown to be relevant to the study of our nuclear future, nor is there anything "empirical" about available studies of "nuclear war."

As for the chief *substantive* contribution of the application of systems analysis to matters of national policy, our conclusion must surely be implicit in what has been said so far. It is extremely difficult to justify the particular exotic nuclear strategies that have sprung out of Kahn's fertile mind and are now generally accepted as realistic options in the community of deterrence theorists. If we were not fairly sure that civil defense would work well, would we dare to think of invoking nuclear weapon strategies such as limited strategic nuclear war, controlled counterforce war, etc., to which the likeliest responses are either surrender or escalation to a higher level of nuclear destruction? Kahn himself, in his latest work, reveals that he doubts the efficacy of these strategies more than most deterrence theorists.[114] But he is always able to find a good word for "limited" nuclear strategies, and that good word is always dependent on the assumption of a workable civil-defense program.

What Kahn has produced is not scientific analysis but prophetic science fiction; unless it strikes our literary imagination it has neither more nor less merit than any other of its kind.[115] How unsystematic does a systems analysis have to be before we balk at taking such uncalculated risks with our fate on the basis of such a "rigorous" method?

I. The Contribution of Game Theory

ANOTHER major attempt to provide deterrence theory with the aura of "science," and one which is perhaps even more well-known among the general public, is that which supposedly involves the use of the theory of games of von Neumann and Morgenstern.[1] The exact relationship between game theory and deterrence theory is certainly much misunderstood, as many deterrence theorists have recently asserted.* In this chapter I shall therefore be making two related points: first, that where there has been misunderstanding it has often been the fault of deterrence theorists, rather than of their critics and the public; second, that often deterrence theorists have been all too well understood in the claims they have made for the relevance of game theory to their work.[3]

*Wohlstetter, for instance, has managed at one and the same time to insist both that deterrence theorists have not, as charged, made much use of game theory, and that it has been very useful to them. His article[2] reminds one of the apocryphal defense attorney's opening address to the jury: "Ladies and Gentlemen of the jury, the defense will prove that my client never saw this woman before; that in any event he did not attack her but she consented; and that furthermore he was temporarily deranged while under the influence of alcohol and thus unable to tell right from wrong or know the nature and consequences of his acts."

As with systems analysis, we must begin by making a distinction between proper and improper applications of game theory. The basic insight that game theory added to classical economic theory was that one cannot always merely attempt to maximize one's expected utilities by proceeding as though inert nature or an impersonal market arrangement is the only thing that stands in one's way. The universe in which one operates consists of other conscious actors, for whom the pursuit of *their* interests may entail the frustration of one's own. (Compare Wohlstetter's definition of systems analysis, above, p. 21). There is conflict; one has opponents; and they will make things difficult for one if they can. (Actually, game theory was not the first branch of economics to take note of consciously conflicting interests; but it represents the first attempt to create a general theory for describing conflict.) Furthermore, in the minimax theorem, game theory provided a specific (suggested) normative rule for taking the actions of conscious opponents into account. Namely, one asks what is the worst that one's opponent can do to one's self, and so defines one's own "best" course of action as the one that is the best defense against the opponent's expected (i.e., best) move; he, of course, is assumed to engage in the same kind of reasoning (and if he does not, so much the worse for him; he cannot gain more than one's own "minimaxing" permits him). As Bernard Brodie writes, "What matters is the spirit of game theory, the constant awareness that we will be dealing with an opponent who will counteract our moves and to whom we must in turn react." [4]

This description obviously might apply not just to economic behavior, but to any form of social behavior under conditions of conflicting interest. One such form of behavior has been perceived to be war between nations, and the academic strategists—by their own account—soon came to make the connection. They realized that, given their intuitive assessment of the problems posed by nuclear weapons, the conservative defensive posture of the minimax rule was particularly relevant. That is, a military strategy that depended on one's opponent's *not* doing his best against one's self was terribly inadequate, not only theoretically but practically, since his best could conceivably destroy one. Although some may be surprised that such a thought had not occurred to military men, that appears to have been the case. Thus, for example, the RAND study of overseas bases for SAC (referred to in the previous chapter) took its particular and noteworthy direction when the analysts found that SAC's plans were based on striking first, and that its performance would be seriously degraded if the Soviets inconveniently—and "rationally"—decided to maximize *their* expected utilities rather than ours by striking first in a crisis.

Clearly one cannot wish to quarrel with the importance for military strategy of such an insight. And if the strategists who first had the insight say that they were helped to it by the example of a theory that dealt abstractly with such situations, then one should not deny the usefulness of the theory to them.* Without doubt

---

*Actually, of course, military men had in the past sometimes avoided the simple blunder of ignoring the enemy's strategic calculations, although "It is amazing how little this simple conception of reciprocal response has characterized war plans in the past." According to Brodie, it was an infatuation with strategic air power that led military men to put on blinders of the particular kind the RAND study uncovered.[5]

the theory is extremely helpful both in suggesting new insights of this kind and in providing an abstract conceptual framework within which traditional concepts of conflict may be formalized and thus seen in a new theoretical light.[6]

But to say this much is not to say that knowledge about, or use of, game theory provides solutions to specific problems that would be unavailable to the non-game theorist;[7] nor is it to say that a statement about a policy problem that has been couched in game-theoretic terms is somehow more valid than one that is not. As we shall see, unfortunately both of these claims have often been implied by prominent deterrence theorists; and it is those implications, along with Kahn's use of systems analysis, that have given deterrence theory the appearance of an incipient "scientific" discipline.

II.   The Structure of Games and the Structure of Politics

Before we undertake an investigation of exactly what claims deterrence theorists have made for game theory in policy studies, it will be helpful to make some general comments about the logical structure of that theory. I shall not attempt here to repeat at length the many varied criticisms that have been made of game theory in its putative role as applied science—criticisms that are apparently accepted by deterrence theorists themselves.[8] Rather I shall outline a few key difficulties, consideration of which will make an evaluation of game theory–oriented deterrence studies easier. Basically, we want to ask whether (or how well) the axiomatic structure and deductive logic of the theory fit what we know, or think we know about international conflict; also, whether that structure and logic are themselves self-consistent.

The game-theoretic version of rationality includes among other, more complicated definitions (or rules) the requirement that the "players" (opponents) calculate both their values and the expected payoffs of the various strategies that are intended to realize those values (that is, each player has a "payoff function" that represents his "preferences"), and that each player, in addition to knowing the properties of the "game"—the formal structure of the conflict—knows perfectly the "payoff function" of the other as well as of himself. Furthermore, the players pursue in modified form the goal known as utility maximization; the preference for maximizing utilities defines the nature of their "rationality." (However, it should be repeated that one special version of utility maximization is particularly associated with game theory; the idea of minimax or what is also called "maximization-of-security-level.")[9] R. Duncan Luce and Harold Raiffa, authors of a standard text on game theory, have asserted that this rule of utility maximization is a tautology, implying only that the players prefer most whatever they prefer most.[10] But this particular postulate is not, as they suggest it is and as the last sentence might seem to suggest, a "weak" one (and thus not in need of criticism?). The point is that whatever choice one makes must be calculated from one's preferences, in a game. No doubt we can reason back from an individual's choices—any choices—and say tautologically that they must have been deduced from some "utility function" and are therefore "rational," even if they do not partake of maximization-of-security-level rationality. We cannot indulge in such *post hoc ergo propter hoc* thinking, however, if the utility function has been *previously specified* by the individual, as it is in the game theory universe, and he *then* does not follow its logic in making his final choice. If such behavior were "rational," there would be no "irrational" or non-rational behavior, and the concept of rationality would be a completely empty one. Luce and Raiffa to the contrary, therefore, this is a "strong" and not a "weak" assumption. Its strength can be seen not only when we try to imagine decision-makers following with rigorous fidelity a previously chosen logic that has dictated the choice of a deterrence strategy, but also when we try to imagine decision-makers coming to the initial choice of any strategy at all on the basis of game theory logic.

Such an act of imagination instantly leads us to the first point that must be made about this definition of rational behavior: it does not at first glance have any real-world relevance. Purely instrumental choice unhindered either by emotional or ideological blocks on the one hand, or by ignorance on the other, exists only in the abstract world of game theory. As Sidney Verba has noted, it is very unlikely that decision-makers can secure the "accurate information, correct evaluation, and consciousness of calculation" and "cool-headedness" that are required by rational means-end calculations. Among the sources of this unlikelihood, the following are basic: (1) The fact of "human frailty," which suggests that "the type of calculation required by the model for anything but the simplest choices is beyond the powers of any individual, group, or presently designed individual-computer system. There may be too many significant variables, inadequate information, variables that are not easily quantifiable, or decisional methods that are not advanced enough. . . . " (2) The frequent occurrence in human affairs of decision-making groups "that [make] no serious attempt to approximate the rationality model in [their] decision-making because of lack of commitment to such an approach. . . . " (3) The frequent lack of clear self-awareness of values, or presence of unresolvable value conflict. (4) The fact that values undergo change during a drawn-out decision-making process. (See below, pp. 108–11). (5) The fact that collective decision-making makes it impossible to arrive at an agreed ordering of goals or interpretation of available information. (See below, pp. 184–85). (6) The informal way in which information is actually acquired by decision-makers, resulting invariably in incompleteness of information. (7) The "interrelatedness of incremental decisions," [11] which so configure the decision-maker's environment that "a new policy will therefore tend to be not the best of all possible policies, but a relatively small variation on a present policy. . . . "[12]

Verba's estimate of the formal notion of rationality is shared by mathematical economists themselves. As Luce and Raiffa put it:

[W]hy does the mathematician not use the culled knowledge of human behavior found in psychology and sociology when formulating his assumptions? The answer is simply that, for the most part, this knowledge is not in a sufficiently precise form to be incorporated as assumptions in a mathematical model. Indeed, one hopes that the unrealistic assumptions and the resulting theory will lead to experiments designed in part to improve the descriptive character of the theory.[13]

Thus game-theoretic analysis quite obviously falsifies the manner in which decisions are often made in real-world political contexts. Conceivably this could be a minor criticism, however. Those deterrence theorists who invoke game theory for their purposes—none of whom, I assume, really believes that human behavior is ideally "rational"—might have in mind that in a situation of all-out nuclear war or the threat of it, the disparities between the different values involved are so immense, and the likeliest course of behavior for both sides so obvious, that one can assume the possibility of a fairly high level of "rational" behavior being achieved. This would be to say that the axiomatic structure of game theory has one real-world analogue in times of drastic international military crisis, if at no other times. But even if we for the moment make this heroic assumption, we soon find out that the assumption of rationality creates no greater a disparity between the game-theoretic universe and the real political world than do some other assumptions that are imbedded in game theory. We may see this by taking a close look at some examples of deterrence theorizing that have seemed to be strengthened by reference to game theory.

Perhaps the most striking instance occurs in Oskar Morgenstern's *The Question of National Defense*. Unlike some other deterrence theorists, Morgenstern has explicitly cast himself in the role of a Cassandra. Yet at a few key junctures it is extremely difficult to dissociate prophecy from theory in his work on defense policy, and not merely because of his association with von Neumann. Thus in *The Question of National Defense* we come across the following at a crucial point in the argument:

The parallelism of these efforts with what goes on in games such as poker is apparent. One should therefore expect that an understanding of these games would be helpful. This is the domain of the mathematical theory of games of strategy. It has, indeed, produced rules of behavior which are directly applicable to military problems of the kind outlined here. We shall have opportunity to draw at least one fundamental lesson later . . . (cf., p. 78). The important point to make at this juncture is that each side will have to choose that strategy which is optimal for him in the sense that it is his best action no matter what the other side can do to hurt him.[14]

If the reader then turns to p. 78, for the "fundamental lesson" drawn from the theory of games, he will discover this:

[The principle that in view of modern technology it is in the interest of the United States for Russia to have an invulnerable retaliatory force and vice versa] sounds paradoxical. It is, however, *possible to give a rigorous proof*. The argument is complicated and difficult; it makes use of notions of the mathematical theory of games of strategy. . . .

Leaving these statements aside, we can argue on an intuitive basis. . . .

In three other places in the text, each involving some key point about the nature and feasibility of deterrence, Morgenstern states the relevance of game theory in almost identical language.[15] The whole is reinforced by an article in the *Sunday Times* Magazine Section entitled "Cold War Is Cold Poker," in which Morgenstern issues a popularized clarion call for more familiarity by Americans with "games" of strategy.[16]

It is thus hardly accidental that if one mentions Morgenstern in casual conversation, one often finds him identified as the man who has helped provide a "theoretical" foundation for an optimal American defense policy. Perhaps this is not wholly Morgenstern's doing, as he cannot help his permanent association in educated minds with the idea of game theory. But if he had intended to discourage excessive reliance by his readers on such a notion of what he is proposing, he would certainly have done well at all costs to avoid the language I have quoted. And in fact it does not seem as though he wished to produce any other result, really: his book opens with the prefatory remark that "This book is based on a long and profound involvement with defense problems, ranging from the mathematical theory of strategy to the logistics of supply. . . . "[17] One perhaps cannot tax Morgenstern with an explicit assertion that these two problem-solving techniques bear the same kind of relation to choice-making in national defense policy, but the implication is certainly there. The same kind of association between grand strategy and scientific theory that Kahn has postulated for systems analysis is claimed for game theory too.

And yet, when we ask what a game-theoretic analysis can actually accomplish for deterrence theory, a different picture emerges. We may bring this true picture into sharp focus by asking what exactly is being claimed.

The key word in Morgenstern's discussion is "invulnerability." If by his reference to invulnerability Morgenstern meant that one should adopt the strategy which assures that one will be unhurtable, the quoted statement would merely be trivial. But Morgenstern does not mean to be trivial nor to suggest that we need game theory to tell us to be stronger than our opponents in every possible way. What Morgenstern *does* mean to say, as his discussion of "The Oceanic System" makes clear, is that the "best" strategy for a nation is the one which makes an attack on that nation most undesirable—that is, which enhances its *retaliatory capability*.

Morgenstern is not alone in associating this proposition with game theory. Although other analysts are more subtle than he, several of them have also made exactly the same kind of argument. Thomas Schelling has written, in his *The Strategy of Conflict*, an essay on "The Reciprocal Fear of Surprise Attack" and a following essay on "Surprise Attack and Disarmament." [18] The first is purely theoretical, the second entirely policy-oriented. The subject of each is the same, though: the perils of a hostility system that is surprise-prone because of the vulnerability of one or both of the parties involved. In fact, one can see Schelling as giving, through an intensive study of different kinds of game situations, the "help" Morgenstern promised, that will show invulnerability to be the "best" posture in certain "games" of strategy. The argument of the theoretical essay is expressed in the statement that "The players may be driven . . . to rely on arrangements that either observably blunt their own capacity for surprise or observably improve their own and each other's [warning system reliability]." [19] This argument is restated in the policy chapter to put the case for preferring deterrence plus arms control to general and complete disarmament; as Schelling asks rhetorically: "Should we instead recognize measures to safeguard against surprise attack [not as first steps toward disarmament but as] an implicit acceptance of 'mutual deterrence' as the best source of military stability we are likely to find. . . ?" [20] From a game-theoretic analysis, then, we generate the conclusion that invulnerability is the best posture we can buy, and may even (as Schelling points out) require increasing our participation in the arms race in order to produce greater "stability." [21]

Similarly Daniel Ellsberg (now an official in the Department of Defense and a highly respected deterrence theorist) has written a theoretical paper on deterrence, published originally by RAND.[22] The conclusion of this paper, to the extent that there is one, is that measures which simply enhance our first-strike capability contrast poorly with measures "for reducing the vulnerability of the retaliatory force";[23] the latter reduce the value to the Soviets of striking first as opposed to waiting for our first strike. This conclusion is presented, however, through a discussion couched almost wholly in game-theoretic terminology, replete with matrices, utility function, payoff structures, etc. According to Ellsberg, he is not trying "to define a 'game' corresponding to this schema, though the format might suggest that interpretation. . . . " But clearly a discussion carried on entirely in terms of a mathematized and deductively axiomatic probability-utility calculation makes such an interpretation unavoidable, let alone "suggests" it.[24]

As for Ellsberg's view of the usefulness of his paper, it is clear that, as stated by the editor of a volume in which the paper appears: "The model is not intended to be rigorous but does provide a useful conceptual schema for analysis." [25] Morgenstern and Schelling might have written the same. Ellsberg adds, moreover, that his discussion "may represent a minimum framework which is an advance over that implicit in much current discussion," which, like Wohlstetter and Knorr, he too scorns: "Unfortunately, there has been a historical tendency on the part of policy-makers to reject the aid of abstract frameworks of the present sort on the grounds that they are 'too simplistic,' and then to make practical decisions on the basis of much cruder, implicit models." [26]

At a lower level of generalization, we note the related comments of Charles Hitch himself on the subject of defense against nuclear attack. "Suppose," Hitch asks, "you have your defenses deployed as well as you can. Now you get more defenses. How do you deploy them?" His answer is prefaced by the remark that his intuition at first told him that you would deploy the additional defenses to protect additional targets, but "game theory says no. You use additional defenses mainly to increase the defense of targets already defended." [27] In context, as we shall see, it is fairly clear that Hitch is talking about defense against nuclear attacks, and his assumption appears to be that one's "most valuable targets"—by which he clearly means chiefly weapons sites—should be as heavily defended as possible. Once more, then, "game theory" tells us to emphasize retaliatory capability.

And yet, despite all this intellectual fire-power—which is clearly the way semi-informed readers must see it—one is forced to the conclusion that the admittedly important proposition about invulnerability and retaliation is not "proven" or "shown" in any way by game theory. Let us assume for the moment (an assumption I shall shortly criticize) that somehow a calculation of our values can be made: that we can have some fairly rigorous knowledge of the choice relevant Americans—and Russians, etc.—would make between surrender and destruction, war and peace, freedom and subjugation, and the various incremental steps toward any of these ends that can take place along the way. We could then talk seriously about our "utilities," and we would be able to discriminate rigorously among various possible outcomes. Let us go on to imagine that for a given situation—say, defense against a potential attack on the continental United States—there are three alternative strategies available to the United States. Given all the information that must need go into such a calculation, we arrive at a description of the "game," in which the strategy that promises to maximize our security level is one of the variants of the strategy of deterrence, as Morgenstern, Schelling, and Ellsberg conceive it.

Have we now demonstrated that deterrence (i.e., maintenance of an "invulnerable" second-strike posture) is our "best" strategy? No, we have not. What we have demonstrated is merely that given certain *conditional* values for all possible (non-negligible) outcomes of the U.S.-U.S.S.R. conflict (i.e., our own best estimates of the gains or losses to us and them from each conditional outcome), a certain strategy is "best." And what a limited meaning this statement turns out to have when we view it in the light of the nature of game theory.

To begin with, let us consider the nature of strategic choice. A strategy, put simply, is a set of rules for making a choice among a series of alternatives, or of discrete choices among alternatives, where there is uncertainty about what conditions will be like when the decisions must be made. Game theory, then, is the theory by which we arrive at appropriate rules; if a game-theoretic analysis is complete, it will provide us with the rules for an appropriate response to every conceivable non-trivial alternative set of circumstances.[28] A decision consisting of the adoption of a strategy always contains a statement of the type: *if* he is going to do such and such, *then* I ought to do such and such. Strategies are therefore sets of *contingent* choices. An operational, or tactical choice, by contrast,[29] is the kind of choice we make in analyzing the circumstances a strategy is supposed to meet, in order that we may know how to implement the strategy. (Another way of putting this is to say that a strategy is merely a verbal instruction to one's self; an operational choice gives the verbal instruction physical content.) A policy, finally, is a choice we initially make among values, or purposes: among, that is, the ends to be sought by means of appropriate strategies and tactics. Thus, in theory one may decide as a matter of policy to keep the lands of Southeast Asia free from Communist hegemony at whatever cost; a strategy is then necessary to accomplish this end. One may then adopt, say, a "limited war strategy," which tells one that in certain circumstances one will (or will not) enter a limited war situation to do this. The use of strategic bombing of North Vietnam then, may be a concrete operation shown by analysis to be necessary for the successful carrying out of the strategy.

In the form I have so far chosen to clarify these distinctions, the choice of an end itself, the choice of an appropriate strategy, and the choice of concrete means to implement the strategy, are each presumably a different and separate kind of decision. However, what the example should make obvious is that, as Charles Linblom among others has cogently argued, these various types of choices are often if not always inextricably intermingled.[30] The policy of "containment" itself implies a strategy, and indeed might not even be adopted in the absence of assurances that a strategy appropriate to its implementation existed. In turn, what looks like a strategy may in another perspective really be a policy; the strategy of limited war may originally commend itself in the form of a policy statement that the nation should not engage in unlimited wars except to defend its own substance. And most important, the tactic of, say, strategic bombing will in some contexts quite probably be seen by either ourselves or others as symbolizing, or eventually even compelling the independent adoption of a new strategy or a new policy; it may, that is, seem to imply the statement of a national purpose (say, "victory") hitherto unstated, rather than the mere preference for a "technique." These terms, then, can be distinguished only formally: "technical" problems of procedure cannot be separated from problems of strategic analysis, nor both from problems of political evaluation.

Furthermore, to the extent that in politics what seem to be strategic or tactical choices always involve policy considerations, the game theorist as decision-maker is faced with an additional problem. He would have to be prepared to supply not only an evaluative analysis of possible outcomes, but also a means of assessing the political values that, if they change, will change the utility of the different possible outcomes to us—and vice-versa! This would not be necessary if the following conditions obtained: (1) we knew that the performance capabilities and the behavioral modes of ourselves and our opponents would not change over time; (2) we had in hand some kind of quantified *and* unvarying national value estimate, a sort of operational version of the Preamble to the Constitution. But both of these conditions are simply antiempirical.[31]

The problem is not merely that we cannot at present quantify our values but, more important, that we cannot do it as dynamically has the interplay between strategy, policy, and tactics demands. Game theory is based on a *static* representation of human behavior. The following statement by von Neumann and Morgenstern makes this quite clear:

> We repeat most emphatically that our theory is thoroughly static. A dynamic theory would unquestionably be more complete and therefore preferable. But there is ample evidence from other branches of science that it is futile to try to build one as long as the static side is not thoroughly understood.[32]

Whatever may come about in the future, there is certainly not yet a dynamic game theory. But then, how can the theory be used to describe the real world in any way? In the real world, there is not an unrelated mass of single-shot "games," but rather many *sequences* of events, which may or may not be unrelated, and each of which may or may not be best described as one multiple-play game or many single-play games. Whenever there are separate sequential groups of events that may be described as "games" but are non-autonomous; or whenever in one game sequence later plays are non-autonomous (with regard to earlier plays), and consequently the potential utilities and payoffs cannot be stated precisely *ab initio*, then a static theory is irrelevant for practical purposes. And the crucial point is that most important real world events are indeed always dynamically structured in the sense that one cannot judge (impute payoffs to) the results of a given situation without knowing—often only by using hindsight—how it affected, and was affected by, other situations of whose existence one may not previously even have been aware. Changing expectations modify values, and changing values modify expectations; short-run results modify the assessment of long-run results. To reify one set of conditional outcomes is to hide this truth from ourselves.[33]

Thus, game theory tells us how to theorize about an extended game but not how to recognize whether we are in one.[34] For example, how does one know that a single game, or even an extensive game, is not really part of a more extensive game, for which the optimal strategy over-all is not at all the same as the optimal strategy for each "game" that composes it?[35] The limited-war game in Vietnam or the Formosa Straits may be part of theU.S.-China deterrence game ultimately; in addition, these may all be part of the U.S.-U.S.S.R. deterrence game, and even part of limited-war games in say Berlin or Cuba. Then again perhaps not. Who can really tell? One would have to be a prophet not only about the evolution of events but of one's own and one's opponents' values to resolve this question. Similarly, the deterrence game may be part of a larger world-peace versus world-war game, or democracy versus communism game; this might suggest to us entirely different estimates of the expected payoff of a given deterrence strategy if we ever thought, as we may in the future think (when it will be too late?) to put the question that way. Furthermore, all these may ultimately be conceived of as part of a human race versus nature game. Which of these is the case we may not find out until we are well into the game (which game?)—and what our values *really* are will of course depend on which game we recognize ourselves as being in. And to mention only briefly a point I shall advert to at length later on, in the real world a given choice may have the political effect of freezing out options that in theory are supposed to be available as a corollary of that choice. Often we need to be extremely lucky to know what the effect of a choice on ourselves will be even the day after we make it —let alone months and years in the future.

It is evident that this is precisely the point that renders Morgenstern's and Schelling's claim and Ellsberg's example meaningless. From what I have said about the static's quality of game theory, it follows that the statement about invulnerability's being the best strategic posture can be true only at a single decision-point—that is, in a single crisis. How far in the future is that crisis to be? *Our* values, and *our* estimates of their values, and *their* estimates of *our* values, may have changed by then (whenever "then" is). Indeed, the adoption of the recommended strategy might be one of the events that leads to a change in the conditional values! Furthermore, we have also seen that the particular kind of U.S.-U.S.S.R. conflict, which the analysts tend to deal with and for which deterrence is supposedly a feasible strategy, may be part of another "game" entirely—a three player, U.S.-U.S.S.R.-China game—and the prospects of maximizing our "security level" in this game may be negatively affected by the adoption of the deterrence strategy for our "military conflict" game; thus, Arthur L. Burns has written that "some of the moves, both bilateral and unilateral, that reduce the attractions of nuclear warfare for the two Super-powers have the unintended consequence of attracting more members into the nuclear club."[36] Within the framework of a single game's matrix, how can we possibly assess the significance of such an eventuality?

Finally, as Karl Deutsch has pointed out, capabilities are not constant but changing.[37] Thus, returning to our other point about the lack of a clearcut demarcation between policy, strategy, and tactics, we see that changes in available tactics as well as changes in policy might also change our estimate of the desirability of a given strategy.

Of course, all this is hypothetical (though no more so than the uses of game theory that we are discussing). But if we analyze the specific proposals involved, these criticisms have a direct bearing. Concretely, the argument for additional increments of "invulnerability" is hedged in by several limiting conditions. On the one hand, "invulnerability" may entail mere deterrence and thus conflict with other military goals, such as "defense," damage-limitation "if deterrence fails," etc. (This is exactly the gravamen of the change that Kahn, Glenn Snyder, and others have made against the version of deterrence theory that is associated with Morgenstern.) On the other hand, the addition of new increments of military strength of *any* kind may interfere—or have interfered—with the attainment of non-military goals, such as general disarmament (e.g., a "soft" bomber base in Turkey is a lot easier to disarm than a "hard" missile site buried somewhere under the Rocky Mountains).

Superficially, we could avoid this logical problem. We could assume that American and Soviet leaders care almost entirely for the value of protecting our (their) retaliatory capability, and hardly at all for the distinct values of, say, being able to "roll back" the "Iron Curtain" (Western "Imperialists"), or doing everything possible to bring about disarmament, etc. But this would be to say that deterrence is the best strategy if one's

chief value is and always will be to deter! No doubt—
but one does not need the help of game theory to arrive at
this useful conclusion.

There is still further reason for being totally skeptical
about these examples of reliance on game theory. In addition to telling us merely that if we want to deter we
should deter, arguments such as these also depend on an
unstated and controversial assumption about the importance of conscious goal-directed behavior in real life.

We begin by observing that, once more, the argument
we are dealing with rests on the "delicate balance of terror" thesis. Ellsberg writes (and clearly Morgenstern
and Schelling would agree with him) that "Perhaps the
most significant aspect of the current [i.e., 1960] strategic
balance is that, under typical conditions of technology and
posture [the value of a strike-first policy is greater than
the value of a strike-second policy to the Soviet Union]."[38]
Therefore, Ellsberg argues, we should decrease the value
to the U.S.S.R. of a strike-first policy (by opting for invulnerability) and increase the value to it of a strike-second
policy (by correlatively putting our own forces in a
strike-second posture). The unstated assumption in this
argument, which is identical with the one Schelling
makes in both his theoretical and policy discussions, is
that there already is (was) a significant (non-negligible)
value in a strike-first policy for the Soviet Union.

But why should we think this to be the case? I can
imagine four reasons: (No. 1) the Soviets want to destroy us if they can, independently of our own behavior
(short of "surrendering" to them). (No. 2) The Soviets
want to destroy us because they think we want to destroy
them. (No. 3) The Soviets ought to want to destroy us
because *we do* want to destroy them. (No. 4) The Soviets

have to assume that we may want to destroy them as long as we have the kind of force posture that looks aggressive; assuming this, their logic must dictate to them a readiness to "go first."

I have no idea which of these assumptions deterrence theorists actually made—which statement is in itself a commentary on their supposedly "clarifying" use of game theory. What we might call the Assumption of *Their* Malevolence (No. 1) is unsupported by any evidence that any deterrence theorist has to offer. The Assumption of Suspicion (No. 2) does not clearly entail a strategy of *deterrence* as compared with a strategy of negotiated disarmament or what are called "unilateral initiatives" by us.[39] Indeed, in this context further militarization of any kind might well have negative effects. The Assumption of *Our* Malevolence (No. 3) is quite obviously not believed in by any deterrence theorist.

As for the Assumption of Reciprocal Fear (No. 4),[40] I am under the impression that some writers such as Schelling believe it to be indicated by the structure of game theory itself. But it is not; rather it is imported from outside. This is so because there is no such thing as a deployment that inherently "looks aggressive." The appearance of aggression-proneness depends on expectations; the insistence that even with a "soft," apparently first-strike posture we could not seem non-aggressive to sensible opponents is sheer dogma, as is insistence on the corollary notion that a second-strike posture *doesn't* look aggressive. Of course in a crisis, as Wohlstetter argues, appearances must be expected to change for the worse and we might not be able to help seeming aggressive, or somehow destructive of Soviet values.[41] But still that does not necessarily indicate a strategy of deterrence (i.e., the development of a "better" second-strike posture) for us.

The problem is one of the autonomous probability of events—that is, the probability that an event will occur no matter what we consciously do about it: a condition that may be true even of events we think of as highly susceptible to rational control.* However, because of its antiempirical assumptions of rationality and perfect knowledge, and because of its static character, game theory cannot take this aspect of real life into account. The basic concept of the theory, which can be seen in the rules mentioned above, is that in a "game" of strategy

---

*In formal game-theoretic terms, "autonomous probability" has no real meaning since the phrase could be taken to stand only for an area of ignorance about an opponent's conditional values, and the formal theory does not allow for such ignorance. We are talking about the real world, however, in which there is ignorance, and "hedges" for ignorance must be made. To refer to the specific case discussed immediately below, there is a (subjectively estimated) probability that the Soviets have adopted a *decision* rule (cf., Luce and Raiffa, *Games and Decisions*, Ch. 13) which they will follow generally regardless of the nature of—conditional outcomes expected from—the specific conflict situation (e.g., attack if attacked, never attack, attack only if provoked as much as x3 on a provocation scale of x10, etc.). This is like saying that Column has decided prior to the playing of a particular game that he will always choose strategy b3 no matter what Row's choices turn out to be (over a broad range of possible outcomes), or will always choose the column that contains the highest payoff for him, or the lowest for Row, etc.

Alternatively, and perhaps even more importantly, there is also a (subjectively estimated) probability that the Soviets will not be able to follow through on their strategic intentions—e.g., will decide not to attack and then attack, or vice-versa; will not follow through on a known decision rule; etc. This very strong possibility in the real world is also not taken into account in formal game theory.

The analysis which follows should be considered in conjunction with the discussion contained in this footnote.

intentions are directly translated into results; the only factor influencing the translation is the strength of a given intention—i.e., the utility to us of a given outcome—compared with the strength of the remainder of our own and our opponent's intentions. But there is no reason to believe that intentions always or even usually produce results in real life (see the note above).

I shall have more to say later about the methodological importance of the possibility that events have an autonomous probability of taking place regardless of what conscious opponents do. Suffice it to say here that in the face of centuries of man's apparent incapacity to control the course of his affairs, the assumption that conflict is rationally ordered, while it may be extremely useful for heuristic purposes of theory-building, is in the context of politics sheer mysticism.

Abstractly, our intentions may not be taken into account by our opponent in his formulation of a rule of choice. Or he may formulate such a rule based on a complete misinterpretation of our future intentions, or based on his intentions in another "game" that are not affected by what we do, except grossly; we may do the same of course. Similarly, he may not be able to translate his intentions into results, nor may we: political constraints generated prior to the particular conflict may warp intended actions from the desired effect.

Concretely, there is a certain autonomous probability that the Soviets (or, someday, the Chinese) will be deterred, or will not want nuclear war, no matter what choice we make over a certain range of choices available to us. Fear of world opinion; their own internal restraints; and simple unwillingness to take a chance on attacking even "soft" nuclear forces are among the elements that might produce this likelihood. At the same time, there is a certain autonomous probability that war —i.e., breakdown in the U.S.-U.S.S.R.-China conflict structure—will come at any state of weapon deployment. Therefore, our judgment of whether the Assumption of Reciprocal Fear compels the adoption of a given strategy (by this I mean both the use of the strategy itself and the public actions involved in adopting it) is incomplete without an estimate as to how the choice will affect those two probability levels. For example, if we felt that the autonomous probability of nuclear war in the cold war era was high, and that a massive increase in our second-strike strength would not decrease this probability, then even though such a strategy seemed the "best" counter strategy to the Soviets' most preferred strategy, we might not (in 1960, say) adopt it. We might prefer (have preferred) to stay at the lowest level of armament consistent with our not being absolutely terrified, and pressed for some kind of disarmament.

That is, we are "hedging" because of our ignorance of our opponents' intentions (and his of ours).[42] What is the best hedge is open to question. If the U.S.S.R. has an information-acquisition rule that all increments of nuclear armaments to us are indications of hostile action,[43] then Schelling's preference for higher levels of missile deployment is self-defeating, as it is also if they have a (secret) decision-rule against first use, or if disarmament is their preferred strategy under any circumstances.

Whether they are in fact likely to have any such rules, or are instead likely to be "aggression-prone," is a matter to be decided by educated guesswork based on a sober, *political* analysis of Soviet intentions (and our own, since we may or may not provoke them by our actions). Sober political analysis is exactly what is not contributed by airy, speculative analyses based on "insights" derived from game theory. Like systems analysis, game theory leads us astray by focusing our attention on secondary problems that happen to be theoretically calculable.

III. *Pseudo-Quantification*

So far we have been considering several deterrence theory formulations as instances of the application of game theory's broad insights and over-all approach to decision-making. There are also deterrence theorists who have used, or pretended to use game theory more directly, by constructing specific problems and demonstrating how their solution indicates the choice of a certain deterrence strategy.

For example, Morton Kaplan has presented his only purely theoretical analysis of deterrence in an article entitled "The Calculus of Nuclear Deterrence."[44] The "calculus" involved is based roughly on the concepts of game theory, or at least on the kind of formal discussion of strategic choice that has developed under the general aegis of the theory of games. The reader is warned by Kaplan that his intention is only heuristic, that his "model" of international conflict is not a rigorous one, and that some major simplifications have been made in developing it. This warning having been issued, Kaplan then goes on to create, analyze, resolve and discuss a "game," the conclusion of which is that given a "game" with the values and payoffs Kaplan has assigned, the strategy of limited nuclear reprisals may very likely be the most effective threat for countering a massive attack on Western Europe. One can, perhaps, on reading through this article keep in mind that Kaplan's calculus is only meant to demonstrate a heuristic model, which according to Kaplan himself has certain definite limitations as a source of data for policy-makers; one can perhaps also keep in mind that the values and probabilities with which he fills in the matrix boxes of his calculus have been made up by Kaplan out of whole cloth. But when one on further investigation finds that Kaplan is the author of at least three independent articles that contain a wholehearted advocacy of precisely that strategy of limited nuclear reprisal, it becomes very difficult to make any distinction at all between Kaplan's theory and Kaplan's advocacy.[45]*

In a slightly different fashion, Glenn Snyder, another writer well-known in this area, mixes abstract theory with practical application. His major work, *Deterrence and Defense,* is subtitled "Toward a Theory of National Security." Three-quarters of the book, approximately, is devoted to a very *un*theoretical discussion of the problem areas of American defense policy: preventing surprise attack, vitalizing NATO, defending the "gray areas," etc.

*This difficulty is heightened by the fact that in a Princeton Center of International Studies Research Monograph, *Some Problems in the Strategic Analysis of International Politics,*[46] which does not deal specifically with deterrence theory, Kaplan engages in much the same process, mingling an essay that is completely game-theoretical in substance and style with an excellent discussion of some of the problems of what might be called military diplomacy. The whole effect of this method is to accomplish an intertwining of game theory and international conflict analysis; and since Kaplan's version of the latter contains many references bearing on the problem of deterrence, and again of limited nuclear retaliation, the idea that that particular subject is peculiarly clarified by reference to game theory is once again reinforced.

The first chapter, by contrast, is set forth under the heading, "Deterrence and Defense: A Theoretical Introduction." Snyder's purpose in this introduction is to show that "deterrence" and "defense" represent different and often mutually exclusive values—the value of being able to prevent attack and the value of being able to counter it effectively—and that in providing for either of these values through the development or deployment of a given weapons system one necessarily foregoes the opportunity to use the expended resources in forwarding the other of those values. At the same time, however, he surrounds this point with a whole battery of matrices such as those used by Kaplan, (incorrect) explanations of "the principle of mathematical expectation,"[47] and other examples of "rational" decision-making discussed in the context of the formal theory of strategy. The idea appears to be that such choices can be rational—and thus one's defense strategy as well. Snyder's subtitle makes clear that he hopes to see the concept of national security considered on such a basis. Similarly, in the last chapter Snyder discusses problems of communication and tacit bargaining with the "enemy," and attempts to develop a theoretical framework for analyzing and choosing among the various practices that are ordinarily called "diplomacy." Here too, Snyder is concerned with the problem of what "moves" are "rational" in the strategic context.

The net effect of these two parts of *Deterrence and Defense* is to surround and infuse the discussion of substantive problems with the notion that formally "rational" solutions to them can not only be found but chosen by policy-makers. The whole purpose of these chapters seems to be to convey the idea that in some way a formal theory of rationality, of the kind advanced in the work of game theorists and those doing related work in the area of "rational" strategy will lend considerable aid to the planner or public-spirited citizen who wishes to deal intelligently with the immediate problems confronting NATO or the Strategic Air Command. Purposeful or not, that is indubitably the notion that is conveyed. Finally, when one is prepared for thinking about strategy in these terms, one comes across in Snyder's concluding chapter a "mathematical example" concerning defense in Western Europe. It is interesting to read Snyder's Kaplan-like assertion that the example "is intended only to illustrate the essential logic and involves no commitment either to the numbers or the results."[48] However, when one discovers that Snyder's game matrices *inter alia* show that massive retaliation would be a "cheaper" response to a surprise attack on the U.S. than would "no response"; that buying more ICBM's would increase the probability of peace (i.e., "no attack" by the U.S.S.R.) and that buying more limited-war capability would be even better; and when one further remembers that Snyder has implicitly and explicitly made all these points earlier in his text,[49] then one must be forgiven for thinking that Snyder's lack of "commitment" to his results is, like Kaplan's, somewhat incomplete.

Such "examples" accomplish a two-fold purpose. First, simply by force of being an "example" the calculation makes certain assertions. One of Snyder's matrices, for instance, reads as follows (this is the limited-war capability matrix, in which the numbers represent—on what scale only Snyder knows—costs to the U.S. of different responses to different actions by the U.S.S.R.).

		U.S.S.R.	
	No Attack	Nuclear attack on U.S.	Ground attack on W. Europe
No response	0*	−500	−100
Massive U.S. retaliation	0	−400	−400
Ground Force Defense	0	0	−30
Probabilities	.80	.10	.10
Expected cost	0	−40	−3 = −43

(U.S. label appears at left between "Massive U.S. retaliation" and "Ground Force Defense" rows)

The whole point of assigning utility numbers to such "values" can only be to convey the impression, first, that these problems actually are calculable; and second, that the risks under discussion really are worth taking. Thus, for example, when Snyder calls the imaginary "loss" to the United States if it fails to respond to a Soviet nuclear attack on the U.S. −500, while calling the cost of "no response" to a ground attack on Western Europe only −100, he is saying that there is a quantifiable relation

*The zeros do not represent expected values, or the example would be absurd. Rather they represent costlessness—Snyder is only considering comparative costs in this example, and thus the example is not really a game-theoretic one. But game theory is the obvious and intended referent for his analytic technique.

from the American perspective between destruction in a nuclear war and the "loss" of Western Europe to Communism.[50] The former is only five times "as bad" (whatever that can conceivably mean) as the latter, which is to say that in some circumstances the difference would be negligible. The result is implicitly and appreciably to increase the favorability of our estimate of adopting strategies in which the United States takes a serious chance of incurring destruction: that is, strategies that propose to defend Western Europe by greater-than-conventional means. Similarly, Kaplan's quantification of the costs and gains of limited nuclear retaliation suggests that these risks too are easily commensurable. Although von Neumann and Morgenstern do not even faintly suggest that index numbers can be constructed for this kind of value, the deterrence theorists blithely proceed to engage in this kind of pseudo-quantification.*

---

*The Von Neumann-Morgenstern utility index does provide a theoretical means of arriving at a numerical utility scale for the individual.[51] But that such a scale could have any meaning for a nation, or that it yet has any practical use in the political realm, is still a dream. No game theorist, indeed, has made a claim stronger than von Neumann and Morgenstern's summary statement about the uses of their index—a statement which with regard to non-monetary calculation is virtually a disclaimer: "How real this possibility [of numerical measurement of the utilities of the individual] is, both for individuals and for organizations, seems to be an extremely interesting question, but it is a question of fact. It certainly deserves further study. . . . At any rate . . . [if] the individual's preferences are all comparable, then we can . . . obtain a (uniquely defined) numerical utility. . . . All this becomes, of course, pointless for the entrepreneur who can calculate in terms of (monetary) costs and profits."[52] Of course, policy-makers undoubtedly do assign utility rankings to their own and others' motives, somehow, else they could never arrive at decisions.[53] The point is simply that they do not do so in accordance with the mathematical logic of the economist: they stab in the dark.

If, on the other hand, we were to take such "values" as the nation, our culture, etc., more seriously, we might *never* be able to justify by calculation a policy that created a serious risk of incurring their destruction. Of course, it might be that, in reality, our instinct would be to value our obligation to Western Europe more highly than our obligation to ourselves. But then we would have to further decide how we valued a Europe that had been the scene of war, as against a Europe that had been "conquered" by Communism, as against the risk of nuclear war, etc. The point is that to call the process of arriving at such judgments "calculation" is merely to ratify with spurious authority the decision to do what one's prejudices lead one instinctively to want to do. To assert commensurability and calculability where they are entirely lacking is to make a hidden value judgment of the most egregious kind.*

The other purpose accomplished by these "examples" is equally objectionable. Analyses of such matrices falsely assert, again *sub silentio,* the static quality of the events we have to deal with in politics—as indeed they must, given the nature of game theory. For the calculations concern (and can only concern) single decision-making moments—and in the real world as we have said, there are no (or few) single decision-making moments. Where did the assigned "values" come from? What concatenation of events, what prior choice among competing strat-

---

*Similarly, one suspects that policy-makers themselves, even when they seem to have engaged in something resembling a process of calculation, will often merely have found a persuasive way of expressing their inmost prejudices (and in many cases it will be themselves they are trying to persuade, not simply those who are questioning their decisions).

egies produced them? Furthermore, since the "game" we are in does not end, as we have seen, with this "decision," what effect do we expect it to have on the future utilities of future outcomes in different games? The questions cannot be answered, of course: because the examples are meaningless.

IV. The Uses of Tautology

In fact, we have really not been talking about "examples" of strategic choice at all, since there is no reason to believe that strategic choices will ever be made in this way (and no reason to believe that if they are made in this way, they are anything but inane). All that a reference to game theory can possibly do is provide an algebraical illustration of a verbal argument that one has already made. The illustration can be no better than the verbal argument; in most of the cases I have mentioned it is actually worse.*

In Ellsberg's paper, for instance, the verbal case for finite deterrence is no less convincing than such arguments usually are. But the "game" representation is extremely poor. The matrix alternatives he shows are "Wait (and strike second if struck)" and "Strike (first)." In reality, though, given his own argument the likeliest alternatives would be that both sides wait or that both strike "first" simultaneously—an option not described in his matrix. Furthermore, the matrix is in any event theoretically worthless in that "Wait" cannot possibly be a "move" in a game: all moves are made

*Not in Morgenstern's case, for his references to game theory are pure hyperbole.

simultaneously and in ignorance of the opponent's "move," so what could one possibly be "waiting" for?

As for Kaplan and Snyder, they make the relatively simple argument for multiple options look even more questionable than it is by giving assigned values for "Europe," "U.S.," etc., that are, to put it mildly, eccentric. And Hitch, whose reference to game theory I have not previously discussed, and who of all these writers ought most to know better, is the worst of all. A strong case for concentration of defense could be made out verbally—if one were talking about protecting prime targets, which are not yet well protected, and if the value to the potential attacker of the already protected targets was in every case higher than the value of any as yet unprotected target. That is, Hitch's statement makes sense only on the extremely dubious assumption that we are chiefly protecting our retaliatory force, which is not yet satisfactorily protected, *and* which requires all our additional defenses to be satisfactorily protected, *and* which we have no reason to doubt is an attacker's sole target until it is completely destroyed.*

But then—and this is a point that finally summarizes our previous remarks—if we know we are making all these assumptions, game theory has not actually shown us anything at all. Our assumptions have dictated our behavior; game theory has merely provided us with a mathematical technique for explicating the meaning to us of our assumptions (which will only be necessary if

---

*To put that point another way, Hitch's conclusion holds only if the attacker will destroy his primary target before he devotes *any* resources to destroying his secondary target, etc.

the calculations are complicated). And if we have made bad assumptions, as Hitch appears to have done with a vengeance—e.g., does "defense" really have *no* diminishing utility at the margin?—then even game theory cannot save us from error. On the contrary, it merely helps us hide our errors from the untutored.

Logicians say that from an empirically false premise any conclusion follows. To use an antiempirical theory—which is how we must describe game theory in the context of international relations—doubles one's chances for arriving at "any conclusion." For one can follow rigorously the premises of the theory; or one can import one's own unverified assumptions into the theory's structure and proudly present their working-out as a "proof" or an "example" of something. In either case, one has merely borne out Alfred Schutz's sardonic remarks about the experimental use of behavioral models:

> A total harmony has been pre-established between the determined consciousness bestowed upon the puppet (the "rational man") and the pre-constituted environment within which it is supposed to act freely, to make rational choices and decisions. This harmony is possible merely because both, the puppet and its reduced environment, are the creation of the scientist. And by keeping to the principles which guided him, the scientist succeeds, indeed, in discovering within the universe, thus created, the perfect harmony established by himself.[54]

He succeeds also, one might add, in substituting a pseudoscientific vocabulary for the simpler, less impressive language of personal belief in arguing about matters of public policy.

I. The Contribution of Thomas Schelling

THERE is yet another and more sophisticated use to which game theory has been put in deterrence studies: that which is found in the work on threats and bargains of Thomas Schelling, whom I have already mentioned.

Schelling's work is crucial for a final assessment of the question of the influence of game theory in this field. It could conceivably be argued—although I think such an argument would totally misapprehend the nature of intellectual influence—that most of the works I have discussed previously are not important; or that their importance has nothing to do with their references to game theory. Neither of these arguments could possibly be made with regard to Schelling, for of all the theoretical works in the field of deterrence analysis his *The Strategy of Conflict* has been the most respected in the academic and research community;[1] and although the relationship of his theoretical to his practical arguments is often ambiguous, there is still obviously an intimate connection between them which has escaped no one's attention.

A caveat, it is true, must be entered about Schelling's use of game theory. *The Strategy of Conflict* is not really a book, but rather for the most part a collection of loosely related articles in which game-theoretic speculation and policy-oriented speculation usually occur under separate titles. However, to think that this separation can be made psychologically is to be very unrealistic. Let us consider, for example, Part III of *The Strategy of Conflict*. A chapter on the concept of "The Threat that Leaves Something to Chance," in which the idea of "brinksmanship" receives a favorable reception, directly follows an entirely theoretical essay on the potential roles of "Randomized Threats and Promises" in formal game situations, in which Schelling attempts to see what insights can be gained by relaxing the rigidity of the "rules" of communication in formal game theory so as to make the sequence of information-receiving, information-sending, and choice-making more true to life.[2] The two chapters are not linked explicitly, but the central subject of each— what happens when the choice of fulfilling a threat or not fulfilling it is out of the threat-maker's hands—is the same; and it is impossible not to come away from one's reading with the feeling that the same expertise has been at work on each subject and has produced the argument in favor of "brinksmanship." In Part IV, as noted in the previous chapter, Schelling follows the same pattern in his discussion of protection against surprise attack. In this case too, the conclusion of the policy chapter—that an arms control system based on the controlled deployment of invulnerable weapons is preferable to general and complete disarmament—thus seems somehow theoretically grounded; in both cases only the most hardened compartmentalizer could manage to ignore the possibly fortuitous conjunction.[3]

Finally, we must refer to the most famous essay of all thost that appear in *The Strategy of Conflict*, that on "Bargaining, Communication, and Limited War."[4] The subject of this essay also does not fall within the theory of games, strictly speaking, but rather is a report of experimental work suggested to Schelling by his dissatisfaction with orthodox game theory. But the whole is couched as part of the development of a theory of bargaining that would be an advance on the orthodox theory, and its patrimony can thus hardly be ignored.

Indeed, a close examination of this essay and the surrounding material reveals particularly well just how Schelling fills his dual role as speculative theorist and hard-headed policy adviser. "Bargaining, Communication, and Limited War" is the final chapter in a section on "a theory of strategy," and is preceded by a purely theoretical chapter on bargaining. The first part of the essay itself describes Schelling's laboratory simulation of "games" of conflict. Here functioning as an experimental social psychologist, he tries to show what happens when certain types of "games," characterized by partial conflict of interest and partial mutuality of interest,[5] are actually played. The problem he deals with is whether his players, prevented from communicating with each other and thus from co-ordinating their behavior, can somehow achieve a kind of *tacit* co-ordination that will enable them, independently, to make choices that have the effect of an agreement that provides some payoff for each player: as compared with the "no agreement" case, which would provide zero payoff for either player, and which one might ordinarily expect to have eventuated because of the prohibition on communication.

For example, two players are asked to agree, without overt communication, on the division of 100 dollars. If they each name the same division, they get 100 dollars each; if their divisions don't match, they get nothing.

This "game," or any similar "matching" game can be varied to observe whether a felt inequality of initial circumstances (asymmetry) will reflect itself in a mutual recognition that an exactly even split cannot be agreed upon as easily as an "unfair" one. Again, two players are shown a map with various landmarks on it. The landmarks include several buildings, hills, etc., but only one river, which divides the map unevenly. The question is whether the players, imagining themselves as military commanders, will agree on a division of the map area—without fighting—at the unique river. Or, two players are told to choose a strategy from a payoff matrix that includes no self-evident choices; the question is whether they will co-ordinate their choices on the basis of their perception of some unique *physical* feature of the matrix.[6]

In all these games what Schelling discovers is the existence of something he calls "prominence" (or "focal points"). This characteristic of game situations is best described as a psychologically distinctive solution point, such as the one equality among a host of inequalities or, as in the last-named case, the pull which the upper left-hand corner of any set of boxes supposedly exerts on Western eyes (all other things being equal). For Schelling, what is significant about this concept of prominence, and what shows the theoretical thrust of his work, is the demonstration that for certain classes of games potential solutions or outcomes exist which are unknown to formal game theory, and which it would not predict. The experiments are thus of obvious importance for theory construction in the area of decision-making and bargaining studies. (In this context, we can see Schelling as attempting partially to answer the complaint of Luce and Raiffa quoted on p. 99 above.)

However, the report of these intriguing experiments is followed, in the remainder of the essay, by an exceedingly practical disquisition on limited war. The purpose of these pages is to argue that prominence may exist in real limited-war situations as well, and the examples of tacit co-ordination on the non-use of poison gas in World War II, and of "sanctuary" agreements, etc., in the Korean War, are adduced. Then the question of nuclear weapons is raised, and it is suggested that without overt agreements such as treaties, we and the Soviets may be able to agree on a non–first-use policy in future limited wars. Finally, the subject is raised again in a completely policy-oriented appendix (Appendix A) in which national leaders are advised how they ought to behave if they wish to maintain the nuclear–non-nuclear distinction which Schelling finds already in existence.[7] And of course these essays are also crucial to the subject of deterrence generally (though perhaps not as much so as those on brinksmanship and arms control), in that one of the conditions that nuclear deterrence must deal with is the necessity of keeping limited wars limited. Furthermore, the concept of tacit co-ordination is actually basic to the central idea of deterrence itself—i.e., the necessity for each side to divine the circumstances under which the other side will or will not use its deterrent, and so inform-ally to treat certain actions as non-provocative of nuclear war.

Thus Schelling, in these pregnant essays, has set the stage for his preparatory remarks to *The Strategy of Conflict* and could hardly disclaim their clear impact.

The subject of the book, he writes, "(s)trictly speaking . . . falls within the *theory of games*." * To this he adds:

> The essays are a mixture of "pure" and "applied" research. To some extent the two can be separated. . . . In my own thinking they have never been separate. Motivation for the purer theory came almost exclusively from preoccupation with (and fascination with) "applied" problems; and the clarification of theoretical ideas was absolutely dependent on an identification of live examples . . . the interaction of the two levels of theory has been continuous and intense.[9]

Finally, an introductory essay that deals mostly with the uses of strategy studies for "theoretical development" concludes with the remark that

> It seems likely that a well-developed theory of strategy could throw light on the efficacy of some . . . old devices [Schelling here refers to ancient and medieval precursors of the exchange of hostages idea in deterrence theory], suggest the circumstances to which they apply, and discover modern equivalents that . . . may be desperately needed in the regulation of conflict.[10]

Thus, despite the ambiguity of Schelling's intentions, we must surely conclude that his accomplishment—the interweaving of theoretical speculation with policy discussion—is what matters. And as to that it is clear that one is constantly being led in the direction of "practical applications" and "live examples."

---

*Later, however, he remarks, ". . . There is scope for the creation of 'theory.' There is something here that looks like a mixture of game theory, organization theory, communication theory, theory of evidence, theory of choice, and theory of collective decision . . . we might call our subject the *theory of interdependent decision*."[8]

In sum, Schelling is important as a theorist at least partly because his theories seem to lead to important and striking proposals; and his proposals are striking and important not merely because of their content but also because they seem to be based on his theories.[11] When he is quoted as an authoritative source by deterrence analysts, it is as the contributor of such concepts as the "reciprocal fear of surprise attack," "the threat that leaves something to chance," "tacit co-ordination," etc., which are thought to infuse more simple-minded ideas of strategy with a sophisticated, "theoretical" content. As the author of academic arguments for the possible desirability of a "brinksmanship" strategy, for the installation of a "hot line" between the Kremlin and the White House, and for stabilizing measures in the arms race generally, Schelling is at least as well known as he is for his work on bargaining and threats; and the point is that he is well-known for all these contributions on the basis of the same book.

II. The Uses of Simulation: Limited War

My purpose in the remainder of this chapter, then— as in the chapters on systems analysis and game theory proper—is to clarify what Schelling's theoretical work actually adds to his policy discussion, and what is the exact nature of the latter with regard to rigor, theoretical grounding, etc. I shall begin with some remarks about the concepts of prominence, co-ordination, and limited war.

That agreed-on limitations in a limited war must be distinct and obvious is a point with which I assume no one would want to argue. Clearly, all who are engaged in the discussion of limited war are in Schelling's debt for making them more aware of this point than perhaps they were before.[12] Schelling himself, furthermore, carefully restricts the scope of his argument: he realizes, that is, that limitations in war do not exist per se, but only (if at all) if we and our opponents very badly want them to exist.[13]

What needs to be pointed out, however, is that Schelling's work, because it is so oriented to the immediate short run—because it is so ahistorical and apolitical —tells us nothing about the prospects of limited war, and thus nothing about the prospects of nuclear deterrence. Specifically, Schelling gives us no reassurance that escalation[14] can be avoided. He offers some grounds for hope that if both sides wish to avoid escalation it *may* be possible for them to do so. Even here he implicitly overstates his case, though. For despite his caution he fails to clarify precisely the conditions under which his experiments are relevant or irrelevant.

Thus, take the following passage, which is perhaps the central one in Schelling's disquisition:

> Let any of us try to cooperate for a prize: we are to sit down right now, separately and without any prior arrangements, and write out a proposed limitation on the use of nuclear weapons, in as little or as great detail as we please, allowing ourselves limitations of any description that appeals to us— size of weapons, use of weapons, who gets to use them, what rate or frequency of use, clean versus dirty, offensive versus defensive use, tactical versus strategic, on or not on cities, with or without warning—to see whether we can all write the *same* specification of limit. If we are in perfect agreement on the limits we specify, we get a prize; if our limits are different, we get no prize. We are permitted the extremes of no limits at all on the one hand, or no atomic weapons at all on the other, and any graduation or variation defined in any way we please.

My argument is that there are particular limits—simple, discrete, qualitative, "obvious" limits—that are conducive to a concerted choice; those who specify other kinds of limits, I predict, can find few partners or none at all whose limits coincide with theirs.[15]

That "no-use-at-all" would be easier to agree on than any other limitation is beyond doubt; but whether it would *itself* be at all "easy" to agree on is a question that is simply not illuminated by Schelling. He appears to suggest that his experiments do illuminate this point, as evidenced by his reference to the appendix from which the above quotation is taken, in the body of the main essay.[16] But in fact they provide little or no help.

The experiments provide no help because there is no reason to believe they replicate any of the conditions of international conflict—and to the extent that they do, the results are unimpressive. In the 50-50 division game, for example, the players have no incentive at all to do "better" than one another, since their chances of losing are virtually infinite if they don't co-operate and their culture is egalitarian; 90 per cent of Schelling's sample chose the even split. In the map-river game, by contrast, only slightly over 60 per cent could agree on the river.[17] It hardly seems surprising that as the games get more complex and conflictful, the incidence of agreement dwindles; or, the less the grounds for conflict, the more the likelihood of co-operation. That is the most one can make of such experiments. Actually, Schelling does not even establish that much. As Martin Shubik has noted, since motives cannot be observed empirically we cannot be sure exactly why the players chose the solution they did.[18] The players may have been tacitly co-ordinating their behavior because their motives were co-operative, or because each was trying to do the best possible for himself. If the latter were the case (and Schelling gives no reason to believe otherwise), then less symmetrical games might produce either a clear winner or a refusal to agree, and more strongly conflict-of-interest games might produce simply a head-on collision resulting in no agreement. The real-world analogues of these latter situations are, for our purposes, "surrender" and escalation to all-out war; neither is an acceptable conclusion to a conflict in the universe of deterrence theory.

Furthermore, Schelling's experiments are culture-bound in that there is no true emotional antagonism between his subjects. Other experimenters have found that when the conditions of such games are varied so as to simulate *hostile* conflict, non-co-operative results are more often produced. Thus Morton Deutsch, working with abstract laboratory simulations similar to Schelling's formal-rule games, but making in addition various attempts to generate hostility and competition among the players of the game, reports as follows:

> . . . Agreement was least difficult to arrive at in the No Threat condition, was more difficult to arrive at in the Unilateral Threat condition, and exceedingly difficult or impossible to arrive at in the Bilateral Threat condition. . . .
>
> . . . .
>
> In our experimental bargaining situation, the availability of threat clearly made it more difficult for bargainers to reach a mutually profitable agreement. Indeed, Bilateral Threat presents a situation so conflict-fraught that no amount of communication seems to have an ameliorating effect. . . .
>
> Everyday observation suggests that the tendency to respond with counterthreat or increased resistance to attempts at intimidation [is] . . . a common occurrence.[19]

In addition, one group of experimenters who set out directly to test Schelling's propositions in varied laboratory settings, observed a tendency of truly *mixed*-motive games—games with some element of co-operation present —to degenerate into zero-sum, or strictly competitive "power-struggle" games, because of the non-rational urge of the players to "look good" or "score points" rather than to understand their opponents' psychology and thus reach collaborative bargains; others have reported that when the players are divided into competing groups, group affiliation tends to affect their understanding of proposed solutions in a biased manner.[20]

These reports, of course, generate their own methodological problems and are not necessarily any more relevant in a broader setting than are Schelling's. Certainly they are no less convincing, though. On the basis of the evidence so far before us, that is, we cannot make the leap and conclude from Schelling's work that the ability of the U.S. and the U.S.S.R. to reach "tacit agreements" has been shown, either by analogy or by isomorphism, to be more likely than we thought it was.

Indeed, Schelling's own interpretation of his work has led him to statements about international conflict that now look dubious, as the following:

> . . . [C]onsider some other distinctions that are significant in the limiting process. We provided much equipment but no manpower to the war in Indochina; . . . (T)he point of all this is that, in limiting war, tradition matters.[21]

Doubtless the nuclear non-use threshold is a more rigid one. But traditions that were much older have decayed before,[22] and nothing that Schelling has written should lead us to the conclusion that this one will be any different in an armed and hostile world.

The comments I have made here perforce apply to writers other than Schelling, of course. There have been produced in the last decade a host of reports of "war games"; informal "simulations"; large-scale computer-programmed "simulations:" etc.[23] Most of these studies make no attempt, or only the most abashed attempts, to justify some kind of policy on the basis of the experiment.[24] Over-all, though, the impression is occasionally given that we are somehow picking up information about the world through these exercises, for those working in any area of public policy hesitate to admit that they are accomplishing nothing at all of immediate practical value. Thus Herman Kahn reports on a game in which by some fantastically subtle political maneuvering the Chinese Communists force both the U.S. and the U.S.S.R. to agree to a poorly policed disarmament scheme; China then reveals itself as the strongest nuclear power in the world and begins to dominate world politics; nuclear war threatens. Kahn then announces, "This game, although it can be denounced as farfetched and gloomy does illustrate a number of problems implicit in presently conceived arms control agreements." Of course it does not; the game only illustrates the players' attitudes toward Communist China.[25]

Whenever, that is, the experimenter arbitrarily chooses the "parameters, rules and structural features" for his experiment to investigate certain variables, the utility of the parameters themselves becomes a separate question.[26] In Schelling's work the most important parameter for "practical applications" is notable chiefly by its total absence: namely, the assumptions we make about American, Soviet, Chinese (and German? French? Egyptian?) *political* behavior. As Verba has lucidly remarked, "That a simulation does not 'look like' the real world is not important. What is important is the question of whether *it operates like the real world in the respects that are relevant to the study at hand."* [27] Where the most relevant feature of the real world is not even considered, obviously we can make little practical use of the study.

Thus we must assert that, once again, the approach to policy that we have been studying is no better than the verbal argument that is given for it. That we can reach tacit agreements on nuclear weapons and nuclear war, being a proposition that is never discussed by Schelling, remains unproved. As for the theoretical experiments, as yet they do little more than explain to us Schelling's thought-processes about limited war. The latter are surely interesting; but any suggestion that the accumulated weight of expertise developed by the growth of game theory and related studies is somehow thrown behind Schelling's policy proposals would be absolutely incorrect.

III.   Games and Threats: The Theory of Brinksmanship

To the complaint that we may not be able to reach agreements on mutual military restraints as long as the arms race continues, and that an attempt at complete disarmament ought therefore to be our most-preferred alternative as compared with various limited-war strategies, Schelling has at various times made answer. The theory of brinksmanship and a theory of arms control, both developed (the latter inchoately) in *The Strategy of*

Conflict represent answers that are supposedly strengthened by insights derived from game-theoretic analysis. The supposition, however, does not stand up under investigation.

I have already mentioned Schelling's notion of stability through arms control, briefly, and will advert to it again later. As for his idea of brinksmanship, it is based on an analysis of threats in the context of game theory. In this analysis Schelling tries to assess what an ability to deliver ultimatums, commit one's self to certain strategies or to the randomized choice of a mixed strategy, etc.—possibilities outside the pale of orthodox game theory—might do to the choice of strategies in a game. His suggestion is that by the successful use of such devices (e.g., getting in one's own ultimatum or commitment to a certain strategy first) one may be able virtually to compel one's opponent to adopt the strategy that is best for one's self.

In other words, Schelling is attempting to argue that threats can be not anxiety-producing phenomena but, in some circumstances, inspirations to correct choice. Deterrence, of course, is tacitly based on threats (and this is especially true of deterrence in limited war or other crises). Schelling is thus implicitly suggesting that deterrence will not look like an impossibly bad strategy if we can learn how to use threats properly; "brinksmanship" is the general theory of crisis threats that he develops.

The idea of brinksmanship as discussed by Schelling has two elements that may seem separate but are ultimately related: the notion of an "irrevocable commitment" and of a "threat that leaves something to chance." The "threat that leaves something to chance" is a threat that puts one in a physical or psychological position such that if the threat is not responded to in the desired fashion one may not be able to control one's counter-response (e.g., by leaving the actual performance of the threat to an independent third party). This kind of "threat" derives its potency from the mutual recognition by opponents that, in Schelling's words,

> . . . [S]ome of the most momentous decisions of government are taken by a process that is not entirely predictable, not fully "under control," not altogether deliberate . . . a nation can get even into a major war somewhat inadvertently, by a decision process that might be called "imperfect" in the sense that the response to particular contingencies cannot exactly be foretold by any advance calculations, that the response to a particular contingency may depend on certain random or haphazard processes, or that there will be faulty information, faulty communication, misunderstanding, misuse of authority, panic, or human or mechanical failure.[28]

The central idea here is that it may be possible to structure a situation so that an opponent is left with only *one* sensible ("rational") course of action: in effect, to give in. But Schelling's development of this idea is most unsatisfactory.

To begin with, a close inspection of the passage cited and of the whole essay from which it is taken suggests the following interpretation: fear of predictable non-rationality is expected (or hoped) to lead the threatened party to respond rationally. (Schelling uses the word "rational" sparingly in the essay under discussion, but in context it is clear that by "imperfect" decision processes he means to denote what he elsewhere implies is irrational behavior; see, e.g., the quotation on p. 164 below.)

However, Schelling is thus caught in a self-contradiction, because he tries to have it both ways. If he were consistent, he would have to admit that it is just as "predictable" that "they" will respond irrationally to our threat, or fail to comprehend its meaning and its possible outcome, as it is that we will "unintentionally" carry out the threat. As Karl Deutsch has noted, "The theory of deterrence . . . first proposes that we should frustrate our opponents by frightening them very badly and that we should then rely on their cool-headed rationality for our survival." [29] Conversely, it is also "not entirely predictable" that we will not make the threat badly, or unconvincingly, or make a threat we didn't intend to make. After all, if our decision-making processes are imperfect, then surely so are our threat-making processes.

These brief comments suggest that the theory of brinksmanship is just a simple play on words. This is clear in John Foster Dulles' version of the theory, in which Dulles seems to say "We acted cleverly and they responded in the appropriate manner."[30] But of course if they hadn't, then we would have acted stupidly. This makes the theory of brinksmanship a *post hoc ergo propter hoc* theory, and thus no theory at all.

Like others I have mentioned, Schelling falls into this confusion because of his own reliance on game theory. In the first place, he forgets that in real life one cannot define one's parameters as easily as on paper. Thus the uncertainties that make brinksmanship such a problematical, if not terrifying, strategy are lost sight of in the theoretical analysis. We know little about the psychology of credibility but for our matrices we simply assume it.[31] Again, we have no reason to believe that there is any such thing as a purely retaliatory weapon,[32] but for our paper chase we state that some of our weapons are retaliatory, and that our opponent knows it: reality disappears in a haze of abstraction.

Moreover, in the game-theoretic universe in which Schelling begins his analysis, paper opponents respond to threats and promises by choosing the most mathematically correct among the strategies that remain to them. But that is not necessarily so in the real world unless one assumes, as all deterrence theorists seem to assume, that decision-makers invariably choose a correct method of forwarding "the national interest" through military means. But that particular predisposition is an essential component of the notion of instrumental rationality that game theory incorporates—a notion which is thus smuggled through the back door into our roomful of supposedly "imperfect" decision-processes. Without that predisposition, without the game theoretic or some other assumption of rationality (see chapters 5 and 6 below), "brinksmanship" becomes meaningless.

If rational choice cannot be expected from *either* party, as must clearly be the case, Schelling's theory leaves us in limbo: brinksmanship becomes just another ambiguous move that does not force a single "correct" course of action. Schelling has merely created a paradox: we must be irrational in order to be rational. Of course, if perfect information were available on both sides, the meaning of a threat could presumably be made unequivocally clear. But in a world where omniscience is granted to few statesmen, the only way Schelling's "threats" or "commitments" can be given an unequivocally clear meaning to a fallible, "muddling" audience, is for the threatened action to be unquestionably and publicly automated.

But then the "threat that leaves something to chance" is turned into an "irrevocable commitment,"[33] and that is an even less cheering prospect. The true nature of irrevocable commitment is indicated quite well in the following passages from Schelling and Morgenstern:

> To illustrate, an instructive model is that of twenty men held up for robbery or ransom by a single man who has a gun and six bullets. They can overwhelm him if they are willing to lose six of themselves, if they have a means of deciding which six to lose. They can defeat him without loss if they can visibly commit themselves to a threat to do so, if they can simultaneously commit themselves to a *promise* to abstain from capital punishment, once they have caught him. . . . If fourteen of the twenty can overpower the remaining six and force them to advance, they can demonstrate that they could overwhelm the man; if so, *the threat succeeds and the gunman surrenders, and even the six "expendables" gain through their own inability to avoid jeopardy.*[34]

> It is sometimes argued that the death penalty is not a good deterrent against murder because many murders occur nevertheless. Therefore one might argue that the deterrent against aggression on this country might not work either. But the parallel is faulty: The murderer has a good chance not to be found, or when found to escape, not to be convicted, or, if convicted, to receive mild punishment, to be granted clemency, etc. All this is different from the present military situation. There the alternative to *not* seeing the deterrence is a very high probability of obliteration. The point is to make this probability "equal to one," that is, to make obliteration certain and automatic.
>
> If every potential murderer were sure that the very moment he commits the murder he too is killed, few murders would occur.[35]

These passages reveal just how unpromising the idea of irrevocable commitment is. The reason no modern society has ever considered investigating Morgenstern's idea is that the idea of automatic retribution seems horrifying to most people unless there is absolute certainty about two things: the guilt of the criminal and the utter wilful unrighteousness of his deed. But such certainty is almost always lacking in a court of law, and so too is it lacking in international relations.[36] (Indeed, if one reads Morgenstern's *Question of National Defense* closely, one can see that although he has relied throughout on the metaphor of instant obliteration in justifying his favored weapon systems as threats, he has with complete inconsistency insisted that those systems must be such as to permit slow, thoughtful decision-making when an actual attack has been made. Surely one does not make obliteration "certain" by being slow and thoughtful.) Furthermore, in actuality there are some "potential" murderers whose propensity for homicide might very well be increased by the existence of a certain death penalty; there are also, in large numbers, would-be suicides.[37] The motives of such persons are no doubt attenuated at the level of international politics; but following Freud, it can certainly be argued that ultimately these are also motives that affect the leaders of nations.[38]

As for Schelling's besieged gangster, although it is not clear from the surrounding text whether Schelling wishes to treat his situation as one analogous to the problem of nuclear deterrence, the reader cannot help but see that in fact the analogy to a pure deterrence situation in some respects holds perfectly. This is only one of many such analogies with which *The Strategy of Conflict* is replete. This one is particularly significant because, whereas the others only suggest relevant questions or hint at possible solutions to such questions, we have here a clear-cut statement, conveying a tone that informs the surrounding chapter and ultimately much of the book: "the threat succeeds. . . ."[39]

In the face of such assurance one is constrained to note that Schelling is clearly relying also on the capital punishment analogy, and his argument is thus subject to the same objections. If one *could* construct a world in which gunmen and victims got into such situations, I can think of no reason to believe that the gunman in this case would (or would not) be especially likely to surrender, rather than to settle for carnage. Furthermore, Schelling's example suggests one immense difficulty of "irrevocable commitment"—the gangster could if Schelling had not so carefully and omnisciently defined his armament make his own threats, such as, to blow everyone up if a hand is laid on him. And suppose he could not convince them that he was not bluffing? The prognosis would then be fairly desperate.

Put simply, the "irrevocable commitment" is (at the level of nuclear war) Kahn's "Homicide Pact Machine"; and the "threat that leaves something to chance" may very well be a delayed-action version of the same thing. The interested, or alarmed reader is referred to Kahn's discussion of such machines on pp. 145-49 of *On Thermonuclear War;* without dissecting the notion in Kahn's comprehensive fashion, we can surely see that this is the most undesirable possible tendency of pure, Type I deterrence. We have, in effect, what promises to be an automatic mutual obliteration mechanism. At what point is it to be set to operate? What reason have we to believe that the choice we make beforehand will be the one we wish we had made afterward? If there is *no way back* from the brink, then one has rendered one's self incapable of rectifying errors of judgment or calculation, and deliberately put one's self in a position where one can be destroyed by a single mistake. If this is the way correct choices are forced by threats, then we badly need less threats and more blundering—and we must also hope, as Karl Deutsch suggests, that the Russians and Chinese will never translate *The Strategy of Conflict*.[40]

At various times, to be fair, Schelling attempts to answer such objections by referring to real-life situations, not merely game theory problems, in which such threats apparently work: criminal law, child-rearing, automobile driving, labor relations, marital relations, and alliance relations are among those he mentions.[41] Such examples of threats, however, although they make Schelling sound more authoritative, really only accentuate the looseness of his thinking.

The differences between the relationships that are described by some of these examples and those prominent in the American-Communist conflict system are so obvious that they need no belaboring. Two are especially worth noting, though. The child-rearing analogy suggests that Schelling's cavalier handling of the "levels-of-analysis" problem is endemic in his thought. If be can suggest that a relation based on love and designed for the education of dependents is analogous to one based on distrust or hatred and designed for the intimidation of equals, we should not be surprised at his manifest lack of interest in discussing such banal phenomena as American and Soviet foreign policy. As for automobiles, Schelling refers approvingly to an astonishing article by C. W. Sherwin, in which the latter compares war-peace decisions with automobile-driving decisions, and finds cause for rejoicing in the comparatively low rate of failure among the latter: "The American automobile driver makes, on the average, between 10 million and 100 million successful decisions before he is killed. . . ." (Later Sherwin remarks, generously, "the calculation, I realize, sounds a little naive.") [42] Schelling praises Sherwin's article as an "excellent example" of the attempt by scholars to go beyond "immediate problems" and create instead a "methodology" for dealing with long-run problems. [43]

If this is Schelling's idea of a "methodology" his lack of care in moving between the world of theory and the world of practice is not surprising. Elsewhere he has written that

> . . . whether deterrent threats lead to desperation, hostility, and panic, or to quiescence, confidence, and security, probably depends on how the threats are arrived at and expressed, what demands accompany them, and the costs and risks of initiating violence or reacting to it.
>
> . . . .
>
> If the participants in a threat system lack the kind of "toughness" that immunizes them to irritation, suspense, and the involvement of personal honor, *substantive* threats are probably best kept for last resort. . . . They should be deterrent rather than "compellent." . . . They should support some fundamental *status quo*, superimposed on which is a system of etiquette, law, ritual, diplomacy, arbitration, or self-restraint. The threat for regular use, then, is the threat that persistent violation of the rules, or persistent bad faith, will endanger the "civilization" that has been built. It takes more than just willingness on both sides to do this, though. It takes skill, and perhaps some luck; tradition and confidence depend on experience, not just intentions. (And many of us are not yet persuaded that the intentions are even there.)
>
> My point is not that it is little white threats that make the world go round. It is that nations needn't give up just because military brute force may have to be replaced by threats as a means of protection. . . . Perhaps as we become less confident of brute force, and more attentive to the role

of threats, we can be more subtle, more careful, more civilized about them. . . . [44]

It is Schelling's prerogative to believe that one can write of the cold war as involving "irritation, suspense, and . . . personal honor," and expect to solve the problems of a revolutionary age by reference to "some fundamental *status quo*." But his notion of the usefulness of threats depends on such ideas; and they are purely political ideas, which he never otherwise discusses. They are also questionable ideas: one never gets the impression from Schelling or other deterrence theorists that they would be willing to put up with constant, irritating, and even humiliating threats from the Russians or Chinese. Our threats are supposed to intimidate them into behavior congenial to us—but what of their threats to us?

Nor is the concept of "learning" helpful here. It has been suggested by some deterrence theorists, Schelling among them, that "rational" responses, which at present could not safely be expected (say, to a limited nuclear attack), may be "learned" under the pressure of events.[45] Generally, though, to expect the "learning" of rational responses to take place in an atmosphere of nuclear violence, is to make exactly the same dubious assumptions about behavior as are made by deterrence and brinksmanship theory in the first instance. Furthermore, while "learning" abstractly requires only stimuli and an organism to respond to them, in the case of deterrence the term concretely seems to suggest the additional element of some kind of teacher-pupil relationship. It is indeed remarkable that in considerations of the prospects for the learning of proper deterrence behavior, it is invariably "we" who teach "them." Schelling's bargaining models, in which the bargainers gradually "learn" what they can agree on, are an exception. But if one thus takes a completely agnostic position about who "teaches" whom, one has no reason to believe that the bargain reached will be acceptable to the American version of deterrence theory. One might ask, what qualifies "us," except our self-love?

One cannot avoid concluding that this whole notion of threats, commitments, etc., depends on an asymmetrical evaluation of the world in which behavior that is reasonable and even educational when done by us is offensive saber rattling when done by our opponents. Indeed, that is the only way one can explain remarks such as this one of Schelling's: "I pay little attention to the Geneva negotiations. The most promising course is to get the Soviets to agree to a fairly expensive inferiority and taper off ourselves."[46]

IV.   The Bias of Game Theory

Having said all this about these various "uses" of game theory and "proof" of the desirability of a deterrence strategy, we can now also see why many observers, whether well- or ill-informed, have been so passionately critical of the resort to game theory by deterrence theorists. The genesis of these criticisms lies precisely in the indiscriminate concentration on conflict that deterrence theorists are so proud of. It is not that, as Wohlstetter claims, game theory is "pro-conflict" and its critics "anti";[47] it is that the use of a game-theoretic format has helped deterrence theorists to describe strategic choice in completely militarized terms, and in an imaginary context of complete insecurity.

All the writers I have mentioned (except Hitch, who is working at a lower level of generalization) do this. Taking the matter of insecurity first, one can see that it is this emphasis that is largely responsible for the "missile-gap" notion that was so central in all these approaches to deterrence. James King, himself an expert of note, has remarked about the "missile gap" that

[E]ven though many of them don't believe it themselves, they insist that our strategy should be formed, and our military plans made, *as if* the Russians will attack the moment a set of conditions can destroy 90 percent of the Strategic Air Command. This is to proceed as though the Soviets were bent on world conquest, like an Alexander. Nobody believes that any more, but the analysts treat it as a conservative and therefore necessary operating assumption. But of course the assumptions we make about the adversary determine our own courses of action and these, in turn, influence the adversary's intentions. The realist assumption, unadorned, therefore, hardly seems the way to get agreement, of the kind we need a lot more than we need additional armaments, with the Soviet Union. The realist assumption, as applied by the analysts, in other words, leads to an unjustified preoccupation with military force. More than that is required for security.[48]

It is the minimax theorem, among other things, that makes this "conservative posture" seem "rational." And it is in the game theory universe that "enemy" advantage, or estimate of gain over cost, is immediately translated into a strategic choice. If deterrence theorists had not been infatuated with this way of looking at the world, they might have made different assumptions about the need to go far beyond a minimum deterrent in the crucial years of the past decade and not set in motion the "self-fulfilling prophecy" that King describes.

As for the militarization of these analysts' thought, it is constantly visible in their refusal to compare military strategies with non-military ones. Again, the intellectual constraint imposed by thinking game-theoretically is one factor affecting this refusal; for in the kinds of schema that Ellsberg, Schelling, and others invent, the two kinds of strategies are not strictly comparable and cannot be rigorously analyzed without so much complication that the matrix model becomes useless.[49]

The worst and most significant offender in this regard is Schelling, who has bolstered his earlier theory of deterrence plus arms control with some further work in which general and complete disarmament is described as just another, poorer example of a deterrence-arms-control system. Having made this description, Schelling feels free to remark that general and complete disarmament is "a fraud." [50]

It is probably true that hostility is endemic, and entails conflict, which entails deterrence, always and everywhere. Indeed, I have said that Schelling oversimplifies his bargaining models by not building hostility into them. But much worse is the way in which he compounds this omission, when, having successfully built (or overbuilt) hostility into his *arms-control* model, he assumes that only militarized strategies are available for expressing it. Why should this be so? Why could not a disarmed world maintain deterrence without nuclear weapons, and perhaps even by means of non-military strategies? [51] In principle, it is surely not impossible; and if the resulting balance would be relatively unstable, one might prefer the potential of that instability to the "stability" of a world armed to the teeth with "second-strike" missiles.

There are sensible (though not necessarily correct) political arguments to be made against the attractiveness of this prospect or the feasibility of reaching it. But deterrence theorists offer no such arguments, and one of the ways in which they avoid offering them is by referring to game theory; that is, they put their conclusion about the primacy of military strategies into a matrix so that they never actually have to defend it.

Of course, the fault is not with the theory but with its *soi-disant* practitioners. There is no need for an orientation toward conflict to produce such a mode of thought.* *Military* deterrent threats are only an example of deterrent threats, not a paradigm for them, and *military* conflict is only an example of, not a paradigm for, conflict in general. But the disposition to think in this way to begin with, combined with the pressure toward oversimplification that is entailed when one attempts to use a theory that really does not yet have practical uses in any complicated context, [53] produces the results we have seen.

All these theorists think that a world can be built on nuclear threats. Schelling gives them the rationale that after all, lawyers, husbands, and mothers build worlds on threats too. No doubt that is so, and in a matrix all threats look the same. And yet, the result of this undisciplined theorizing is to obscure the terribly important possibility that those other threats work, not because they are like H-bomb threats, but because they aren't.

*The attempts of welfare economists and mathematicians to produce definitions of "co-operative rationality," plausible schemes of social arbitration in semicompetitive situations, and other forms of theoretical escape from zero-sum competitiveness, show that game-theoretic research need not take the direction it has taken in the deterrence context.[52]

THE FIRST PART of this discussion has dealt with the contribution to deterrence theory of specific analytic techniques that have been developed by social scientists. The remainder of this study deals not with techniques but with an obviously related concept: the more general and informal notion of decision-maker rationality that I have already mentioned from time to time.*

In a way, it could be argued that this notion, rather than the methods of analysis so far discussed, is the major contribution from modern social science that has been put to use in theorizing about nuclear deterrence. For recent developments in all the social sciences—and some not-so-recent developments in one of them—have been heavily weighted with the vaguely specified congeries of ideas that is subsumed under the phrases "rational behavior" and "rational man." Not only in eco-

---

*More general and informal, that is, than the rigorous version of rationality developed by game theorists. It could be argued, perhaps, that game theory is the only genuine theory of rational behavior in all cases of interdependent risk-taking action, since it is the only formal theory of what constitutes utility maximization in such situations. From here on, therefore, I am assuming that by "rationality" we refer only to the *intention* of maximizing specified utilities, and not necessarily to the formally correct method for doing so.

nomics but also in political science, sociology, and social psychology, as well as in that interdisciplinary field now called "decision-making" (of which game theory is a signal instance), new conceptions more and more concern the observable or theoretical effects of something called "rational" or "non-rational" behavior. Thus there has been a proliferation of attempts to show how the prospects for various kinds of goal-attainment can be calculated, or at least will seem more calculable than they did heretofore, if only some model of rational choice can be constructed.

Moreover, in some more positivistic versions of social science, "rationality" is proffered as a weapon with which to break through the barrier of the "fact-value" distinction: the assertion is made that while "value statements" about society are only subjective and thus not systematically analyzable, the social scientist can contribute studies that demonstrate the most instrumentally "rational" method for attaining agreed-upon or "given" ends.[1] This particular kind of argument about value judgments and rational discourse appears to have had a major effect on deterrence theory, although it is now somewhat dated in professional philosophical discourse.

In deterrence theory, the general "assumption of rationality" takes the concrete form of the assumption that if policy-makers will only make correct choices (i.e., be "rational") all-out nuclear war will be averted or at least its consequences mitigated.[2] We have seen how this assumption is heavily relied on by Kahn, by Glenn Snyder in his theoretical framework for discussing national security policy, and by Morgenstern in his use of the capital punishment analogy. This explicit reliance on a notion of decision-maker rationality is found again and again in the literature, as the following quotations indicate:

> Deterrence may be defined as a method of forcing good (or more accurately, rational) behavior through the fear of self-destruction . . . nothing is required of the opposing sides except self-interest and a certain amount of rationality.[3]

> It is sometimes said that strategists and systems analysts must (or, at any rate, do) assume that preparations for wars and wars themselves are conducted in a perfectly rational way on both sides. This sounds rather foolish and, in fact, would be. . . . [T]here is nothing in the nature of a conflict system design which forces the analyst to assume that the opposing parties are perfectly intelligent. A candid appraisal of our own history and that of our allies, to say nothing of what we know of enemy institutions and history, quickly establishes the likelihood of irrationalities.
> Nonetheless, the possibilities of rational behavior have a large if not an exclusive role in a systems analysis. If men are not always rational beings, they are the only beings who are sometimes rational.[4]*

> . . . The rationality upon which deterrence must be based is frangible.[6]

The likelihood of rational decision-making under conditions of limited strategic war—as indeed, in any kind of nuclear war, or in any kind of serious war in the nuclear age—is another problem about which little, in fact next to nothing,

*Kahn has made a similar comment: "These worries are, in fact, based on an important phenomenon: in normal circumstances, as well as under stress, decision-makers may not behave in an entirely rational fashion. However, researchers who study these problems do not really assume that decision-makers are wholly rational, but rather that they are not totally irrational—which is quite different from the assumption of rationality." Earlier he writes: "An understanding of the need for control, caution, prudence, understanding, restraint, and rationality is widespread in the U.S. . . . "[5]

is known. . . . We are not justified in concluding that rational decision-making will be hopelessly degraded. Beyond doubt, however, here is another built-in-risk of limited strategic war. This is a risk we need not run if better alternatives obtain. Only if they did not would it make sense to take advantage of the possibility that both our opponent and we would be reasonably rational in limited strategic war.[7]

The actual calculations of key decision makers may be less systematic than the logic this [i.e., his] calculus requires. . . . [8]

Deterrence demands hard, continuing, intelligent work, but it can be achieved. [It is t]he job of deterring rational attack by guaranteeing great damage to an aggressor. . . . [9]

Deterrence, to be effective, has four requirements: . . . 3. The opponent must be rational, i.e., he must respond to his self-interest in a manner which is predictable. 4. In weighing his self-interest, the potential aggressor must reach the conclusion the "deterrer" is seeking to induce. In other words, the penalties of aggression must outweigh its *benefits*.

. . . .

At the very least (all countries) should strive to make certain that war, if it does start, is the result of a deliberate decision and is not produced because the opponents, in taking measures which they deem to be defensive, push each other into an attack in self-defense.[10]

A deterrence policy . . . constitutes a special kind of forecast: a forecast about the costs and risks that will be run by the party to be deterred, if certain actions are taken, and about the advantages that he will gain if those actions are avoided.[11]

There is . . . a constellation of studies, all concerned with various aspects of policy, or rational decision, and of conflict of purpose; all interpretable as attempts to work out the implications of various strategies being adopted by participants in one or another of the several spheres of rational decisions. . . . [12]

Deterrence . . . is concerned with influencing the choices that another party will make, and doing it by influencing his expectations of how we will behave.[13]

A few remarks about the relationship between deterrence and behavioral theory are in order before we proceed to a discussion of the assumption of rationality. First, several of these quotations would seem to suggest that deterrence theorists do not really expect rational behavior but rather are merely hoping for it. Some of my comments will be addressed to the hope rather than the expectation, therefore. However, although few deterrence theorists are sanguine about whether rational action will indeed take place, all assume that it *can* take place—and this assumption is really the subject of the following chapters.* Indeed, there are grounds for asserting that deterrence theory *in toto* is nothing more than one kind of theory of rational behavior. At least this is true as long as one puts at the heart of one's analysis a systematic behavioral generalization, rather than a vague hunch or intuition on the one hand or an analysis of the behavior of concrete individuals on the other. And although many laymen and even policy-makers may indeed accept deterrence on the basis of merely a formless hunch or intuition that "the bomb *can't* go off," no prominent deterrence theorist has ever done so;[14] nor has any deter-

---

*I have found few deterrence theorists to be consistent in their pessimism about rationality. See, e.g., Kahn, *On Escalation*, p. xi.

rence theorist produced an analysis of American and Soviet social patterns that show deterrence behavior to be a cultural norm in the two societies.* On the contrary, what presents itself to the academic world and the informed public as deterrence theory is based precisely on generalized, rather than individualized, statements about decision-making.

It is true that some deterrence theorists have outrightly denied reliance on the rationality concept and said no more than that as a rule fear and uncertainty may be expected to prevent the outbreak of nuclear war.[15] But they too are ultimately thrown back upon that concept. For such words as "fear" and "uncertainty," when generalized beyond an analysis of specific decision-makers, merely establish a certain (theoretically quantifiable) relationship between a general assumption of decision-maker rationality *and a subassumption of information* (without which any theory of rationality is in any event incomplete). Thus, when one says that uncertainty helps to prevent all-out war, one simply says that in any decisional calculation that envisages a potential response of all-out nuclear war to certain courses of action, one so weights the calculation against those courses of action that only a very little expectation of

*On occasion a few writers have seemed to predicate the stability of deterrence on the special rationality of Soviet Communists. However, that idea is so palpably biased that one cannot take it seriously as an attempt to concretize the general assumption of rationality—especially since no attempt is made to show that the leaders of other nations are less rational. I think such interpretations of Soviet behavior are based on a misuse of Nathan Leites' *The Operational Code of the Politburo* (New York: McGraw-Hill, 1956), in which he emphasizes the tactical flexibility of Communists. But mere tactical flexibility is not necessarily the same thing as "rationality" in a given context.

such a response is necessary to make them seem undesirable. (But one cannot eliminate the need for knowledge altogether without asserting that one would never under any circumstances court the danger of nuclear war. This would be a strategy not of deterrence but of bluff or of unilateral disarmament.) [16]

Actually, if decision-makers were generally moved by non-rational criteria, then no matter how fearful and uncertain they were, their uncertainty and fear would be irrelevant, for those are words suggesting consequence, and non-rational actors are either heedless of consequences or unable to perceive them accurately in an empirical sense—that is what it means to be non-rational.[17] If, for example, one is to induce desired behavior by threats—to deter—then one must be capable of the reasoning necessary to predict which threats will induce which behavior. Or, if one is the object of threats, one must be capable of the reasoning necessary to determine the proper response to them. Merely conscious behavior is not enough, for it is compatible with unreason, as witness the behavior of, say, the paranoiac. Deterrence, moreover, is basically a matter of successful prediction— or, to be less formalistic, of plausible prophecy; and over the long run only the processes of "rational" thought make this possible.* Irrational or non-rational decision-makers can avoid catastrophic decisions, but only by accident, not because they have any principle of decision-making—such as withdrawal from positions of dangerous uncertainty—that will help them to avoid it.

*There is such a thing as predictable irrationality; psychoanalysts deal with it regularly, for instance, or like to think they do. But they deal with it on a rational basis, for in the analyst-patient relationship, the former is manipulating the situation on the basis of a "rational" analysis of the latter.

In fact, it should be emphasized that no qualification of the notion of rationality can be fitted into deterrence doctrine and leave that doctrine standing whole as an explanation of the successful avoidance of nuclear war —as more, that is, than a frantically hopeful hunch. If it is diluted with any really non-rational propositions, its logical structure, at least, must begin to collapse. It is important to make this point because some prominent deterrence theorists, wary of reliance on the assumption of rationality, have claimed, or seemed to have claimed, that deterrence theory is not necessarily a theory of rational behavior.

Thus Schelling has argued that a rational strategy can under some circumstances be used by otherwise irrational persons, and Kahn has suggested that a rational strategy may also work vis-à-vis normally irrational persons.

> . . . [E]ven among the emotionally unbalanced, among the certified "irrationals," there is often observed an intuitive appreciation of the principles of strategy, or at least of particular applications of them. I am told that inmates of mental hospitals often seem to cultivate, deliberately or instinctively, value systems that make them less susceptible to disciplinary threats and more capable of exercising coercion themselves.[18]

> Moreover, we want to deter even the mad. It is sometimes stated that even an adequate . . . deterrent would not deter an irrational enemy. This might be true if irrationality were an all-or-nothing proposition. Actually, irrationality is a matter of degree and if the irrationality is sufficiently bizarre, the irrational decision maker's subordinates are likely to step in. As a result, we should want a safety factor in . . . deterrence systems so large as to impress even the irrational and irresponsible with the degree of their irrationality and therefore the need for caution.[19]

As for Schelling's point, one can only say that anything is possible but that ordinarily we hope for a little more assurance about the way the arts of statesmanship are being practiced than we would find in an institution for the mentally ill. Kahn's hortatory argument is, by contrast, well taken, but he is not really diluting the rational element in deterrence theory, as some have thought;[20] he is merely saying that even the mad may be pressured into rationality by the sheer obviousness of the deterrent threat. Quite so; that is what deterrence is all about.

More interestingly, Glenn Slyder has pointed out that emotional values may be built into a rational calculation, so that various weights may be given to the satisfaction of emotions such as honor, prestige, etc., in the decision-making process.[21] However, he goes on to note that if the process itself is distorted from "rationality" by the experience of such emotions at the time of decision-making or planning (for instance, if "honor" compels the making of a threat that sober calculation would show simply cannot be made credible), then the process can no longer be described as a rational one.

These attempts to imply a limit on the scope of the assumption of rational behavior, therefore, only make clearer than ever the strength of the relationship between a coherent behaviorally generalized deterrence doctrine and the concept of rationality—that is, the hope that things can be arranged so that rational decisions will be made.

II. The Ambiguity of Deterrence Rationality

One way to begin a consideration of the rationality assumption in deterrence theory would be to ask what specifications it consists of. One would have to make up a catalogue of such specifications one's self since no deterrence theorist has offered one.[22] Presumably one would have to include, in some cases argumentatively, such requirements as cost-gain comparisons of all options in a given situation, complete knowledge of the options, non-involvement in policy-making of those not interested in such an approach, etc. However, I think it is more useful to start merely with a broad statement: "rationality" in deterrence theory refers to the making of policy decisions that correctly balance a nation's efforts in pursuit of the dual deterrence goals of preserving national (or alliance) integrity and avoiding (high-level) nuclear war. In pursuing an investigation into the prospects for, and problems of, consistently making such decisions, we shall find out just what specifications the assumption of rationality can in fact meaningfully include.

The first point I shall discuss here concerns the effect on the way we conceive of certain strategic problems that involve long-run versus short-run considerations when we adopt the notion that strategic behavior is best thought of as rational behavior. The problems I have in mind are those of limited war and technological progress.

Deterrence theory tells us, essentially, two things: first, that limited means of defense or limited deterrent threats are appropriate as responses to limited provocations (it is the insistence on this point that distinguishes advocacy of deterrence from advocacy of "massive retaliation"); second, that the ultimate deterrent threat (or response) of all-out nuclear war should be reserved for those provocations that cannot be deterred or thwarted by limited means. The key to these two components of deterrence doctrine is the idea of *credibility*. A rational man does not (a) make threats that are not credible, or (b) allow himself to be deterred by threats that are not credible or (at least) are incredible. The notion of non-credibility is tautological, and does not necessarily have any empirical referents; but it is assumed by everyone who has contributed to the development of deterrence theory that there are indeed some potential provocations that should not be met in theory, or could not be met in practice by the ultimate threat of all-out countervalue war.[23] What exactly these provocations may be is a matter of internal doctrinal dispute that is not of major interest here; the point is simply that every deterrence theorist posits the need for some kind of limited war capability, even if only the capability for fighting, à la Kahn, a "controlled counterforce war" that avoids the destruction of cities.[24]

Thus the rational decision-maker, when confronted with a limited threat, according to the theory of deterrence counters it with limited means—and in short-run terms it is always "rational" for him to do so. If a nation can prevent an incursion on its interests, *as it defines them,* by fighting a limited war of greater or lesser intensity, then it should "rationally" do so. If a limited war is being lost and the question of "escalation" arises, a rational decision-maker will weigh the worth of the interest being defended and the probability of successfully defending it against the ultimate probability of a destructive war and the worth of what would be destroyed by it; if on the basis of current information the expected payoff of the first calculation is higher than that of the second, escalation will logically follow. If this logic is unsound, then there is a dangerous contradiction in deterrence theory.

Unfortunately, that is indeed the case. I have already pointed out, in my remarks on game theory, that it is theoretically possible for a series of "correct" short-run decisions to add up to an "incorrect" long-run decision. (The reverse is probably also true.) In practice, this is to say that the idea of rational decision contains an essential ambiguity when applied to repetitive events. The example of limited war is a case in point.

There are two problems involved here: the problem of escalation and the problem of continuing cold war. As to the former, it is "rational" to escalate so long as two conditions exist: (1) any counterescalation can be "overbid"; (2) the process does not lead to all-out nuclear war. Unfortunately, the conditions are mutually incompatible. Eventually, if no counterescalation by the opponent can be successful, the only riposte left to him is all-out war—or "surrender." [25] And "rationality" has no principle for choosing between the two, since they are both rejected as goals.

There is a possible answer to this dilemma as posed. It might be asserted that "rational" action in such a situation is to press for a negotiated settlement at a point where the escalation spiral is not yet out of control.[26] That is an unsatisfactory solution, however, *unless one side is clearly superior at all levels of escalation, including that of all-out nuclear war*. If the question of superiority and will is uncertain, negotiation is not *ipso facto* a preferable alternative for the side that happens to be losing at the moment.

Of course, we could strive to make the question of superiority and will certain: that is, to make the United States decisively superior to the Communist nations at all the levels of the "escalation ladder." But if this "negotiation through strength" is "rational" behavior for the United States, it also is for the U.S.S.R. (and China). Here then "rationality" depends on establishing asymmetrical rules of behavior, or asymmetrical levels of achievement, for us and our opponents.[27] But such behavior is insensible unless we have empirical evidence to support the proposition that such an asymmetry exists and can be made to continue to exist. The obvious difficulty with such a proposition is the *hubris* that is required to assert it—which perhaps explains why no deterrence theorist has (wisely) ever been caught asserting it in public.[28]

Failing some such "rule of the game," which would proclaim the U.S. (or its opponents) permanent "winner," the dilemma of our so-called rational decision-maker persists. He may think his side is permanently the "stronger," but he must convince the opponent of this also. Since strength is a matter of will as well as resources, this may be very difficult to accomplish; the more continual one's own success, the more one's opponent is led to redouble his efforts in order to stop "losing." A desperate gambler betting double-or-nothing on "heads" and steadily losing thousands of dollars, will find it easy to convince himself on each successive throw that the odds in favor of "heads" have gone up—though a moment's thought would show him that before each throw the odds are still 50-50. And, conversely, his winning opponent, though he knows full well that over a lengthy series of throws the odds against continued "tails" are astronomical, will comfort himself with the thought that on each single throw they are, after all, 50-50. Gamblers often work themselves into such disastrous situations, where they become unable to stop; the difference between their situation and ours is that ordinarily the loser does not have the capacity to blow them both up if he can no longer sustain his losses.

The point is that there are two "logics" to this situation; one short-run and one long-run. It is "rational" to choose either logic; but if the opponents make different choices or if they both choose the short-run view, they are headed for trouble. The latter eventuality seems especially likely in that it is natural to discount the future about which one knows so little, as against the present about which one has so much more information. And the analogue of the coin that must fall "heads" sooner or later is the opponent who must "win" a battle sooner or later—but whose future needs we are unlikely to worry about when there are obvious victories to be won in the present.

Indeed, Levine has written about deterrence theorists that they "have the shortest time horizons of any group [in the arms debate], giving the greatest relative weight to the present as compared to the future"; that "they want to buy time"; and that "they will almost always opt for short-run stability, for 'next year's' fulfillment of their major goal of keeping the peace [i.e., nuclear peace]." [29] Such a preference is no doubt defensible. But from a different—equally "rational"—point of view it can also be impeached. The impact of events over time may change value patterns, or expectations, or both (see my discussion of game theory, above), and thus change someone's perception of what is an "obvious" or "acceptable" victory—or defeat. And the result may be a *long-run* disaster.

For example, Sherman's march through Georgia, a marvelous exercise in military strategy, contributed to "winning" the Civil War—and also contributed to "losing" the peace for the next century or more. What was conceived of as "victory" then came to seem like a kind of defeat when reconciliation rather than subjugation became the North's goal—but it was too late to take back Sherman's march. In a world full of nuclear weapons, similar miscalculations could produce a much more devastating result than lynchings and other forms of racial oppression. For a great power that was continually losing in the cold war might finally feel it necessary to make a surprise attack, or find some other method of initiating all-out nuclear war, in order to "redress the balance" or merely to achieve some kind of perverse psychic satisfaction.*

Other kinds of potentially disastrous misperception or miscalculation of one's true interest in the outcome of a certain event are equally imaginable. Richard Rovere has written about the Korean War that "it was the most hated war in our history" and that "it was so divisive and so productive of hatreds and bitterness that it might very well have been better never to have become involved in it." [30] Ultimately that war may not turn out to have been harmful at all. But the point is that if even the war described by Herman Kahn as "the right war in the right place at the right time" [31] can be so judged, to call the process of making decisions about entering such wars "rational" is to say nothing at all.

To see more clearly the impact of the long-run–short-run dilemma, we can turn to no better example than to what is so far the only serious attempt by an academic theorist to show that deterrence theory has "worked" in

*It is a common explanation that the Nazis' proclaimed goal of revenge for Versailles was an important element in their rise to power.

practice, not just by luck or accident, but because of the relevance of its descriptive categories.

The study to which I refer is Charles McClelland's analysis of the Quemoy-Matsu crisis of 1958. In this analysis, McClelland concludes about Secretary of State Dulles' handling of the crisis:

> Opposition behavior, largely, was to look back with disfavor on the general course of American policy in the Far East before the Quemoy crisis and to call for a shift in the line of current action as a prelude to some future reforms of policy. The more plausible interpretation of the Opposition role is that it was, in the main, ineffective in influencing the direction of the Administration's crisis policy because it failed to follow and exploit the specific "logic of the situation" in the succeeding phases of change and development in the crisis arena. . . . Opposition's watchdog responsibility should develop in international politics into the careful tracking of the particular path being trod by the Administration and the criticizing and reporting of mistakes and missed chances *within the bounds set by the decisional opportunities of passing international situations.*[32]

Now what must be noted about this analysis is that it is precisely the definition of rationality in terms of "the logic of the situation" that can generate the process of self-contradiction I have described. *Our perception of the logic of the situation itself may be unsatisfactory.* "Rationality" may require "exploiting" it (see the quote from Kahn on p. 182 below), but a different kind of "rationality"—the "rationality" of survival, for instance—may require changing it. Robert Wolff has noted one of the many ways in which that fear might turn out to be well-grounded:

Some while ago, a high Chinese official was reported as saying that China could profitably fight a nuclear war, because even if the United States killed 300 million Chinese, there would still be (at that time) 300 million left. This statement, whether genuine or not, sent shivers through the western world, for it opened up the horrifying prospect of an enemy who could not be deterred. . . . Should the United States ever confront a China armed with nuclear weapons and possessed of so grim a value scale, it will literally be faced with annihilation or surrender. There will be no defense, and deterrence will have failed.[33]

Similar considerations pertain to other cold war crises. American escalation in Vietnam may be "rational" if the Vietnamese, Soviet, and Chinese turn out to have less of the necessary kinds of resources for such a struggle than we do. It also may not, for like Sherman we may "win" the war but lose the peace. And of course our escalation will have been decidedly "irrational" if in the end they turn out to have more of those resources. Nor can we really make any predictions in this regard, since we don't even know whether the necessary resource for such a struggle will finally be military muscle or emotional resolve.

Again, in the case of the Cuban missile crisis of October, 1962, the general impression in the United States following the withdrawal of Soviet missiles from Cuba was that the administration's policy had been "successful" in forcing the withdrawal without enlarging the crisis—just as Dulles' policy in 1958 was "successful." But a number of such successes, or a similar "success" in a situation in which the opponent suddenly decided he was valuing his cause too lightly, and our victory may be Pyrrhic indeed.

Of course deterrence theorists have tried to cope with the problem of escalation in the cold war. Thus Schelling and Kahn argue (very tentatively, as I have noted earlier) against any first use of nuclear weapons in limited war:[34] we should be wary of pushing our opponents too hard. But their argument, to the extent that they really mean it, is political rather than logical; and since they rate political considerations inferior to logical ones, that argument may always be overturned by a new calculation. If national leaders decide they can gain an advantage by using nuclear weapons in a limited war, and that the chance of counter escalation is so low as to make the move worthwhile, then they will "rationally" (by Kahn's or Schelling's standards) use them[35]—and be almost exactly in the situation of the gamblers in my example, if the enemy does "raise the bid." If we rely, as does deterrence theory, on rationalistic logic rather than subjective insight, then only perfect knowledge of the future could help decision-makers to avoid such a prospect with certainty—and perfect knowledge does not exist in human affairs.

Nor do Schelling's bargaining games offer a way out of this theoretical impasse, even were one to concede their relevance. As long as those games are being played co-operatively, both players should "co-operate" on the "rational" solution: meet at the river that divides a territory unevenly, divide a dollar unevenly because one of the players has made and can enforce a "brinksmanship-like" commitment to accept only such a division, etc. But it would also be perfectly rational for the losing player to decide he didn't want to "co-operate" anymore and try to kill the other! For the winning side, it is "rational" not to use nuclear weapons in a limited war, since escalation might otherwise be unstoppable. But is it for the losing side? Not if "he" decides it is no longer worthwhile to keep the war limited—and nothing in Schelling's or anyone else's theory of rationality can tell him not to reach such a decision, for that is a matter of values, which according to such theories are determined a priori, and which in real life can be changed at will. If one can't stand losing a small war, who knows, one might win the large one—why not escalate?*

It is no answer to say that ultimate escalation will be irrational because the winning side, if it has been rational, also has an invulnerable countervalue deterrent. As Kahn points out, no deterrent can be assumed to be *completely* invulnerable, beyond question; there are always bound to be uncertainties that reveal themselves only in execution. And since the preattack environment is more familiar than the post-attack environment, those uncertainties are likely to favor the first attacker.[36] By the same token, Kahn has assured the world that "annihilation" is not inevitable. He can imagine situations in which it does not occur; so may a potential loser, with his back to the wall. If one is fairly sure of losing what one values anyhow, why not do it at a time and place and with means of one's own choosing?

Furthermore, the possibility of some such outcome could conceivably be greatly increased if the concept of "rational behavior" is applied in the same way—as it must be if it is applied at all—to the cold war's technological as well as to its political problems. The inherent self-contradictions of that concept operate similarly in this area. In a world based on mutual deterrence, the

*Or, as Senator Goldwater has asked, "Why Not Victory?"

possibility of technological breakthrough in either offense or defense such as to upset the deterrence balance is also either a limited or ultimate threat, and it is "rational" to counter that threat by appropriate means. These means are, of course, to make the breakthrough one's self, either before the other side or so soon after that its momentarily sole possession of the new "weapon" is not yet decisive. Thus, if a new type of bomb or missile poses the possibility of a more devastating or more unstoppable attack, each side must "rationally" strive to develop it first. The same is true for defensive weapons, such as antimissile missile systems, massive civil-defense programs, etc. It is also true for radically divergent types of weapon systems, such as those meant for biological and chemical warfare (and thus, the United States is currently engaged in rationally building up an extensive arsenal of such weapons).[37] And, of course, if a "destabilizing" breakthrough can be achieved by the mere addition of greater numbers of a weapon already in inventory, each side must strive to see that it makes the addition in time.

A recent article by Clark Abt lists weapon-system innovations that will be feasible in the next decade. Most of the horrific ones are considered by him to be not worth the cost of developing them; that is, he assumes that that is the way American and Soviet policy-makers will perceive the situation.[38] But the costs we are willing, or even eager to bear vary with the way the world looks to us. If either side's perception of the threats to its well-being changes radically—which is not out of the question, given the Vietnam situation, for example—then it may come to seem rational to build some destructive devices even at a very high monetary and social cost. At the very least, on past performance no deterrence theorist will find himself able to say that it is irrational.

The result is that rational behavior may (and probably does) posit a continuing "arms race," both qualitatively and quantitatively, wherever there is a potential gain to be realized.[39] What Arthur Herzog calls the "pure deterrence attitude" results in the following typical comments by a government official: "There is safety in the research race. . . . The arms race is a dynamic thing. . . . By maintaining our research we can make sure that asymmetries do not occur." [40]

The possible consequences of such an attitude are two-fold. First, to the extent that arming against each other exacerbates tensions between opponents, one or both sides become more likely to find themselves in the presence of so implacable a threat that only war can eliminate it. Second, the arms race itself greatly increases the likelihood that one side, in a situation of tension bordering on desperation, will perceive (or misperceive) its enemy as being likely to take advantage of a breakthrough in the arms race (and of course also increases the possibility that the perception will actually be correct). The effect of the combination of these two possibilities is to increase the probability of escalation in a limited war, or simply of "pre-emptive" attack—all in the name of "rationality."

An instructive recent example of potential long-run irrationality based on rationalizing short-run calculations is the American decision to possess a clear first-strike capability against the Soviets, who are felt to be incapable of matching our effort.[41] And so they are, probably; so the next logical step for them is to move the arms race up a notch by developing some new super-weapon that will be destructive enough, and "invulnerable" enough, to unbalance the arms race all over again by destroying the security of America's "secure" retaliatory force, and also of any conceivable civil-defense plan. They may not, but we will only know after the fact—and will they have been "rational" not to do so? Not by our standards, apparently. Again, Freeman Dyson has argued that an American decision to push ahead with the development of an antiballistic-missile missile system would give a disastrously forward push to the arms race, but no deterrence theorist has seen fit to oppose the tentative decision to do just that.[42] In fact, Kahn has written that "Perhaps the most significant value of [an ABM] program would be that it would give the U.S. the kind of capabilities and understanding of ABM that can come only from actually being in the ABM business."[43] This indeed is a kind of "long-run" thinking that we could do with less of.

Similarly, the failure by the major powers to agree on and enforce a world-wide general disarmament system before the "Nth Country" situation gets out of control— with all the threats of accidental war, catalytic war,[44] etc., that that event may entail—is a further example of the possible "irrationality" of rational strategic thought. But it is hardly a surprising one, since, if rationality is our guide, we have no principle for deciding whether proliferation is a good thing. Herman Kahn, after much agonizing, has recently decided that—like first use—it is not. But he sees the other side of the argument too: by some standards, which are perfectly compatible with nuclear deterrence, proliferation (to our allies at any rate) might be a good thing. Suppose, for instance, our NATO allies, or the West Germans, insist on proliferation for themselves? Even if we don't want nuclear proliferation, we also don't want to fracture NATO, or force the Germans to carry out their threats to arm themselves with nuclear weapons if we will not arm NATO.[45] What are we to do? One thing is certain: rationality does not tell us which course to pursue.

The impact of these major ambiguities in deterrence rationality is especially striking when we consider the doctrine of arms control, which I have already discussed briefly in Chapter III, above. (I use the phrase "arms control" to imply a type of proposal that is both distinct from, and opposed to, proposals for "disarmament.")[46] As we have seen, some deterrence theorists seem to say: *If* agreement is reached on proposals to police limited war, to guard against surprise attack, to keep communications channels open in the event of unintentional threats to the peace, and to limit technological research and development;[47] *and* if those agreements are workable, *then* within that framework a deterrence strategy would be clearly indicated to rational men. The question that arises is: is it consistent "rational" behavior for the same men both to engage in the militarily hostile, occasionally combative conduct that deterrence strategy permits *and* to keep arms control agreements workable?

There are several reasons for thinking that at best those two modes of conduct cannot, with any confidence, be expected to occur together over the long run. At the worst, it can be claimed that they are definitely incompatible, and that Schelling's theorizing in addition to being methodologically inadequate, is again self-defeating. As John Polanyi has argued:

> Can we really hope to reach and maintain agreements which have sufficient substance that they significantly diminish the "dangerous arms competition," and yet are so neutral in their effects, and *remain* so neutral, that they do not run

afoul of the "intensive struggle and conflict among the participants"?

Partial measures of arms control will be hard to obtain and hard to maintain in force, for two reasons. The first is that mutual assurance against the dangers of cheating will be extraordinarily difficult to achieve in a world of intensive struggle and (military) conflict. The second reason has to do with the changing military requirements in a fully armed world; a world in which technological revolutions follow one another with unprecedented rapidity. These military requirements are of two kinds: requirements for the maintenance of effective tactical forces . . . and requirements for the maintenance of invulnerable strategic forces. The latter constitute the essential element in stable deterrence; a concept which lies at the heart of arms control.[48]

Polanyi then points to several ways in which the requirements of "mutual assurance" and of military security may be expected to conflict with each other (e.g., inspection vs. secrecy; controls on strategic arms vs. the need for improved tactical arms that differ in degree but not in kind; efforts at production control vs. efforts at "preemptive breakthrough; etc.). "In the long run," he concludes, ". . . the demands of stability, which take precedence over the need to control the arms race, will come into conflict with the provisions for arms control."

This is to say that rational men with some common and some hostile interests, will only co-operate when there is an enforceable payoff for co-operating. When they perceive a better payoff for hostility, they will be hostile. The only way that this dilemma can be eliminated is by eliminating opportunities to be (militarily) hostile—but that is exactly what "arms control" does not do. As one deterrence theorist nicely puts it:

[I]f, for reasons connected with its desire to stabilize the strategic balance or to enhance long-range political objectives, the United States should accept an arms-control agreement which reduced the likelihood that a nuclear war could remain limited or which suggested that the use of nuclear weapons in local war would be inhibited by the fear of disrupting the arms-control agreement, then the United States should alter its strategy for local defense to take account of these facts. However, equally, if not more, important is the effect decisions on military policy should have on arms-control agreements and negotiations. If the United States settled on a nuclear local-war strategy, it should use arms-control negotiations to facilitate this strategy and not to hinder it.[49]

Nor should we be surprised by these remarks if we consider the philosophical background of arms control theory. The doctrine of arms control, like the deterrence theory of which it is one aspect, and like that traditional balance-of-power theory of which deterrence theory itself ("the balance of terror") seems to be one aspect, is an example of a broad theoretical outlook that has been of tremendous significance in Western thought. I would call this outlook "the general theory of competitive equilibrium"—the most well-known case of that theory being, of course, the classical economist's theory of general economic equilibrium. All such theories are subject to the objection that no one has ever observed a competitive equilibrium to exist for very long in human affairs of any kind, except where the competitors surrendered their means of violence and social dissolution to a political authority that they had created external to themselves.*

The very opposite of that situation exists in the deterrence–arms control world. To find an analogue in the eco-

---

*It is almost impossible to talk about the relationship between civil society and political authority without falling into the language of social contract theory. My use of such language is due to this difficulty, not to any desire to endorse the casual explanations inherent in that theory.

nomic realm we should have to imagine a free market economy in which the forms of political authority were non-existent and every entrepreneur and worker was armed with a machine gun. We should have, in other words, to imagine a situation very much like Hobbes' state of nature: which is precisely the image of "rational" human behavior and world order that deterrence theorists seem to have. In this world, arms control becomes perfectly compatible with the attitude revealed by Kahn when, writing about the development of new weapon systems, he states that "where there is good evidence of a lead it is probably a mistake not to exploit it." [50]* With that remark we say farewell to arms stabilization.

A host of other dilemmas of deterrence rationality could be discussed, of which I shall briefly mention just two. The idea of "fail-safe" mechanisms is one. Suppose we decide that only the President should have the power to push the ultimate button. If our fail-safe system is perfectly safe, his sudden death will render SAC inoperable. If the system can be "go" after his sudden death, then there must be at least one loophole in our fail-safe procedures, and all the elaborate complexities in the world cannot render it any the less a loophole.[51] Which choice do we make? Is it rational to opt for safety? No more than it is to opt for capability. We had better forget about being rational and make our choice—or find a better way to order international politics, perhaps.

Another problem is that of communication. Communication between hostile nations is for purposes both of

*Presumably he and other deterrence theorists would say the same about opportunities to cheat; the same reasoning certainly applies.

reassurance and of manipulation. If we were absolutely determined to avoid war all manipulative communications (e.g., lies) would be irrational. But deterrence theory only provides us with a *conditional* determination to avoid war. Do we use our communications as a weapon, or not? If so, to what extent? Again we are confronted with the long-run–short-run dilemma. In any given situation manipulation of an enemy may seem the best choice; yet in the end, if we are found out, we may create a worse enemy than we already had by engaging in such behavior. Should we discount the future? There is simply no "rule" of rationality on the subject. Without such a rule, arms-control techniques like the "hot line" become ambiguous in their purpose—as will be obvious if we try to imagine a "hot line" between Tokyo and Washington on December 6, 1941.[52]

In all the cases I have mentioned, to sum up, the notion of deterrence rationality is useless because of the existence of duality in our goals—*peace* with *honor*—and multiplicity in the means potentially capable of attaining them. Of our dual goals, any mixture is rational as long as it does not completely traduce the idea of nuclear deterrence. Of our multiple means, any one may turn out to be the correct one. Once again if we had perfect knowledge the latter problem would not arise. But once again, inarguably we do not.* We are thus stuck with

*One definition of the notion of rationality is indicative of its emptiness in concrete situations. Marion J. Levy defines logical (rational) action as action that an all-knowing observer would say is logically linked to an (empirically) desired end. Since there are no all-knowing observers, there seems to be no logical action. One is reminded of Bishop Berkeley's taking refuge in God to escape the logic of solipsism.[53]

our assumption of rationality, which can lead us to think in endless circles but can never help us to make any but the grossest, most obvious choices.[54]

III. The Problem of Policy-Making

Another (and similarly) crucial problem in the theory of deterrence rationality concerns the ways in which we actually make our policy, rather than difficulties in choosing among policies. What first comes to mind in this regard is the problem of governmental organization, which is often summed up in the aphorism that a camel is a horse created by a committee. That is to say, what are the implications of the fact that government, even in a totalitarian society, may to a large extent be described as a kind of bargaining process—the result of the continual bargaining being continually changing policy.

Two aspects of this process are particularly noteworthy here. The first, which is probably most relevant in democratic societies such as the United States, is the sheer number of individuals and institutions concerned with policy formulation in a given field. Congressmen who are locally, nationally, and institutionally oriented; the President and his entourage; departments and agencies at or near the Cabinet level; the military establishment as a unit and the three branches taken separately; and the influential opinion elite [55]—all have a contribution to make, and all must be placated in an area such as national security policy. Often, too, policy is finally approved in special committees, such as the NSC or the JCS, made up of formal delegates from various of these institutions. The result is that the kind of legislative maneuvering, parochialism, and power-seeking that textbooks associate with legislatures actually characterize policy-making in the executive branch as well.[56] In the 1950's especially, the result of failure somehow to control this bargaining process in the policy community led analysts with such disparate views on other matters as Generals Maxwell Taylor and James Gavin, Robert Gilpin, Bernard Brodie, Glenn Snyder, Thomas Finletter, Saville Davis, Amitai Etzioni, and Arthur Waskow to bewail the results; many of these critics would surely have agreed with Waskow's complaint that ". . . adherents of each service have in mind its own continued power and prestige, rather than any independent assessment of proper defense policy for the United States." [57]

In addition to the difficulties caused by the involvement of decision-makers in the bargaining process (difficulties which, to repeat, must be immense even in the Communist nations), there is also the problem that decision-makers are faced by difficulties inherent in the collection and interpretation of intelligence—of knowledge. Under the best of circumstances, the course of information flow from the field through information analysts to policy-makers will be tortuous, bedevilled by the demands of any complex communications process (such as the desire to conform analyses to one's expectations of what one's superiors desire to hear). As Harold and Margaret Sprout have argued, although politics is generally supposed to be the art of the possible, the assumption that policy-makers can really find out what is possible is a dubious one:

> The higher one moves in the hierarchy of a great power's government, the more one is impressed by the remoteness of executives from the operational environment in which their decisions are executed. What passes for knowledge of the

situation at the higher levels consists mainly of generalized descriptions and abstracts, several degrees removed from on-the-spot observations. On most issues the individual or group responsible for decisions will have little time and only the most general knowledge for checking what is prepared at lower working levels of the organization.

. . . To what extent is a top-level executive a virtual prisoner of the civil and military officials who provide data for him? On the other hand, how may his known preferences affect the substance and coloration of what his staffs decide to tell him? To what extent may their own attitudes and preferences bias their observations and calculations? In other words, to what extent is the "wish father to the thought" in statecraft as in other walks of life? And to what extent do such considerations affect the whole chain of communications in a complex foreign-policy-making situation?

. . . The common sense assumption of adequate environmental knowledge . . . is no more than a hypothesis to be confirmed—rarely, if ever, an assumption to be taken for granted.[58]

But there are also some special difficulties in the intelligence and scientific community. Information gatherers and analysts are the only group involved in policy-making whose major professional responsibility is to adopt the analytic attitude—to be relatively free of interested political or organizational involvement. If they are not, then it must be questionable whether decision-makers will have "the best" or even "adequate" information, or any real "information" that can be distinguished from their own or someone else's prejudices. However, the almost universal underestimation by Americans of the length of time it would take the Soviets to develop A- and H-bombs suggests the extent to which cultural attitudes replace dispassionate analysis even under conditions that make the latter especially urgent.[59] Other examples of such failures of expertise are contained in Robert Gilpin's full-length study, which analyzes the process by which American political decision-makers have received technical and semitechnical information from scientists in the nuclear era.[60] The issues Gilpin studies—the main one being the question of nuclear testing—directly relate to the whole problem of deterrence strategy. In his concluding remarks he notes that "Due to their strong and understandable desire to solve the security problem facing the United States and, of course, all humanity, scientists have too often permitted dispassionate and rigorous analysis to give way to nostrums, oversimplifications, and pre-conceived solutions." [61] Gilpin's exhaustive treatment of the recent work of American scientific advisers is even more suggestive when taken together with C. P. Snow's account of the British intragovernmental disputes over radar and strategic bombing in World War II.[62] The conclusions of each reinforce those of the other. The question they both ask is, how can the scientists, whose expertise is supposed to be rational calculation or the analysis of data designed to forward rational calculation, be distinguished from the politicians, who attain their official positions on entirely different grounds? Maneuvering over the test-ban issue among U.S. governmental agencies following the publication of Gilpin's book, and the public dispute among analysts of the U.S.S.R. civil-defense effort in 1962—both episodes produced virtual charges of lying against official or semi-official sources—only add to one's doubts about the nature of the data "inputs" to the policy process.[63]

Furthermore, it must be strongly emphasized that unlike more ordinary areas of administration, national security analysis is a field in which important information is often deliberately hidden from the view of information-gatherers. This is but a restatement of the dilemma of arms-control systems that I have already discussed: one must communicate to the other enough information to stabilize deterrence, without communicating so much as would destabilize it by making one's forces vulnerable and one's bluffs transparent.

National security is also perhaps the only field in which there are special doctrines of information analysis —notably the attribution to an opponent of all his capabilities—that are antiempirical and therefore may, if adopted, continually and tendentiously distort the truth. Adherence to this "capabilities not intentions" perspective, and perhaps also an element of the scientist nonrationality noted above, offers a partial explanation of the uniform adoption by the intelligence community of the "delicate balance of terror" approach in the late 1950's. Similarly, NATO strategy since 1948 has been based almost entirely on the notion that the Soviets would attack Western Europe as soon as they could feasibly do so; that they have not done so indicates to our analysts that we succeeded in "deterring" them. But suppose they failed to attack not because we denied them the capability, but simply because they lacked the intention! An entirely different perspective on NATO would be indicated—yet "rationality" would be asserted to prohibit our adopting any other perspective than the one we had and still have.[64]

Even more important is the problem that we confront if we try to change to an "intentions rather than capabilities" estimate. How can such a change rationally be justified? As long as we lack considerable information about our enemies' intentions, and cling to the Hobbesian view of the world, rationality would seem to compel us to focus chiefly on capabilities. Suppose the achievement of some kind of détente, or halt in the arms race, might require us to take a chance on intentions? Then we would either have to give up rationality, or give up détente. Whichever choice we made, the idea of rationality would have been less than helpful.

It should be remembered, moreover, that we have been talking only about the behavior of *American* decision-makers. Communist decision-making, as I have said, is also without doubt a conflictful process rather than a monolithic one. For example, in 1963 Sidney Ploss wrote:

> Rarely have Soviet pronouncements on politico-military affairs been as discordant as in the months . . . surrounding the Kremlin's risk-fraught decision to emplace intermediate-range ballistic missiles in Cuba. . . . [I]t is evident that late in 1961 and early in 1962 a consensus had not been reached on the capability of the Soviet military machine. . . . [65]*

Furthermore, since Communist intelligence may be in an even worse state than our own because of the blindness brought about by the wearing of self-imposed ideological blinders, the likelihood of arriving at mutually correct perceptions seems almost remote.[67] In any event, Bernard Cohen's comment about our knowledge of Soviet behavior would probably apply at least equally well to their (and Chinese) knowledge of ours:

> . . . While it might seem to make sense to assume that the Soviet Union is rational and that it makes rough calculations of probabilities, it must be said again that we simply do not know the values, preferences, calculations of gain and

*Ploss adds that the presumably technical dispute over Soviet missile strength actually "had strong political overtones."[66]

loss, and so forth, in the Soviet Union that would give content to these modes of analysis. (Was Hitler really a madman—that is to say, irrational—or was he rational?) We do not even know all that we would like to know about the policy-making system in the United States, to know whose values are relevant, and how they get compromised and combined. Nor do the Russians know these things either![68]

IV   The Problem of Politics

It is imaginable, of course, that dedicated politician-statesmen in any kind of society might create structures to quell the excesses of the bargaining process (though one suspects the methods would be different in democratic and totalitarian societies), and that the application of sheer unfettered intellect might considerably ease the information problem. Indeed, it appears to be the judgment of some deterrence theorists that President Kennedy and especially Secretary McNamara definitely succeeded in doing the former, and it could easily be argued that in the past few years assessments of each other by the U.S. and the U.S.S.R. have increased considerably in sophistication.*

This is to say, in other words, that in order to carry out a certain policy it is rational to choose as policy-

---

*W. W. Kaufmann makes a very strong case that McNamara has succeeded in pulling the strands of policy together so that the United States now has a consistent stable deterrence plus all-level limited-war capability. That is not the judgment of all observers; one critic remarked on McNamara's testimony at a Defense appropriations hearing: [I]t seems . . . The Administration *has no defense policy*, at least not one that I have succeeded in extracting from Secretary McNamara's recent testimony before the HASC. There are moments, like the present one, in which to engage defense politicians—for politicians they are . . . not men formulating a policy rational enough to serve as a basis for meaningful debate . . . in a discussion of strategy seems . . . tantamount to jousting at windmills."[69]

makers men who are "best" qualified to perform such a task. A theory that thus depends for its successful implementation on choosing good men is of doubtful long-run practical value. No doubt, in principle, the problems discussed so far remain soluble ones (and each of us must judge for himself how likely the principle is to be translated into fact). However, what has been said above about choosing the "best" men suggests an additional problem—the problem of politics—and in considering that problem we discover further theoretical difficulties in the concept of rationality that cannot be overcome by any stretch of the imagination. To put it simply, there is and must be a hidden political bias in deterrence theory, and the nature of this bias has serious consequences.[70]

To deal first with the existence of bias, we need only note that not all members of society have a common purpose. However, by their own lights they will all be rational, for, it must be remembered, the concept of instrumental rationality *in general* does not require a commitment to any *particular* purpose, or, in the case of national security policy, to any particular version of national interest (or even to *national* interest at all).[71] Nor will simple exhortation (not that the works of Kahn, Schelling, *et al.* could be so described) suffice to bring about a change in this condition to produce an agreed-on national purpose; at least, the history of past attempts to do so has not been a happy one.[72] Thus, the failure of deterrence theorists to point to any kind of "national value set," that could supply even a rough means-end calculation as the agreed-on end of the society is because no such national value set exists.[73]

To gain some further insight into this problem, we may consider Glenn Snyder's reply to this kind of argument, in his review of Samuel Huntington's *The Common Defense:*

> Consensus is important in domestic legislation because the stakes are the conflicting values of subnational groups. . . . It is true, as Huntington says, that "divergent interests" are at stake in the military policy-making process, but these interests do not diverge over ultimate values except as they reflect different conceptions of how much of the national resources should be devoted to security as opposed to non-security values. Within the over-all allocation of resources to security, the diverging interests center on different conceptions of the means proper to realizing agreed goals and values. . . .
>
> To a much greater degree than in most other policy areas, military policy is a problem of factual analysis, informed prediction, and logical deduction, although value questions cannot be entirely excluded. Of course there is plenty of room for disagreement, and when the disagreeing parties possess both particular organizational interests and power, "politics" is bound to take place. But it is not clear why a compromise representing the relative power of the various interests will produce a policy closer to the logical imperatives of the national interest than an authoritative decision by "one man" or several men whose interests and outlook are truly national. The normative problem is one of *reconciling* politics and logic in such a manner that the inherent logic is not wholly submerged in a welter of conflicting parochial pressures.[74]

This quotation reveals all the pitfalls of deterrence rationality *in esse*. The "ultimate values" which Snyder insists are agreed on, are agreed on (if they are) only when stated so grandiosely and abstractly that they are non-operational.* Snyder himself nowhere comes close

---

*Here and in the following paragraphs I do not mean to adopt the naïve positivist view of insisting that there is no such thing as "the public interest" or "the common good." I do believe that one can distinguish between actions that are "in the *public* interest"

to stating what the "truly national" national interest is, except in terms of military operations based on a short-term and low-level—not "ultimate"—idea of "national security." But it is precisely the political question of how and where to devote resources that engages the operational values of a society. More, those values are emergent; they are actually created by the decisions he thinks are merely "instrumental." Can we say that "national survival," for example, is an agreed-on interest, and all-out nuclear war, surrender, limited war, and protracted war are but differently conceived "means" to that end? Hardly—those strategies themselves embody values that, if not "ultimate," are as basic and troublesome as any that men of affairs ever have to deal with. Indeed, it is because such questions are so troublesome that Robert Levine and Arthur Herzog have been able to write books about *an* arms *debate*, rather than *the* arms *policy*.

In the absence, furthermore, of any clear statement about how one deduces "the logical imperatives of the national interest," or knows whose outlook is "truly national" and whose is not, Snyder's "inherent logic" becomes sheer mysticism (if not partisan prejudice; see my comments below, pp. 247–48). In this context it is worth quoting at length Bernard C. Cohen's comments on the attempt by deterrence theorists to assign priorities to strategic choices without reference to any theory of politics:

> . . . In the search for a science of military policy, the intractable political problems of military policy-making are being skirted or ignored. . . .

---

and those that are not. But to say that the distinction is meaningful is not to say that there is one and only one acceptable version of the public interest (or the national interest) in a given situation.

Military policy-making, like all public policy determination in the American political system, is marked by . . . necessary compromises of value and policy preferences among large constituencies, inside and outside the structure of government, in order to reach decisions that seem as if they can be implemented; and by continuous efforts by various participants in these processes to alter these decisions once they have been made. . . .

[Snyder] . . . sets for [the] decision-maker a mode of rational calculation that may be suitable for the decision-maker in his private capacity but which in our larger democratic political system is wholly dependent for its value-inputs on the structure of value compromises that emerges in specific situations. . . . [75]

. . . Values and preferences may be easily determinable for individuals . . . but for a political system like ours they can be established only by the workings of the political process after it confronts a concrete problem. Hence they are not available ahead of time as inputs for the "rational" solution of the policy problem.

. . . Even more to the point, however, the subjective probabilities that individuals attach to outcomes may be influenced by the values which they believe to be engaged in the issues themselves. . . . Calculations . . . thus can be made to come out the way people's preferred inputs—in the form of probability assessments—want them to come out. The assignment of the most likely probabilities, then, can and often does become a way of making an argument in the policy debate, rather than a way of solving the policy problem . . . [W]hen the analyst has made *his* determination of what the probabilities and values are *likely* to be for the contingencies he is considering . . . his analysis embodying his conclusions is still only one element in the political debate itself, subject to contest at any point by the host of practitioners of the art of political representation (and by other policy analysts as well!).[76]

Thus, the injunction to prospective decision-makers to be "rational," or to plan for possible "rational" behavior must be seen as empty given multiple political options, just as it is empty given multiple strategic and tactical options. We can, of course, enjoin them to share our particular deterrence rationality. But then, there exists an infinity of possible ends for human actors to choose among. Not all decision-makers in our nation, the Soviet Union, China, Germany, or "catalytic" small powers [77] necessarily believe in the exclusive rightness of deterrence. To hope that they would do so is to replace analysis with utopianism—and the latter is not one of the virtues that deterrence theorists claim. Deterrence theory then becomes a kind of hypothetical imperative: "If you want to deter, act so as to deter." But suppose you want not merely to deter?

Moreover, entirely aside from the element of bias involved, there are in fact further political consequences of the choice of deterrence as one's end. And these consequences suggest the existence of one more major inconsistency in the notion of deterrence rationality.

Deterrence theorists have on the whole entirely neglected the political context of their ideas. Of course, that does not mean that they think "politics" cannot have any influence on the decision-making elite. They may, perhaps, feel that such factors can be asimilated into their picture of decision-making without adversely affecting the achievement of the goals of deterrence strategy. But if this is what deterrence theorists feel, they have not said so. Perhaps the most striking feature of the literature of deterrence is that internal political occurrences are hardly ever mentioned as possible destabilizing factors in a deterrence system. (We might contrast this omission with the attention paid such supposedly worrisome problems as erroneous information, Communist ideological aggressiveness and moral recklessness, technological breakthrough, the N*th* country problem, escalation from limited war, etc.)*

The one exception to this generalization is in Levine's *The Arms Debate* (which is only a summary in any event). However, his discussion of politics merely demonstrates one of the worst pitfalls of deterrence theory.

A key component of rational deterrence theory as represented by Levine is the assumption that commitment to deterrence policy is a particular kind of political act. To be precise, it is supposed to be along the American political spectrum a moderate, or "centrist" act, falling in-between the commitment of those who say, "Better Red than Dead!" on the one hand, and "Why Not Victory?" on the other.[79] And to this ideological interpretation of deterrence theory is added the further descriptive point that, as Levine has asserted, "extremists," *particularly anti-Communist extremists,* have little or no influence on national security policy-making.[80] The particular way in which these assumptions are incorrect points up the weakness of deterrence rationality.

The policy process that is implicit in such rationalist theory, which is depicted or suggested by analysts such as Levine, Glenn Snyder, and Kaplan, is one in which policy-makers freely draw on the best available analyses of a situation, freely choose their values from a supply

---

*This omission has been made with deliberation in several of the formalized analyses of deterrence theory. Kaplan, in his "Calculus of Nuclear Deterrence" makes use of the following one among a host of assumptions in building his deterrence model: " . . . no consideration [is] given to internal developments within nations. . . . " And A. L. Burns excludes anthropology, sociology, and psychology from his formal model of international relations, as well as all non-rational elements that might ordinarily be thought of as part of the study of politics.[78]

of relevant values, and freely arrive at the policy that can be shown to be the logical result of combining the preferred analyses and values. For better or worse, however, leaders in a democracy—and perhaps to some extent in any stable polity—are often unable to act with anything resembling the freedom that is here attributed to them. The choice of policies rather moves in incremental steps. Policy-makers tend to start with past choices—past analyses, values, and recommendations—and modify them in marginal ways.[81] This is partly due to inertia—in the complete absence of which political life would become chaotic—and partly due to the fact that past choices represent *commitments,* which must be at least partially honored as long as those to whom (and by whom) the commitments were made retain any political influence.

Now one of the least tangible but most far-reaching of the commitments that political leaders can make is their commitment to be responsive to the attitudes of their constituents. If the attitudes are rigid, therefore, the commitments will also tend to be relatively rigid, and policy-makers will be "unfree" in the most important respect of all: their ability to choose direction for society. Karl Deutsch has suggested as a hypothesis for research on internation conflict that "governments frequently decide to go to war when they believe themselves to be constrained by the lack of any acceptable political alternative to war . . . they lose their freedom."[82] And a critic of deterrence thought notes the relevance of this hypothesis to deterrence theory:

> . . . implicit in the concept of deterrence is the idea of being able to use it as a shield for pushing an adversary to political extremes, safe in the knowledge that as long as he remains sane he will not use his nuclear weapons. However,

an enemy could be pushed so hard and into such an inextricable corner that he may well be forced by the nature of his commitments to act regardless of the consequences.[83]

When speaking of policy-making, therefore, we should ask not only for what values policy-makers have indicated a preference, but also to what values they are publicly committed. And when we do this we see that the rationalistic deterrence theory to which American leaders are supposedly committed is not unrelated to the "irrational" (i.e., non-deterrence-oriented) views of other groups in American society.

Indeed, the notion that the two kinds of thinking are totally unrelated is not only false but dangerous. It is dangerous because Levine's other assertion, concerning the non-influence of the right is also incorrect. The key point here is that, with regard to the cold war, national leaders in the United States have steadily committed themselves, since approximately 1946 (and especially since the fall of China to Communism), to a series of public attitudes that, to use Levine's terms, often look much more like "anti-Communist" than like deterrence attitudes.[84] No doubt the Kennedy administration did much to dampen the heated public spirit which led to such phenomena as "McCarthyism." But it can certainly be argued that the national consensus on the cold war is still vulnerable to the extreme anti-Communists: that they play an important role, even if only a subterranean one, in setting the permissible limits of innovation and reform in national security policy-making.

Some examples of this phenomenon of "limit-setting" are the hostile response of Republican spokesmen to Senator J. W. Fulbright's "old myths and new realities" speech, as well as Fulbright's own unwillingness to disavow certain cold-war attitudes;[85] the failure of *any* liberal senators or representatives to defend the Democratic Study Group's *The Liberal Papers* against the savage, red-baiting Republican attacks on it;[86] the successful efforts made by the Kennedy administration in the summer of 1963 to justify the nuclear test ban treaty in terms that would appeal to strong "anti-Communists;"[87] and most important, the way in which the Johnson administration's attempt to steer a course between "right" and "left" opposition in the Vietnam crisis has often brought it closer to the former than the latter.

In the cold war era the United States has become a nation in which strong anti-Communism, even in periods of "thaw," seems to be the only enduring and safe political attitude in the area of foreign affairs. Thus the "moderation" of deterrence theorists must be seen as fitting into a policy process in which dedication to an anti-communism more immediate and stronger than their own is an important element; a policy process which is so subject to ideological pressures that one noted critic has been led to remark fearfully ". . . it may be easier in the short run to contain the Soviet Union than to contain our own allies or the American energies mobilized behind the cold war."[88] I have already referred to the case of the Cuban missile crisis: whether or not "history" judges Kennedy's strategy to have been successful, the fact that the U.S. was in such a dangerous situation to begin with can easily be laid to exactly the kind of cold war ideological and emotional rigidity that Riesman describes.[89]

The independence of deterrence doctrine is further compromised because, despite being what Charles Osgood calls a security-oriented concept, nuclear deterrence still rests primarily on militarized threats.[90] Thus, unless one is an extreme advocate of minimum deterrence, and probably of sheer bluff in the end, as a deterrence theorist one is most often committed to military modes of thought. This is especially true of the particular mode of thought known familiarly as "toughness." In all crisis situations where nuclear weapons may have to be called into play, "toughness" is indeed almost a synonym for that credibility upon which successful deterrence depends. Therefore, in a given situation most deterrence theorists (as even such a sympathetic observer as Levine admits) invariably seem to concentrate on the military options such as limited war, low-level nuclear war, etc., that are available. (See my further comments on this subject in Chapter VI below.) In doing this they willy-nilly partially align themselves with those other forces in society that also vaunt "toughness." * No doubt "rational" hardheadedness is preferable to "irrational" spleen; but no deterrence theorist has thought to ask whether there may

---

*For example, a sometime collaborator in the production of "Radical Right" literature, Chester C. Ward, has recently published a scholarly analysis of national security problems in the journal *Orbis*.[91] The military strategy content of his analysis is little different from that which one finds in the work of Kahn, Glenn Snyder, and many other deterrence theorists: rejection of a "minimum" or "finite" deterrence strategy in favor of a plausible first-strike plus civil-defense strategy. But Ward varies one—and only one—assumption of the deterrence theorists. Rather than describing the Soviet posture as conditionally hostile, he describes it as secretly "genocidal." The result is a denial of the whole *political* content of deterrence theory: of the need to reach agreements on arms control, to maintain a détente, to keep limited war limited, etc. It is, rather, a win-the-war strategy and as such it is, from the standpoint of deterrence theory, non-rational. But to anyone who rejects the cold war perspective in American thinking, the line between these two modes of strategic doctrine will seem perilously thin.

not actually be a symbiotic political relationship between the two and what its implications might be.

This question is given further importance by the fact that in the world of nuclear deterrents it is necessary to maintain a delicate psychic balance in which such an immense threat is seen as essentially peace-preserving—sometimes even in times of actual warfare. Whether this balance can be maintained will depend on the answers to many further questions: who are the kinds of people who tend to come to power in such a situation? How much does the accumulation of massively destructive arms lead to an increase rather than a decrease in international tensions? How easy will it be for people who think they are capable of fruitfully putting nuclear weapons to coercive use continually to refrain from doing so?

Although an assessment of the real implications of deterrence theory is utterly dependent on the kinds of answers we give to such questions, once again no deterrence theorist has attempted to provide them. Critics, especially social psychologists, have suggested many tentative—and pessimistic—answers. For example, Thomas Milburn has asserted that the idea of deterring someone from a given course of action by threatening to punish him ignores some fundamental insights into human psychology: "[O]utside threat tends to increase the cohesiveness of a group. . . . Punishments (or the threat of them) . . . serve little to change underlying motives" but rather "increase anxiety and hostility." Most important with regard to nuclear deterrence, "[S]evere stress . . . decreases one's ability to use perspective and judgment." [92] Similarly Kenneth Boulding has suggested that it is the perception of hostility that tends to make a conflict system unstable by causing overtures of friendliness to be consistently disbelieved, and that this is especially true in the area of interstate conflict, which is ordinarily built around "images" of an "enemy" that constitute "the last great stronghold of unsophistication." [93] This observation, furthermore, has been strengthened by the accounts of authors such as Raymond Bauer and Ole Holsti. Bauer, a professional Sovietologist, describes how experts and scholars themselves, in both this country and the U.S.S.R., in their attempt to create "models" that will sort out relevant information tend to focus on those characteristics of "the other" that feed national prejudices and increase the probability of mutual misperceptions of aims and actions.[94] Holsti, more rigorously focussing on the specific instance of John Foster Dulles' perceptions of Soviet policy, concludes:

> To the extent that each side undeviatingly interprets new information, even friendly bids, in a manner calculated to preserve the original image, the two-nation system is a closed one with small prospect for achieving even a desired reduction of tensions.
> . . . [P]erceptions of low hostility are self-liquidating and perceptions of high hostility are self-fulfilling. The former, being associated with weakness and frustration, do not invite reciprocation; the latter, assumed to derive from strength and success, are likely to result in reactions which will increase rather than decrease tensions.[95]

Charles Osgood has argued, finally, that in the semi-militarized world of nuclear deterrence one may not be able to institutionalize the threat of military force without also institutionalizing the "bogeyman" view of a "diabolical" enemy; extreme ideological hostility and rigidity especially in periods of severe crisis or hot war; and finally a kind of "moral deadness," which sees no standard for judging any issue except sheer self-protection through military means. The result, he postulates, is likely to be that the "security" of A comes to be the chief cause of the fears of B, and vice-versa, so that a condition of anxiety is created on all sides—anxiety that creates in both leaders and followers neurotic tensions: and these tensions may come to demand reduction by resort to preventive war or lesser but still dangerous acts of irrationality, as the self-imposition of an inability to perceive the existence of options that are relatively nonviolent.[96]

To say that such arguments have been made is of course far different from saying that they are correct.[97] The important points are, first, that on occasion the rhetoric of deterrence must emphasize the reliance on force and extreme distrust of Communism to which more militant groups in American society are so attached;[98] and second, that deterrence theory may be liable to distortion owing to its entanglement with attitudes that breed further cold war instability. In so far as deterrence proposals are dependent upon, as well as contributing to, the broader political setting in which they are made, a strong possibility exists that they will be implemented in a spirit different from the spirit in which they are made. Once again it is clear that in its own terms rational deterrence logic may just as likely be self-defeating as productive of its desired ends.

V. Rationality in International Conflict

The concept of rationality as used by deterrence theorists is neither self-consistent in meaning nor unambiguous in its implications for action. Deterrence rationality requires both continued technological progress in the arms race and, on occasion, arms stabilization; short-run decisions favoring the national interest, conceived in narrow military terms, and long-run decisions favoring the "interest" of international integration; the maintenance of feelings of hostility against a threatening enemy, and willingness to compromise with the enemy in order to avoid catastrophe. These requirements are not always compatible with one another. Absolutely contradictory courses of action are equally "rational," depending on what perspective one adopts, or how one chooses to define the word.

There is one way, perhaps, in which the idea of a consistent use of the rationality assumption could conceivably be salvaged for deterrence theory. It might be claimed that all the criticisms I have so far made have been process-oriented criticisms; that is, they have been based on the observation that the process of policy formulation is not compatible with whatever behavioral requirements one can deduce from an assumption of rationality. It could be argued that the literature of deterrence is largely *decision-* rather than process-oriented, and that the elements that go into the making of a unique decision are largely independent of the elements that have preceded the concrete event requiring a decision. Quite probably this is the way that some deterrence theorists, especially those who have engaged in the pseudo-quantification of game theory in their analyses, have conceived of the problem they are dealing with: we have been attacked; what do we do?

We must explicitly reiterate, therefore, what has so far only been implied: there is a defect in the whole notion that policy is created by, and progresses through, the making of "decisions"—a notion that necessarily inheres in rationalistic deterrence doctrine. The "decision-making approach," as exemplified for political scientists in the pioneering work of Richard Snyder, Bruck, and Sapin has much virtue in isolating relevant actors and aspects of their actions in a specific situation.[99] But that virtue lasts only so long as we realize that a "decision" is only a part of a decisional process that began long before the specific decision was made. What has been said about the incremental nature of policy is crucial here: the analysis of possible actions is always drastically limited with regard both to the number of alternative actions actually studied and the consideration given to potential subsidiary results of alternative policies; the theory is subordinated to *ad hoc* short-run comparisons of proposed policies; the test of final correctness is simple "political acceptability." [100] Thus a series of "decisions" can be taken that add up, in the end, to what I have previously spoken of (and Schelling also speaks of) as a *commitment*. What would have seemed an extremist policy years ago will now seem unavoidable and even "right"—i.e., demanded by the situation into which we have fallen. (It hardly needs saying that this is the way many advocates of the administration's cause in Vietnam describe the sequence of events there, and the present "necessities" of policy).[101] The momentary act of decision, on which so much of the literature of "decision-making" focuses, may be little more than *pro forma*.

Furthermore, if we leave the narrow realm of policy, we see that on a broader scale the notion of "decision-making" begs the whole question of historical causation. As I have noted in my discussion of game theory and the "autonomous probability" of events, often it is not clear whether theories of conscious choice are relevant to what we find ourselves doing. For example, the kind of conflict that makes war a likely recourse may be, as Boulding calls it, "epidemiological," so that its etiology may be described as we would describe that of an infectious disease.[102] We would then be postulating a condition exactly like that to which Herman Kahn ascribes the explosion of World War I:

> [T]he more historians examine World War I, the more it seems to be clear that this was a war none of the responsible governments wanted, a war set in motion by relatively trivial circumstances, a motion which given the state of the world, could not be stopped. . . . [103]

That is, what we mean by the incremental element in policy-making is "increments" not only of prior formal decisions arrived at by formal governmental agencies but also "increments" of change and influence in the whole historical and social context within which a given "decision" is imbedded: the influence of broad, long-run historical forces, and the "subterranean" effects of social structures and ideologies, on the ultimate products of the so-called policy process.[104]

At the very least, surely we want to consider the possibility that detailed analysis of the history, politics, and social structure of ourselves and our opponents would show that we would meet the same fate Kahn describes if we follow on our present course. Along a given pattern of action or events, there always exists a limiting boundary at which we begin to perceive that whatever "good" intentions we may have at some future time of action, we cannot readily expect to be able to implement them. Where may that boundary be crossed, or approached? Most important, will the adoption of a strategy of nuclear deterrence bring us to that dangerous juncture more quickly than would the adoption of another strategy?

Deterrence theorists have almost unanimously neglected to ask this question. None of them has referred to either theories or empirical data about organizational and political structure, and historical and social forces, that would be assimilable to a picture of rational decision-making (by any definition), or that might enable us to feel we are in a historical epoch in which the notion of rational deterrence is and will continue to be a useful one.*

On the contrary, what they have done is to adopt a vocabulary that implicitly settles the question without ever giving critics the chance to argue it. I refer especially to their constant use of the words "aggressor" and "defender" to describe the parties to a war, which gives the clear impression that war is always something someone "starts" (as in the phrase, *"You* started it!"), and can thus be avoided if we can get "potential aggressors" not to "start" anything.[105] Perhaps the influence of game theory as well as simple political bias has contributed to this vocabulary: although in formal game theory moves are simultaneous, it does seem as though most analysts can't even draw up matrices without conceiving

*In fact, some deterrence theorists, Kaplan and Burns most notably, have, as I noted earlier, deliberately excluded such references from their treatment of deterrence problems. Of course, other writers are not bound by this choice; but the importance of formal "models" such as those created by Kaplan and Burns is that they draw out the implications of an idea, and this particular implication about deterrence theory is hard to deny, I should think.

of an "aggressor" and "defender," that is, a first "mover" and a second "mover." But whatever the genesis of this approach, the result often verges on mere chauvinism. (Oddly, that this vocabulary of "aggression" and "defense" may not be the relevant one with which to describe the onset of international hostilities is a thought that occurs to deterrence theorists when they are discussing the problem of dealing with Communist "subversion," but hardly ever when they are discussing the idea of nuclear war.)[106] Here again, the idea of rationality is just a hindrance.

Does the "rational man" concept have any conceivable use in policy analysis? It seems doubtful, since we have seen that it means only that we say before the fact that we will make correct choices, or after the fact that we have done so. The first statement is simply wild prophecy; the second is denied by almost any historical investigation one cares to make. G. Lowes Dickinson, Sidney Fay, A. J. P. Taylor, Herman Kahn, and Robert North on World War I; Taylor, Kahn, Roberta Wohlstetter,* and Herbert Feis on World War II; and Allen Whiting and Morton Halperin on the Korean War—all testify to that effect.[108]

Schelling and others [109] have, at times, referred to the non-use of poison gas during World War II as possibly a successful instance of deterrence based on tacitly

---

*The preface to Mrs. Wohlstetter's book is written by Thomas Schelling, who remarks on the great difficulties inherent in the task of deterrence, and asserts a need for continuously more rigorous thought about how to structure deterrence for the cold war. His conclusion that there must be a policy of nuclear deterrence to begin with has presumably been suggested to him by some source other than his reading in histories such as Mrs. Wohlstetter's.[107]

understood "ground rules" for limiting war. The case of poison gas, though, is only doubtfully relevant to a consideration of nuclear deterrence. Poison gas was not an "ultimate" weapon; it was not even a strategic weapon; it was a tactical weapon of dubious battlefield value to its user. There would have been no reason for a "madman" to use it on the battlefield—it was not that orgiastically destructive a weapon. (And the horrible fact is that where it could be used without costs of the kind a "madman" could recognize, it was: several million Jews were killed with it.) Similarly, because of its limited value there was no reason why a simple miscalculation should have been likely to result in its use. Indeed, when strategic weapons with the potentiality for damaging the nation-state in large were available—long-range heavy bombers targetted on cities; V-2's; atomic bombs—they *were* used, despite the possibility (in the first two cases) of retaliation in kind. Much has been written about the decision to employ these various weapons.[110] The conclusion that is more or less implicit in all these analyses, as stated by George Quester relative to the "breakdown" of limits on bombing in the European theater, is that "this example discourages any over-confidence about our ability to find easy solutions to the problem [of controlled and limited use of strategic nuclear weapons]."[111] None of this or any other available evidence can lead one to disagree with the conclusion that the evidence of human unwillingness to use neat prescriptions of reasonableness during periods of crisis is overwhelming.

Occasionally, it is argued in response to this kind of comment that the "nuclear era" is a "new" era, in which the very nature of the forces "let loose" will enforce a kind of sensible or conservative calculating behavior on decision-makers. This position is implicit, for instance, in the suggestion that the spread of nuclear weapons may induce more rather than less responsible behavior on the part of those who join the "nuclear club." [112] However, one can find few grounds for claiming that nation-state behavior in the cold war period has been more sensible than at other times. It will hardly do to rest that case on the mere absence of general war since 1945. Twenty years without general war is hardly a long enough time to suggest anything at all. The arms race continues; great power hostility remains; crises recur. The most recent of these have seemed, at least superficially, to open as many avenues to general war as did the crises, say, of 1956; if "nuclear learning" is really taking place, its signs are not evident. Hedley Bull's judgment still remains sadly relevant:

> . . . A great deal of argument about military strategy . . . postulates a rational action of a kind of strategic man, a man who on further acquaintance reveals himself as a university professor of unusual intellectual subtlety . . . where rational action is defined to exclude the deliberate choice of military catastrophe, this is not a notion in terms of which it is possible to account for any great part of the history of international politics, or to base any confident prediction about its future. The idea that war is a catastrophe which no government will choose to bring about has been a commonplace of writing about international relations since the turn of the century. The decisions of governments on matters of peace and war . . . do not always reflect a careful weighing of long-range considerations, or a mastery of the course of events; the questions which strike the historian of these decisions a generation afterwards as important appear crudely answered or, more often, not even asked: the governments appear to him to stumble about, groping and half blind, too preoccupied with surviving from day to day even to perceive

the direction in which they are heading, let alone steer away from it.[113]

We are led, finally, to the suspicion that "rationality" is a cant word, implying the possibility of giving a set of self-consistent instructions to decision-makers when, in the context of international conflict, no such set exists. Those who talk about rational behavior have merely found a high-flown way of justifying the policy they favor, while ignoring any discussion of important political problems, and of the possibility that their policy may ultimately be self-defeating. And in that case, if our analysis of the future is different from theirs we might as well conclude that they have done no more than to find a sophisticated way of restating a bad argument for a bad policy.

6   Deterrence Rationality and Ethical Choice

I.   Instrumental Rationality as an Implicit Ethic

To SAY that deterrence rationality is logically inconsistent, and in practice quite possibly self-defeating, might be considered a decisive criticism. However, I do not think it sufficient merely to suggest that defense policy expertise is to a large extent malexpertise, for even that may be considered better than no expertise at all. In this chapter, therefore, I shall take up one further consideration, perhaps the most consequential of all: that the traditional claim of technical expertise to be morally neutral is in this context a false claim. For deterrence theory is not merely a theory of rational behavior which assumes that the practice of rational behavior, and the assumption of rational behavior for purposes of analysis, will be fruitful. In adopting the stance that there is an *enemy,* or an opponent,[1] and that whenever there is a choice between maximizing our values and his, we maximize ours even if that involves injuring him, the theory stands forth as an instance of moral philosophy, and demands to be considered as such.

Since a good deal of modern social science is based on the unspoken notion that the assumption of rationality is ethically neutral, the implication in the above sentence may seem questionable.[2] Economists, for example, might

question whether it is possible to conceive of any definition of "rational" that does not mean "maximizing self-
interest." They would be quite right, of course, if the
term self-interest were taken as a tautology, so that one's
own "self-interest" might equally include one's devotion
to the interests of others: so that, in other words, one
could value co-operation more than competition. But deterrence theory does not so take the concept of national
self-interest. When deterrence theorists talk about the
mutual interest of the United States and the U.S.S.R. in
avoiding nuclear war, they mean that this is an acciden-
tally mutual interest that will only mitigate the impact
of what are otherwise assumed to be strongly and properly conflicting interests. That is why the discussion of
deterrence is replete with references to theories of conflict, limited war, arms control, etc.: to all those aspects
of international affairs which go to make up what is still
referred to as "the Cold War."

Certainly armed anti-Communism is not unreasonable
per se. On the other hand, it is not necessarily reasonable
in every situation. One can think of many instances, such
as the "space race," or the Vietnamese question, where
a strong case can be made out that maximization of our
interest as opposed to theirs is *not* reasonable. Conversely,
for them to be "anti-us" is not always reasonable either.
In each case, arguable political ethics rather than sheer
unarguable necessity often determines the choice to pit
"self" against "other."

Moreover, even if the choice in favor of perceiving
conflict could in some neo-Hobbesian manner be defended
as compelled by the state of affairs and thus ethically
neutral (neuter would be a better word here), there
would still be important distinctions to make in choosing

the kind of conflict we wished to emphasize. However, as I have said in earlier chapters, deterrence theorists such as Kahn, Schelling, and Wohlstetter do not make that distinction: wherever one writes "conflict" or "hostility," they read "military." But there is no general warrant for the assumption that hostility must be militarized. One could indeed try to make an empirical argument—an absurd one, I think—that the Soviet Union is militarily aggressive every time it perceives a possible advantage to be gained from such behavior. But no deterrence theorist has in truth done any more than assume that state of mind among Soviet leaders. Such an assumption is simple anti-Communist bias—which is hardly the same thing as "rationality." Alternatively, deterrence theorists might claim to borrow from game theory the conservative definition of rationality and define "rational" as expecting and planning for the worst.[3] Of course, anyone is entitled to his definitions, as long as he is willing, like Humpty-Dumpty, to admit that they are eccentric. The game-theoretic definition of rationality is no less eccentric because it appears in a theory. Most of the time in real life we do not plan for the worst unless we expect it, and we do not assume we expect it unless we really *do* expect it. To say that we ought to expect the worst regardless is to say we value our personal safety above any possibility of co-operation, social amelioration, etc. Such an imperative cannot be disguised as other than what it is, an ethical choice—and a strange one indeed.[4]

A more relevant objection that deterrence theorists might make to treating deterrence theory as a moral theory, is that those who advise on the logic of strategy are not competent to pass judgment on the values they must work with, nor should they be required to do so:

that is the job of those with the specific responsibility of articulating national values.

There is, however, a deep flaw in this line of reasoning, which becomes apparent when we ask exactly what is meant by rationally "maximizing self-interest." Does the phrase refer to the means we choose to maximize our interests, or to the particular interests we choose to maximize? Is a flagellant who carefully arranges to have himself whipped to death as economically as possible, "rational"? In talking about the relationship between values and the means of maximizing them, that is, we are in the presence of one of the deepest philosophical difficulties: a difficulty that can hardly be resolved as simply as modern instrumental rationalists sometimes imply.

For the word "rationality" can be used in two different senses. Karl Mannheim used the phrases, "functional rationality" and "substantial rationality" to distinguish these senses.[5] By "functional rationality" he meant rationality in the choice of means to an end—what the writers quoted earlier call, simply, rationality, or logical action.[6] By "substantial rationality" Mannheim meant *rationality in the choice of ends themselves*. Some (though not all) of the academic schools of modern philosophy would deny that the italicized phrase can be assigned any meaning if it refers to the realm of moral judgment and has no empirical referent. But leaving that argument aside, one can give a more limited meaning to Mannheim's category by asserting that, at the very least, one kind of substantial irrationality consists in choosing mutually conflicting ends. To take a gross example, perhaps it is true that one can argue neither with the desire to live nor with the desire to kill everybody that one dislikes if those are presented as moral choices.* However, one can certainly argue with the attempt to maintain both these values at the same time, for they are almost certainly incompatible.[7] What happens when one limits one's self to the notion of functional (or instrumental) rationality is that any analysis of ends becomes impossible. That substantial rationality,† which the act of setting values calls for, is left to those who set values; in this case, to leaders. The strategy analysts, then, have nothing to say about this. But if that is the case, then whatever inherent contradictions the leaders' values may contain will be worked into the very tissue of policy analysis.

This is exactly the case of nuclear deterrence theory. In the previous chapter we have seen that one of the logical difficulties with deterrence rationality is that it is dual goal-oriented. A deterrent is supposed to keep the peace and preserve national values against Communist encroachment or attack through means of military threat and action. All other goals must either be ignored by the policy-maker or considered subordinate to these, if he is to be considered "rational." Deterrence theory is concerned only with the functional rationality of decision-makers; whether the substance of what they are trying to accomplish has been "rationally" arrived at is a question that is ignored, or else the answer is taken for granted.

*My own view is that this kind of extreme moral relativism can quite reasonably be argued with; but that would be the subject of a separate essay.

†Or intelligence, since we might prefer to drop the word *rationality* altogether.

Thus a serious problem is generated. In the sense in which scientists try to be neutral, no one can really be ethically neutral in a social action context such as that within which advisers, consultants, and propagandists are placed. For the scientist to be indifferent among ethical principles is for him to accept and endorse the ethic that is presented to him as "given." To be specific, let us suppose the possibility that continuing and successful prosecution of the cold war, which appears in American politics as a virtually unmediated goal, is not compatible with the preservation of other American values. This might be the case for any or all of several reasons, some of which I have already suggested: that the Communist bloc (or part of it) may be driven to desperate action in a limited war or series of limited wars; that the same thing might happen to the United States; that one or a series of technological breakthroughs might irretrievably destabilize the arms race; that the U.S. might turn itself into a kind of "garrison state;" that the attempt to stabilize cold war hostility, even with the most complicated arms control measures, might only generate greater hostility. Suppose, that is, that in the vocabulary of deterrence theorists, the "cold war game" is somehow a *losing* game (has a negative payoff) in the nuclear age, and another "game"—say a disarmament "game"—might not be. Perhaps more relevantly, suppose that cold war attitudes and values are ultimately self-defeating.

What we are considering here, in other words, is not a grandiose pacifist notion that conflict and violence are always self-defeating, but rather the prospect that certain kinds of conflict taking place under existing conditions may be self-defeating, regardless of how useful they might be under different historical circumstances.[8] What "antiwar" theorists [9] object to in deterrence theory, more than anything else, is precisely the empirical assumption that attitudes and values do not interfere with the selection of actions and choices. Their argument is that those national decision-makers who share the attitudes and values of deterrence theory cannot in the long run be trusted to behave "well," regardless of their commitment to functional "rationality." Certain attitudes and values are thought to derange, so to speak, the intellect and make correct choice even in the *real-politik* sense unlikely.

Perhaps it is not the responsibility of mere consultants —which is the position of most of the deterrence theorists —to give advice about the propriety of American political values or to judge the state of their employers' intellects. But if that is the consultant's position,* it is his responsibility not to offer a spuriously authoritative formula for justifying national strategies: a formula which lulls his audience into thinking that all relevant information

*Most deterrence theorists are in fact not in the position described here, for most of them independently agree with the American government's over-all perspective; on this point see Levine's "Open Letter from a Military Intellectual to a Sophisticated Liberal Leader."[10] What I shall be discussing in the following pages is not simply the content of their commitment but their habitual pretense, through their emphasis on the concept of rationality and other objectivity-creating devices, that they are mere scientists who have no moral commitments. It is only fair to say that even though he too makes use of the rationality assumption, Levine is less subject to these strictures than most, for he at least has written openly on the subject of nuclear morality.

can be considered in a "rational" analysis, when perhaps the most important information of all is studiously and deliberately ignored by the very definition of "rational." In using their functional concept of rationality to do exactly that, the deterrence theorists have, *sub silentio*, set themselves up as ethical philosophers, and it is therefore most important to see what their ethic turns out to be.*

In pointing to the ethical questions that the reliance of deterrence theorists on mere instrumental rationality obscures, we need not resort to flights of personal moral fancy. Rather, we can point exclusively to questions that are raised by traditions of ethical thought which are more or less legitimate in the West: most specifically, Christian ethical thought. Those readers who are dubious about the exact relevance of this enterprise should consider that together with the right to maintain a certain kind of political order, the right to uphold and occasionally live by these particular standards make up a good deal of that "national integrity," "Western civilization," etc., that a deterrence strategy is designed to protect. What needs to be discussed, then, is the following question: if it can be "rational" to use nuclear weapons, what is implied about the ethical content of such rationality?

---

*In a *Commentary* symposium from which I have frequently quoted below, Sidney Hook, on being asked what traditional ethical code justified some of the peculiar aspects of deterrence morality, replied, in effect, "the will of the majority." But this is not an ethical code for the individual, it is merely a method for legitimizing social choices, chosen because of its inherent fairness. To say that what the majority says is always right in any context is not to provide an ethical code, but to do away with ethics altogether.

II. Ethical Considerations in Nuclear Deterrence Theory

1. *Deterrence theory* presumes that no conduct is absolutely prohibited.* In Chapter IV above I discussed the convention that values such as "the nation," "our civilization," etc., can be given weights in a probabilistic calculation and pointed out that that convention of commensurability is not only absurd but also tendentious. That comment deserves some further elaboration here.

It is true that, having reminded economists of their limitation in this regard, one cannot really object in principle if they go on trying to make such calculations, for *in principle* all representations of physical well-being can be numerically evaluated. But if ethical principles are so treated, they stop being principles. If we say, for instance, that "not committing murder" is worth +100, we shall feel free to commit any murder that promises a payoff of +101: and thus is generated the attitude that various kinds of nuclear attack may be "rational": that is, sensible: that is, *something that any reasonable man might do.* We are in the presence of a kind of absolute utilitarianism that reaches its height in these candid phrases of one prominent deterrence theorist:

> My own bias rears itself in the view that, strategy being essentially the pursuit of success in certain types of competitive endeavour, a pragmatic approach is the only appropriate one. The basic pragmatic principle is, I suppose, that 'Truth is the idea that works'. Thus, one weighs a strategic concept or idea by investigating as thoroughly as possible the factors necessary to its successful operation.[11]

*From here on we speak only of the kind of deterrence theory which makes claims to be peculiarly scientific, objective, rational, etc., as compared with other instances of policy analysis.

We may leave aside here the question of the revealing distortion of pragmatism,* and merely note how repugnant is this conception to most of the traditional moral codes that have been developed in the West. Of course, anyone is free to assert that he does not recognize the existence of moral prohibitions. However, one is not free to hide such assertions when they are an integral part of the propositions one is advancing. We want badly to know, after all, what is the supervening "higher morality" that dispenses with traditional prohibitions, or whether there are any limits at all on our efficient pursuit of sheer self-interest. No doubt it is not the fault of deterrence theorists that these questions are begged: not they, but the economists, from Ricardo to the game theorists, are largely responsible for the modern social science tradition of sweeping such questions under the rug. But the result is the same.

We may wonder, furthermore, whether there is not some evidence that deterrence theorists themselves recognize the inadequacy of this kind of ethic. I am thinking here of their frequent use of euphemisms to describe the destructive aspects of nuclear war. For example, deterrence theorists invariably favor the term *countervalue* warfare to describe what is after all *counterpeople* warfare (thus using the word "value" in its economic rather than ethical sense the one time that

*By "the truth of an idea" Dewey at least (Brodie, the author of the quotation, is referring to James) meant not *that* it works but rather *the way* it works; that was his operational test of truth. (E.g., in *1984* the "truth" of the abstract idea of freedom is actually slavery.) Admittedly Dewey was rarely clear but the distinction, which is obviously of immense import for both ethics and epistemology, is there to be found in his work.

they do not treat it as suspect). Other examples of euphemism abound in the literature. Thus, in his discussion of limited strategic war, Schelling asserts our need for a "richer menu" of strategic possibilities.[12] Kahn, who is a master of this kind of vocabulary, acknowledges that destruction is "likely to be greatly intensified at the upper end of the escalation ladder," which is a restrained way of saying that if a limited war gets out of hand it may lead to the deaths of millions and catastrophe for whole societies.[13] However, Kahn is more interested in the "lower end" of the "escalation ladder," and here he refers to "sanitary" campaigns in which an occasional missile base may be "taken out." [14] This last phrase, suggesting as it does the relative good humor of a clean body-block in a football game, is one of which deterrence theorists have become particularly fond (along with "cracking up" launching pads, presumably with a pneumatic drill).

More than any other aspect of the thought of deterrence theorists, perhaps, this reliance on euphemism reveals the deep problem of ethical justification which is central to their writings. And indeed, when we note some of the more specific moral questions which their theory evades, we have a glimpse of why this has been so. Perhaps they are unwilling to face those questions directly.

2. *Deterrence theory treats all violence and destruction as qualitatively indistinguishable.* The basic impulse of deterrence theory is to defend American society—or "the West"—by threatening or committing any violence necessary to accomplish that task. There are only two grounds on which deterrence theorists appear to be capable of condemning a given proposal: (1) it would not

"work" as well as some other proposal; (2) the end could be achieved with less loss of life.[15] But any level of violence necessary to protect a given interest is approved, up to and including total annihilation of the enemy; as long as calculation is competitively self-interested, this is bound to be so.

Thus deterrence theory is the obverse, so to speak, of pacifism. To the pacifist's absolute prohibition against killing, deterrence theory responds with an absolute dispensation for killing.[16] Nowhere is this seen more clearly than in this comment by Sidney Hook, one of America's most distinguished ethical philosophers and a "lay" supporter of deterrence policy:[17]

> . . . If you were prepared to support the Second World War, then you were responsible for a decision which destroyed the lives of people who had no choice in making that decision and who did not want you to fight for them. . . .[18]

In context Hook's reference is to the area bombing (and A-bombing) which the Allies used against Germany and Japan. Later in his remarks he refers to the "logical inconsistency" of those who supported World War II but opposed such actions, thus indicating his belief that the question of violence is a matter of kind, not degree: if one approves of an act of war, then one must *ipso facto* approve of an act of *total* war. *Inter armas virtu silent*: one is unhappily reminded of Ivan Karamazov's observation, that a moral relativist will inevitably be forced into the position that "anything goes."

3. *Deterrence theory makes moral distinctions between weapons and targets difficult to justify.* This conclusion follows from the above argument, and is perhaps the most important ethical issue implicitly raised—and

implicitly dismissed—by deterrence theory. Actually the problems of weapons and targets are one, for prohibitions on specific weapons have usually reflected fears about who the likely victims of those weapons would be. In many parts of the world it is legal for a private citizen to own a pistol or rifle, but nowhere may he own a machine gun. The reason for this universal prohibition is that the only thing one can do with a machine gun is commit a massacre; the means are disproportionate to any end private citizens may safely be allowed to contemplate achieving. But in the world of deterrence theory, pistols, machine guns, 100-megaton bombs and poisonous viruses are all alike. It is true that total war is not an invention of the Manhattan Project; and that, as some have argued, many weapons originally intended for self-defense or the use of professional armies have been used as weapons of extermination throughout history.[19] But the obvious distinctive feature of *nuclear* weapons is that they are almost necessarily weapons of mass destruction—that is what they are for.*

To be blunt, deterrence theory justifies the indiscriminate killing of innocent persons under certain circumstances. The English philosophers G. B. Anscombe and Walter Stein call this mass murder. The American theologian Paul Ramsey, agreeing with them, writes:

> Acts of war which directly intend and directly effect the death of non-combatants are to be classed morally with murder, and are never excusable.[20]

---

*This may not be true of some so-called "tactical" nuclear weapons. However, so long as strategic nuclear weapons exist as the *ultima ratio regum*, tactical weapons do not pose a separate moral issue. On the question of "damage-limiting" nuclear war, see below, pp. 232–39.

One does not have to insist on that word; but to use a vocabulary that contains no word to indicate the true nature of what is called for, in relation to traditional ethical standards, is to seduce one's readers into mistakenly thinking that one's theory is ethically neutral. When Klaus Knorr writes that *"On Thermonuclear War* is not a book about the moral aspects of military problems," he has got the truth of the matter exactly reversed, for all deterrence theory is fundamentally concerned with moral issues.[21]

To this insistence that there is a hidden ethical stance in deterrence theory, and to this description of the nature of that stance, several answers have been offered at various times by the supporters of a nuclear deterrence policy. They are all unsatisfactory or evasive (with one exception, which I will discuss at the end of this chapter and which does not apply to most deterrence theorists).

First, it is sometimes claimed that the United States proposes only to use nuclear weapons in self-defense, and self-defense does not raise the same moral issues as does wilful homicide. With regard to that assumption about the motives of the United States, one might make the cynical statement that war usually consists of a fight between two opponents each engaged in an act of self-defense. However, I shall let that point pass, and treat the claim on its merits. Thus Sidney Hook reasons as follows:

> As I read the history of Western culture it seems to me that survival at all costs is not among the values of the West. . . . I would . . . like to point out that in terms of the Western tradition, the view that it is not life but the good life which is the highest ideal . . . was not restricted merely to cases of individual heroism. Total war was also waged in

the past. Let us stretch our imaginations a little. Imagine that
we are living in Carthage and the Romans are at the gates.
Carthage fought a total war. So did Judea. Many illustrations
can be cited of cities and entire settlements which went down
to destruction fighting for what they thought was the good
life. . . . If we surrender our values, we open the floodgates
for totalitarianism to sweep through the world. . . . (W)e
bombed the Japanese islands, but what was the alternative?
The alternative was defeat, and acceptance of a system of
infamy. . . . As a theoretical possibility, no matter what kind
of moral economy one adopts, one can conceive of a situation
in which the conditions of life for a people, like the conditions
of life for an individual, would be unendurable. This, as I
have said, was the decision made historically by Jewish people
in fighting against Rome. It was made by many communities
in fighting against Hitler.[22]*

Such an argument answers itself. To present "total
war" as the decision of a suffering community to martyr
itself *in toto* is such a distortion of the actual situation
that it is difficult to imagine how a distinguished philosopher can possibly have come to make such a statement.
Deterrence theorists may incidentally propose that
Americans fight to the last man (though I cannot think
of any who actually do so), but that is obviously not the
issue raised by deterrence theory. The prospect that nuclear weapons place before us is that our fighting *in extremis* to the last Russian, to the last Chinese, perhaps to
the last European, perhaps to the last of some other
peoples as well. The prospect, that is, is one of destroying
objectively innocent persons in response to an attack
upon ourselves. We propose to engage not in an act of

*I have made no attempt to analyze Hook's history, not being
knowledgeable enough in that field. One can only hope his other
references to historical events have more substance than his
remarks about the war with Japan.

self-defense, but in an act of punishment, and the punished may be legion.

The terrible fact is, as deterrence theorists themselves constantly point out, that the advent of strategic nuclear weapons has made complete defense of any kind almost impossible.[23] There are only three ways in which one could defend one's self against someone who proposed to attack with strategic nuclear weapons. (1) One could defend against the weapons themselves. (2) One could attack those responsible for making the decision to attack before they had carried out their plan. (3) One could threaten to destroy those persons *after* they had implemented their attack.

The first alternative is generally agreed to be at best only a partial solution to the problem posed by strategic nuclear weapons. There is no antimissile weapon in sight that promises to do anything but make an attack more expensive—and after all, if there were a perfect defense, we would not need the deterrent.[24] The other two alternatives require a discrimination in choosing victims that nuclear weapons do not possess. Thus deterrence theory proposes that we "defend" ourselves not by any of these means, but by the threat or reality of nuclear retaliation against the enemy, destroying indiscriminately those engaged in attacking us, and those who are not so engaged in any meaningful sense of the word. To equate such an event to the traditional morality of "heroic" self-defense is to commit a solecism. No one has described this situation of nuclear deterrence better than John Bennett, who remarks:

> When men in the West say "give me liberty or give me death" they rightly evoke a dual response. War is not likely

to save liberty. And when men say this in the United States and in a few western nations, they hardly realize that they may be dooming hundreds of millions of people who never made any such choice. . . . [I]t would be well to ask a larger representation of mankind to have part in this decision since it may mean death for them before they have ever known the reality of liberty . . . I think that it was A. J. Muste who coined the phrase no "annihilation without representation" to indicate what is here involved.[25]

The next three arguments I shall discuss are all attempts to salvage the claim that nuclear deterrence is clearly a form of legitimate self-defense and thus does not raise the grave ethical issues that are suggested above.

First, it is often assumed that since we will be "in the right" in a nuclear war, questions of ethical propriety will not arise. Such reasoning misses the point, however. The question whether one's cause is just is analytically separate from the question of what one may do to assert that cause. There is a difference too obvious to be ignored between shooting a man who is about to shoot you (unjustly, we assume), and throwing a bomb at him that can be expected to blow up six or seven million other people. In the latter case major questions of morality are present.

Second, it has at times been claimed that in modern warfare no one is "innocent."[26] Now undoubtedly it is hard to draw a line, under conditions of modern warfare and particularly of nuclear warfare, between combatants and non-combatants. But this difficulty has lost most of its relevance for theory in the nuclear age, for in talking about the strategic use of nuclear weapons we are talking not merely about the slaughter of non-combatants in a warring nation but also sometimes of peoples who have never at any level of decisions opted to go to war.

In any event, even if somehow one manages to ignore this fact, the claim that the distinction cannot be made is still obviously false. Indeed it is so clearly false that it seems to be nothing but a transparent excuse for fighting those total wars that the authors of such statements wish to be morally free to fight. If we say that there is "no" distinction between combatants and non-combatants, this can only be a prescriptive statement, never a descriptive one.* The distinction may be unclear; but in the words of the English Catholic philosopher Walter Stein:

> It is common, indeed usual, to be uncertain of a boundary but quite certain of what lies well to the east or west of it. . . . Now the line between combatants and non-combatants is one of those which it is difficult to fix exactly . . . yet, nevertheless, there are large areas which unquestionably lie on either side of the line . . . a high proportion of any population consists of children, full-time mothers, pensioners and sick people. Of course, if someone is so inclined, he can reply that mothers rear children . . . that children will one day be workers or even soldiers . . . and that sick people frequently get well again. Moralizing can have its moments.[28]

That is to say, we need only know that there *is* a fundamental moral difference between limited war and total war, to justify our insistence that the distinction be made —however difficult that may be.[29] Indeed, the difficulty of "drawing the line" in modern war is precisely an argument, not in favor of fighting total wars, but in favor of *not* fighting them.

---

*Unless, perhaps, one reifies the abstract concepts "state" and "nation" to an almost unimaginable extent. At least one noted deterrence theorist, Herman Kahn, has indeed accomplished this end by referring to the nation as "he."[27]

A variant on the argument that war has become "objectively" total is the argument that war has always been so. It follows from this, presumably, that a condition so ingrained in human affairs need not be considered to raise moral issues by a realistic person. This view is suggested, for example, in Sidney Hook's statement that "Every war that has been conducted in the West in the history of mankind has involved this morally tragic situation."[30]

This argument, however, is but another instance of the inverted pacifism of those who support the notion of total war uncritically. Put in syllogistic form the argument goes: (a) All war is immoral; some wars are necessary; therefore some immoral things must be done. (b) Violence is a feature of war; war is, to begin with, immoral; therefore there can be no sensible moral restraints on violence in a "necessary" war. But this reasoning both falsifies history and distorts the nature of traditional ethical thought. Unless one has had a personal revelation of divine will, it cannot meaningfully be asserted that all war—or all violence—is immoral, for there is no major Western religious or ethical tradition that condemns war and violence *as such*.[31] Furthermore, Hook's asserted fact is clearly incorrect. War is only "tragic" in his sense when *both* sides are forced (or desire) to engage in a "massacre of the innocents," and we can easily think of wars even in modern times in which that has not been the case.[32]

And even were one to agree with Hook's statement as a general rule, one would hardly have established the grounds for disavowal of the need to consider ethical questions; one would still be confronted with a choice. For as Walter Stein notes:

We may see the H-bomb and other atomic weapons as a final revelation of total war—and in the light of this, revise many of our past judgments and tolerances. Of we may swallow this *reductio ad absurdum* for the sake of absurdities swallowed long ago. How often do we hear of the Allies' saturation raids of the last war, or, say, of the behavior of mercenary armies of the Middle Ages—triumphantly pointed to as brutal and atrocious—as though they were bulls-eye proof of the righteousness of the H-bomb.[33]

Thus the wish to assimilate total war to various traditional aspects of righteous action, such as self-defense or the defense of others, is unfulfillable. An alternative ground of argument suggested by some commentators is to deny that *nuclear* war need be *total* war. This is done either by postulating a kind of war called "counterforce war," or by asserting that a deterrence policy can be based purely on the *possession* of nuclear weapons, and not on their *use*.

The concept of counterforce or controlled nuclear war is certainly an interesting one. Deterrence theorists believe that they have found in it a morality for the nuclear age. Thus Alain Enthoven, a Deputy Assistant Secretary of Defense and a noted defense analyst as well, claims that

According to traditional Christian doctrine, the use of force to repress evil can be justifiable under certain conditions including the following: First, the use of force must have a reasonable chance of success. Second, if successful, it must offer a better situation than the one that would prevail in the absence of the use of force. Third, the force that is used must be proportional to the objectives being sought (or the evil being repressed). For this to be satisfied, peaceful means of redress must have failed. Fourth, the force must be used with the intention of sparing noncombatants and with a reasonable prospect of actually doing so.

It is interesting to observe that the potentially catastrophic character of thermonuclear war has forced practical decision makers, reasoning in a secular context, to adopt a set of criteria very much like those of the traditional Christian doctrine and to apply them to the design of the military posture of the United States.

. . . [O]ur defense posture is being designed to make war less likely and less destructive. I am not suggesting that we can make war and violence desirable. The question is whether we have a better alternative.

Tonight, I have defended our policies on the grounds that they make sense. Can they also be defended on the grounds that they are moral? Viewed with perspective, the two should be the same.[34]

However, Enthoven's assertion is not, on inspection, warranted. "Making sense" and being "moral" might mean the same thing in his perspective, but that they do so in the perspective of "traditional Christian doctrine" is doubtful. It would be different if Enthoven and his colleagues proposed counterforce strategy as the exclusive strategic weapons' doctrine for the United States. This has been done by Thomas Murray (among others), who views that strategy not as a method for making nuclear deterrence more consonant with traditional ethical codes, but as a positive alternative to nuclear deterrence. Thus, Murray condemns the idea of deploying a strategic deterrence force targeted on cities.[35] Deterrence advocates like Enthoven on the contrary propose counterforce strategy as part of an over-all deterrence strategy. As Secretary of Defense McNamara put it, "The very strength and nature of the alliance forces make it possible for us to retain even in the face of a massive surprise attack, sufficient reserve striking power to destroy an enemy society if driven to it."[36] And as a theorist of controlled nuclear war writes:

> In addition both sides may have a positive incentive not to strike at each other's cities. If central war comes there should be concern with utilizing strategic forces for the important task of destroying enemy strategic forces or for threatening punitive damage in the event of destruction of one's own cities.[37]

The essence of this doctrine is to rebut the notion that, if struck in a surprise attack, we must retaliate with an "annihilatory" blow. No doubt controlled counterforce war would be more humane than all-out countercity war. But the latter is not foresworn. Far from it: the idea is that we can "prevail" in a counterforce war, and if we cannot, or if the enemy refuses to accept the result graciously, the countercity strategy remains to discipline his enthusiasm or his imagination. Obviously then, this concept does not do away with the ethical questions raised by the prospect of counter*people* warfare, for it is simply impossible to imagine any objective to the seeking of which all-out nuclear attack could be "proportional." A totally destructive victory over the infidel may have been one Christian doctrine, but I do not think it is what Enthoven and others mean when they talk about the notion of the "just war."

In addition, the very idea that nuclear weapons have a "counterforce" use is dubious and is typical of the distortions to which formal deterrence theory leads. To make simple quantitative comparisons, it is necessary to have a simple "model" and to keep one's categories limited in number.[38] Thus in "model-building" it may be quite reasonable to represent a continuous spectrum of events, which differ from each other only in degree, by a dichotomization that divides the spectrum into two broad types of events that are made to appear as though they differed in kind. The danger of this procedure is that one is prone to fall into the trap of reification, and treat one's own abstract categories as though they correctly described reality.

This is what has been done by those deterrence theorists who write about counterforce warfare as though it were literally that—as though the killing of non-combatants, the destruction of resources, etc., were somehow excluded from it as a matter of definition. Like most reifications, this one misstates the case, for no one has yet managed to imagine any possible nuclear war that could be so described. Even Kahn writes that "In any case, if intrawar deterrence broke down, or 'bargaining' seemed to require it, cities might get hit," and adds that counterforce strategy would be aimed "[m]ainly . . . though not necessarily completely . . . [at] military targets."[39] We need only remember, after all, that his definition of a "counter-force plus avoidance" war is one in which casualties would "almost certainly be less than five million so long as the attacker is careful, no weapons go disastrously astray, and we have a modest civil-defense capacity."[40] And the impact of this description is strengthened when we note the Soviet view, as quoted by Kahn, that "the majority of [military objectives] are located in large or smaller cities and populated places. . . ."[41] That statement, whether it is true for the Soviet Union, is certainly true for the United States.[42] And after all, to make notions like Enthoven's untenable, the Soviets would merely have to refuse to play the counterforce game—to announce that they would treat their own nuclear weapons only in an "all or nothing" manner. What price the counterforce strategy then?

Deterrence theorists who deal with notions such as "counter-force plus avoidance" are fond of positing mythical attacks on naval fleets at sea; Kahn's favorite example is the placing of a missile on a gaseous diffusion plant, which is geographically isolated, employs few workers and has "relatively few emotional or cultural associations."[43] But if such events were the sum total of a conflict it would be duello, not war, and if we were *certain* that "counterforce" war would not pass this point, we would not need nuclear weapons at all, since other means exist of destroying such targets. Indeed, it would be most "rational" then to revive Erich Maria Remarque's notion of putting all the premiers and presidents into the middle of a field, and having them go at it with clubs before a cheering world; after all, no resources would be committed, and thus there would be no investment that one losing side had to recoup by escalation (as long as there was a fresh supply of healthy leadership timber). If the "theory" of "limited strategic war" has not developed past this point, then it must be taken as an attempt at whimsy rather than as a serious discussion of nuclear war.

In any event, ultimately the theory of controlled counterforce war raises more ethical problems than it dispels. The reason that counterforce theorists have been able to convey the impression that they are offering a more "moral" alternative to minimum deterrence is that they have put their argument in life-saving terms. This implies that "massive retaliation," or what Kahn calls "spasm war," is the logical result of minimum deterrence. However, such battles with the shade of Dulles have been irrelevant in the arms debate for some years. The people who criticize counterforce strategy from an ethical perspective are not economy-minded (or bloody-minded) right wingers. Most of them probably literally believe, deep down, that a minimum deterrence strategy raises fewer ethical questions, because *the deterrent will never be used.*

It is, after all, simply impossible to imagine circumstances in which an annihilatory counterstrike makes any sense at all, by any standard of "rationality" that is not equivalent to sheer vengefulness. Of course, a minimum deterrence strategy would entail the great dangers attributed to it by deterrence theorists if it were unaccompanied by any doctrine for dealing with low-level provocations except by "surrender" or all-out war. But advocates of minimum deterrence—mostly those whom Levine calls "antiwar marginalists"—invariably tie their deterrence posture proposals either to some kind of conventional limited-war posture or to proposals for thawing out the cold war and thus decreasing our expectation of the kinds of provocations that deterrence theorists fear (i.e., by eliminating the predisposition for pushing our opponents too hard in the cold war).[44]

On the other hand, the more we move toward a counterforce posture, the more nuclear war becomes "thinkable." The whole point of the Kennedy-McNamara strategic reform was to give the United States more "options" in the use or non-use of nuclear weapons. The choice of a countercity strategy may therefore be somewhat less likely than before; but there is a greater probability of our adopting lower-level nuclear (or even nonnuclear) strategies. And they all kill large numbers of people, as events in Vietnam are demonstrating.

In fact, if the minimum deterrence posture is intended by its proponents as sheer unmitigated bluff—and its great virtue is that it would be so likely to wind up as a bluff no matter what our intentions—then *it* is the posture most consonant with the traditional moral codes that nuclear weapons call into question.* The point, however, is that J. David Singer, Amitai Etzioni, Charles Osgood, Michael Brower, *et al.*, are not deterrence theorists (in Levine's terms, they are "antiwar marginalists" rather than middle marginalists"). No *deterrence* theorist has advocated bluff or even, in recent years, finite deterrence.[45]

Nor, indeed, could any deterrence theorist who is committed to the idea that the assumption of rationality is useful propose the adoption of such a posture. For if rational, hostile, competitive men are making threats at each other, then the idea that we may ever use our countervalue forces is not credible *"unless we really intend to do it.* If we are only *pretending* that we would do it, the credibility and therefore the deterrent value of our force is almost certain to be lessened by the automatic and inevitable leaks."[46] Furthermore, we can reverse that dictum and make the obvious point that given the traditional human manner of responding to aggressive violence, the only way an intent not to use nuclear weapons under any circumstances could be given psychological meaning would be for national leaders of all factions and parties inextricably to commit themselves to such a policy. That would be not deterrence, but unilateral disarmament. As to what is the present commitment of the American government to which so many deterrence theo-

---

*The morality of threats which one has absolutely no intention of executing is a question that need not be discussed here.

rists are advisers, we have the late President's word for it:

> In the event of a major aggression that could not be repulsed by conventional forces we must be prepared to take whatever action with whatever weapons are appropriate."[47]

Once one admits that the ultimate deterrent is not absolute bluff, therefore, the ethical issue is reinstated unchanged. We may see this most clearly in the following graphic example that has been thought up by Paul Ramsey:

> . . . [S]uppose that one Labor Day weekend no one was killed or maimed on the highways; and that the reason for the remarkable restraint placed on the recklessness of automobile drivers was that suddenly every one of them discovered he was driving with a baby tied to his front bumper! That would be no way to regulate traffic *even if it succeeds* in regulating it perfectly, since such a system makes innocent human lives the *direct object* of attack and uses them as a mere *means* for restraining the drivers of automobiles. . . .[48]*

To put it simply, most traditional moral codes forbid treating human life as a mere object of policy, and that is what deterrence theory—the "exchange of hostages"—proposes to do.[49] That theory, to repeat, is *not* ethically

---

*Compare C. W. Sherwin's traffic analogy (above, pp. 149–50). Ramsey has obviously caught the essence of deterrence, whereas Sherwin has not. Anatol Rapoport, discussing this question, notes that the crucial point about violent death is that human beings usually would rather put up with a great number of deaths not caused by wilful human agency than a much smaller number for which human agency is deliberately responsible; for his examples, see pp. 88-91 of his *Strategy and Conscience*.

neutral about the question of violence: of the kinds of wars we have a moral right to engage in.[50]

III. The Political Ethics of Deterrence Theory

The remaining propositions that I deduce from rationalistic deterrence theory are of a slightly different order than what has gone before; they raise questions of what might be called political or social, rather than individual, ethics.

4. *Deterrence theory assumes that a deep psychological and physical commitment to the possibility of wreaking destructive violence on foreign populations is morally neutral.* At the very least this assumption ought to be made explicit and discussed as such. If it is false, then a "rational" deterrist would again be caught in the same trap of self-contradiction that is characteristic of the commitments to limited war and technological progress in the arms race. And it is quite easy to conceive of this assumption's being false. In John Bennett's words:

> . . . [W]hat will it do for us if for generations we live with the expectation that at any moment we may become total destroyers? I am not dogmatic about the precise moral effect of this situation. . . . Is there not a great unexplored danger to our moral sensitivities, to our habits of feeling about the meaning of life . . . ?
> . . . No political system involving police power or collective security can take the place of this moral inhibition [against becoming wholesale destroyers] which has been strengthened by our religious traditions. During the discussion of the problem of Laos the remark was often made by journalists that the Laotians are Buddhists and because of the compassion of Buddhism they had an inhibition against killing each other. This was cited as defect that was inconvenient for our western strategy.[51]

More specifically, when one speaks of the "values" that
deterrence policy is supposed to protect against Communist "provocations," surprise attack, etc., it is usually
the political system of Western democracy that is most
prominently in mind. A rational analysis of strategy is
self-contradictory if it concentrates on "defense" but is
willing to surrender the values that are being "defended"
in the first place. On the other hand, a rational analysis
of strategy that allows for such considerations might
have to sacrifice "defense" to these values if the two con-
flicted. To repeat an earlier point, "rationality" does not
tell us what to do when ends are inconsistent. Levine has
suggested that we may optimize among conflicting desired ends, but he is using the concept of optimization in-
correctly. One can optimize among alternative means
(strategies) to a single end, but ends themselves are
given. If one decides they are not actually in unalterable
conflict, one has not optimized—one has changed one's
values or one's estimates of the strength of one's values
from what they were before. And if the ends truly conflict, *one must choose.*[52]

In practice, most deterrence theorists do choose: they
simply do not worry about such problems as the threat
of the "garrison state," maintenance of our libertarian
culture, etc.[53] Kahn, it is true, has written that the United
States economy could if necessary stand the impact of a
defense budget of 200-300 billion dollars a year.[54] But
that is not a very helpful passage. One must understand
him to be not proving a point (his source of information
is purely personal) but to be demonstrating ignorance of
what is at stake. The tyranny of "national security,"
were it ever to come, would presumably be a function not
of the money, but of the thought that we devote to

national security.* Again, not to include this consideration in any analysis one makes of the costs and benefits of a given strategy is implicitly to make a highly controversial value judgment and practical political prophecy as well. Both may be correct, but they should be made out loud. No deterrence theorist (except, briefly, Levine)[55] has bothered to do this.

5. *Deterrence theory tends to subordinate all political considerations to military ones.* Although theoretically any consideration can be quantified, or at least treated rigorously, in practice problems of military operations are much more susceptible of this kind of analysis than other aspects of policy. As Levine notes:

> . . . there is . . . a tendency [among deterrence theorists] to base arms-policy recommendations almost entirely on military power-as-coercion. . . . Pure deterrence analysis makes its determinations solely by the calculus of national advantage and disadvantage. Although contrary to some . . . accusations, the deterrence calculus does not assume absolute enmity between the United States and the Soviet Union . . . it does not include the noncoercive sort of power which might accrue from such things as international appreciation for our adherence to the "concepts of justice and freedom," or "the habits of democracy and fair play." . . . [A]rms recommendations are seldom made on the basis of deterrence alone, but there is some tendency in this direction because the analysis is available and tangible. . . . Thus for many [deterrence theorists] the implicit analysis of power becomes . . . that . . . power is force and toughness.[56]

*My own view is that the economy would probably be a much healthier economy with an arms budget such as Kahn postulates; poverty might very well be eliminated entirely. Of course that is not the point.

The tendency that Levine correctly discovers (see my discussion on p. 200 above) explains, I think, Klaus Knorr's forceful argument against the United States' adopting a "no first use" policy for nuclear weapons.[57] It also explains Kahn's inability in his latest book to announce, finally, where he stands on this issue, even though he obviously favors a "no first use" declaration. The military objections are too obvious; the deterrence theorist who insists on viewing the world primarily in terms of rational moves and countermoves is unable to give what weight he would like to moral considerations.[58]

Thus, for example, if the military disadvantages of a test ban treaty were found to outweigh its benefits to a large degree, it would be difficult for deterrence theorists to favor the signing of such a treaty: they would invariably adopt Secretary McNamara's posture that "we should engage in [disarmament and arms control] agreements if and when, and only if and when, we can do so without reducing our power advantage."[59] The tendency of deterrence theorists will always be in this direction since military calculus is the calculus that deterrence theory makes most familiar. If one wanted to support, say, a test ban treaty that might weaken our military posture, the only method of doing so open to those with such a psychology would be to intensify other military operations so as to right the "power" balance.[60] As I have said earlier, this is what the Kennedy administration did—or pretended to do to protect itself against such arguments—in the summer of 1963; and the effect of its actions, however nobly inspired, may very well be to have made it difficult for any future administration to put forward a cold war policy that is not justifiable in strictly military terms. This development is directly traceable to the same ethos of which deterrence theory partakes.

6. *Deterrence theory is culture-bound; it shares the most important American cold war biases.* On the question of the nature of Western-Communist relations, the bias of deterrence theorists ranges the short distance from Morgenstern's racial nightmare of conquest by Mongol hordes to the more standard Sovietology of Henry Kissinger.

> . . . [T]he basic relationship between the two camps is one of inevitable conflict. . . . [R]elations between the Communist and the non-Communist world always have some of the attributes of war whatever form the contest may take at any given moment. . . . "Until the final issue (between capitalism and communism) is decided," said Lenin, "the state of awful war will continue. . . . " . . . [thus] the only safe United States policy is one which is built on the assumption of a continued revolutionary struggle.[61]

As Anatol Rapoport points out, these authors all seem to mean "that there are no apparent limits to *how much* power the U.S.S.R. and China will try to attain."[62] There are Sovietologists—George Kennan and Fred W. Neal, for example—who either doubt the present significance of this classical Leninist model of world struggle, or attribute to it a different meaning than it is usually construed to have.[63] But the possibility of making and acting upon such a distinction is either rejected or ignored by deterrence theorists; as I have suggested, their anti-Communism is completely indiscriminate, and simply upholds the feeling of constant competitiveness.

A related, but more subtle form of ethnocentrism consists in the attribution to the Soviet Union (or Communist China) of a "rational" strategic doctrine that significantly differs from that which "rational" American decision-makers are expected to employ. Thus, for example, the Soviets (and the Chinese, but with more reason) are said to be willing to accept much greater damage than we would in a nuclear war. The conclusion sometimes drawn from this analysis is that any arms control agreement must be asymmetrical in favor of the United States: we must be allowed to retain a larger missile force than the Soviets.[64] And as J. David Singer points out in discussing Kahn's proposals, the development of a massive civil-defense capability and not-incredible counterforce capability, which would be considered a most serious provocation if undertaken by the Soviets, is urged on the United States as the most "rational" strategy available to it.[65]

Similarly, Glenn Snyder and Henry Kissinger propose a strategic doctrine according to which the United States should treat attempts by the Soviets or Chinese to insure "local preponderance" around their borders (as in Southeast Asia) as acts of belligerency, although a simlar attitude on the part of the United States and its NATO allies should be thought of as merely keeping the peace.[66] More subtly, Morton Kaplan, following Schelling's dictum that "the status quo is more obvious than change,"[67] proposes a doctrine of limited strategic war built around the notion that the status quo ante is always the logical end of hostilities; this is to say, presumably, that at the point of a gun (or a nuclear bomb) a "rational" Soviet man will always see revolutionary claims as legally inferior to status quo claims.[68] This notion is parallel to Glenn Snyder's generous suggestion that the "enemy" who has violated the status quo can always end the nuclear punishment he has brought down on himself, by surrendering.[69]

One can see, in reviewing such statements, that the formalistic conception of "aggression" which I briefly discussed in Chapter V serves a dual purpose. It enables the theorists not only to talk about war as a rationally explicable "game" played with distinguishable "moves" but also to make the American stance in the cold war one that must be espoused by any "rational" man. Thus a Soviet first-strike capability would suggest the possibility of a surprise attack, and so be terribly destabilizing, whereas an *American* first-strike capability exists only as a potential response to "aggression," and so is not destabilizing at all. In Wohlstetter's classic remark that "When not coupled with the ability to strike in retaliation [a first-strike] capability might suggest — erroneously, to be sure, in the case of the democracies — an intention to strike first," one is reminded of Lenin's dictum that a gun in the hands of a policeman is an instrument of capitalist oppression, but a gun in the hands of a worker is an instrument of liberation.[70]

This aspect of the "theory" of deterrence seems not much different from what any patriotic American military planner might arrive at without benefit of any concept of "rationality." Thus Glenn Snyder writes: "The worth or utility of military forces is, of course, ultimately political, if 'political' is defined as advancing or preserving the values or objectives of the state in international politics, the prime value being, of course, the survival of the state itself."[71] In the context of post–World War II discussions of collective security, "world government," the United Nations, the obsolescence of nationalism, etc., Snyder's second "of course," which is constantly echoed by other deterrence theorists,[72] conveys the air of a roomful of furniture being shoved under a very small rug.

Indeed, as one surveys the development of thought about the uses of nuclear weapons, from "massive retaliation" through pure (type I) deterrence plus limited war, to counterforce capability plus limited strategic war, one wonders if there is really any deterrence theory at all; if the "theory" has not really consisted of a series of rationalizations designed to make the best that could be made out of the state of the American nuclear arsenal at any given time.[73] In any event, the narrow nationalism implicit in the deterrence theorist's concept of national security may be "rational" in some sense, but it hardly exhausts the possible interpretations to be given to that word. It would be easier to argue, I think, that in the nuclear age the basic concept of national sovereignty must be either partially of totally rejected.[74]

7. *Deterrence theory has an antipopular political bias.* What is at stake, finally, is the compatibility of the "rational" analysis of strategy with the postulate of free political choice in a framework of representative government. Are those members of the body politic who, for example, reject the doctrine of "peaceful coexistence" with the Soviet Union, or who advocate a "forward strategy" or an even more aggressive anti-Communist policy, to be considered "irrational"? It seems clear that the answer must be affirmative, since from the point of view of deterrence theory the idea of rationality can hardly be associated with a tolerance for the prospect of

nuclear war as broad as the one that was expressed by the Republican candidate for President in 1964.[75] Nor is it merely the so-called far right (and, of course, the left) that must apparently be excluded from the councils of government in a "rational" state (all the while exerting, as I have noted, a subterranean influence in the case of the right). Writing about the change-over from the Eisenhower to the Kennedy administration, Glenn Snyder quotes Samuel Huntington as saying that "the record of 1945 to 1960, however, suggests that its political system and ideology might well hamper the United States in playing a more positive and creative role in world politics." Snyder then adds: "One can only suggest that an analysis of the record of the Kennedy Administration since 1960—in such fields as limited warfare and unconventional warfare capabilities, trade and aid programs, and firm, careful diplomacy, might have produced, on the whole, a somewhat more optimistic appraisal."[76] One can only reply, not by Mr. Eisenhower. It is hard not to believe that Snyder is speaking for almost all deterrence theorists in this passage,[77] in which "hard-headed" power-oriented moderates somehow become the only true custodians of the national interest, while persons such as H. Stuart Hughes and Senator Goldwater (and Eisenhower himself?) are thrust outside the pale.

To the extent that the political process affects political decision-making with a serious element of "irrationality," national security policy-making must be depoliticized if it is to be "rational." Even Congress, with its umbilical attachment to parochial interests and its short-sighted constituent concerns, must be more or less excluded from a direct say in national security policy. Perhaps it is not necessary that one advocate popular control of foreign and military policy in order to qualify as a democrat. But as de Tocqueville long ago suggested, there is a tension in American democracy between the demands of its populist political theory and the apparent demands of a stable overseas policy. That tension is resolved by deterrence theorists without qualms—and without argument. *Raison d'état* becomes their inspiration; executive leadership becomes their guide; and democracy must look out for itself.

IV. The Ethical Root of Deterrence Theory

I have implied throughout that the attempt of deterrence theorists to be neutral in a situation in which ethical choice is absolutely essential is a pretense, masking their adherence to the ethical values held by their employers or clientele.[78] What is this collection of values? Are the implicit judgments discussed above all there is to deterrence morality? When one probes beneath appearances, one discovers that that is not the case.

It is not, after all, that deterrence theorists deny the importance of the considerations discussed in this chapter — Kahn at least does his moral agonizing in public on occasion—but that they give the particular moral and political questions I have raised less weight than they do another, conflicting moral demand. This point has been made angrily by Levine, Wohlstetter, and Brodie among others.[79] I think their anger at being considered "immoral" is partly justified: the choices I have described here—targeting of innocent persons, no absolute prohibition against certain kinds of killing, etc.

—can be consciously *moral* choices and deserve consideration as such (though not, in my opinion, agreement). But one of the reasons that scorn was aimed at deterrence theorists on this subject is that for years most of them were (most still are) egregiously guilty of avoiding the moral issue altogether, or misrepresenting it.

Essentially, it seems most reasonable to understand deterrence theorists as elevating one value to a position superior to all others: the value of resisting Communist expansion and the diminishment of human freedom, which must ensue on such expansion. Levine has argued rather oddly that the major value of deterrence theorists is the wish to avoid war, and that their anti-Communism is only secondary in this regard.[80] But clearly the position of deterrence theorists is that a properly implemented deterrence policy will as a matter of hypothetical fact avoid all-out nuclear war, while it is at the same time necessary as a matter of moral obligation to avoid Communist expansion, conquest, or attacks on the West. If the hypothesized fact turns out to be not a fact in the end, and the Communists attack us, deterrence theorists are prepared to punish the Communists *in whatever manner* is necessary to fulfil the obligation. Levine's mistake is to confuse prudence with ethics. Deterrence theorists are "antiwar" in the sense that they do not wish the United States to be bombarded with nuclear weapons if it can possibly be helped; but they are *not* "antiwar" in the ethical sense of being themselves committed to some kind of non-warlike stance.[81] On the contrary, although many deterrence theorists have expressed unease over the nature of nuclear war as an international social fact, hardly any have ever expressed real unease about the nature of nuclear war as something one does to others.* At the same time, most (if not all) deterrence theorists have adopted a definitely moralistic stance vis-à-vis the potential and supposed aggressions of international Communism.[82]

Whether resistance to Communism is so fundamental a requirement of survival that all other moral considerations must ultimately be made secondary to it, is a question that needs a lengthier discussion than would be relevant here. This much can surely be said, though. The principles of action described in this chapter seem to be so questionable, by any reasonable standard, that to adopt them one must meet the most stringent demands of ethical reasoning. One must establish beyond doubt, to paraphrase Enthoven, the nature and extent of the threat to be resisted, the necessity of particular military means to resist, and the unlikelihood of accomplishing that same end through other means. Having done this, one must also give reason to believe that in any event the end can be accomplished in the prescribed way without incurring unbearable costs, not only physically but above all ethically.

Deterrence theorists, to repeat, have hardly done this (in the case of Kahn we have seen in some detail just how far his systems analysis was from making this kind of investigation). To the extent that they have not, their theory has come to look like an unhappy mixture of moral relativism and sheer chauvinism.

Yet the task set out here is not an impossible one (though it is, I think, extremely difficult). Among those

---

*In a letter to The *New York Times*, October 13, 1961, Thornton Read did express such a feeling.

concerned with the problem of resolving these conflicting ethical claims, for example, Richard Falk has attempted to outline such a position, arguing that the use of force is justified to the extent that it is necessary to preserve the existing system of international order. Hans Morgenthau and Louis J. Halle have also rather agonizingly presented a similar case for a deterrence strategy, even while asserting that that strategy is morally indefensible according to the traditional ethical codes.[83]

However, neither Falk nor Morgenthau nor Halle is a deterrence theorist; none of them supports counterforce nuclear war à la McNamara; and none of them suggests that the kind of "rationality" that enables decision-makers to make optimal decisions has anything to do with his own ethical position.[84]

V. Summary: The Misuses of "Rationality"

As long as we conceive of choice as being at least subjectively "free," then to call a given decision "rational" merely implies that it is the decision we prefer to see made because we would have made it ourselves. Nothing has to be done unless we desire to do it. For deterrence theorists, the dangers of an uncontrolled arms race make arms control "necessary."[85] Similarly, according to Levine (and I think he speaks here for all rationalist deterrence theorists), it is an "analytical" proposition that "Weapons are primarily to deter war but we may *have* to strike [first or second]. . . . (Italics added).[86]

But for others, disarmament or even "surrender" of some kind might instead be seen as ultimately "necessary." And the truth is that none of these necessities is truly necessary. To use the language of obligation in such a context is to make one of the worst confusions of all: the confusion between "objective" analysis and "subjective" judgment.

The concept of instrumental rationality must almost certainly always have a normative element in it.[87] It must be someone's rationality, to achieve his own purposes, that is called to mind by the use of that word. We could say that rational decisions are those that are inevitably going to be taken anyway—but then there would be no need to write books on the subject. To argue as do deterrence theorists—to equate their ethic, or the American cold war ethic which they accept, with the "rationality" and ethical neutrality of the scientist—is thus permissible only if one clearly admits that there are other, equally valid "rationalities," which could be used to justify strategies other than deterrence strategy. To say that rationality justifies *that* strategy alone, without being explicit about the fact that one has given a special meaning to the idea of rationality, is to mislead all those who follow the discussion of nuclear strategy. It is to suggest to the interested public that somehow nuclear weapons have a "rational" use in strategies such as limited nuclear retaliation, controlled counterforce war, etc.—when the equally likely case is that any use of nuclear weapons will ultimately be self-defeating.

I.   Recapitulation: The Non-Political Character of Deterrence Theory

SEVERAL CARDINAL POINTS emerge from this study of the methodology of theoretical deterrence studies. First, the questions that deterrence theorists seem habitually to ask—whether "rationality" can control the arms race, and whether "scientific" analysis seems to favor certain kinds of wartime strategies rather than others—are of the most limited value. It is important to understand just what that value is and to see in what way it has been oversold.

If one accepts all the assumptions that go into a deterrence study or into the verbal presentation of deterrence logic, and *if* one feels that the analysis has been truly rigorous, *then* one will be prone to accepting the conclusions generated by the analysis. This is to say that like-minded people will reach the same conclusions if they reason logically. No doubt; but the statement is trivial, for why should we all be like-minded? Let us consider a number of propositions concerning international policies, suggested by my earlier discussion, on which we may *not* be like-minded.

A. The Communist powers will seize and exploit every military advantage we allow them, even

outside the peripheries of their own borders—or
they will not.

1. The German problem can be "solved" only
   by military deterrence strategies—or it can
   be "solved" by political accommodation.

B. The arms race can be stabilized through arms
   control—or, within the presently anarchic international system, it cannot.

C. Continued prosecution of the cold war is in our
   interest—or it is not.

1. The West German demand for nuclear proliferation of one sort or another[1] presents a
   problem soluble by strategic means — or it
   does not.

2. The continual fighting of limited wars, such
   as that in Vietnam, probably will not lead to
   all-out-war—or it probably will.

D. The Soviets are not serious about disarmament—
   or they are.[2]

1. The world would be a worse place after the
   conclusion of a "bad" disarmament agreement—say one based on Soviet proposals—
   than it would be given the prospect of a
   continued arms race—or it would not. (Another way of putting some of the implications
   of these first four points is to say that, in
   Aaron Wildavsky's terms, the *greatest* danger
   of the present confrontation may be seen as,
   on the one hand, appeasement of an implacable enemy à la 1938, or as, on the other
   hand, the prospect of getting into an uncontrollable, spiralling arms race with an

opponent who could be dealt with successfully on a non-militarized basis.)

E. The domestic political, social, and moral effects
of a continual emphasis on anti-Communist
ideology can be controlled—or they cannot.

F. It may be worthwhile going through the uncertain catastrophe of nuclear war at some level
to attain our policy ends—or it may not.

G. The use of nuclear weapons is morally support-
able in some instances—or it is not.

H. It is not reasonable for the United States unequivocally to adopt a no-first-use policy—or it is.

I hope it is obvious that these are among the crucial
propositions one can make about world conflict in the
nuclear era (doubtless there are several others I have
left out). The point is that deterrence theorists have
simply not discussed these propositions. They have, on the
one hand, wasted their time and ours by asking what
we have seen to be essentially meaningless questions
about the prospects for something called rational behavior. Even worse, they have, on the other hand, settled
matters regarding the specific propositions presented
here by making either explicit or implicit assumptions
about them. Thus, the argument that the balance of
terror was delicate directly depended on an assumption
about Communist aggressiveness. But this is to say that
Wohlstetter did not really show the balance of terror to
be delicate; he merely assumed it. Again, Kahn's civil-
defense-not-incredible-first-strike strategy depends directly on assumptions about Communist aggressiveness;
the lack of a political solution in Europe; the neutral
long-run political effects of the cold war; the potential

utility of nuclear war; the morality of using nuclear weapons; and the reasonableness of a first-use policy. He does not show it to be a feasible strategy, as he claims to, but merely tells us what we have to believe to think it is. Similarly, Schelling's theory of brinksmanship depends on assumptions about the uses of limited war and the prospective feasibility of nuclear war; in the long run, his views on arms control and the prospective stability of limited war depend on additional assumptions about most of the propositions listed above. In fact, the whole notion of the workability and preferability of a deterrence strategy depends on the making of assumptions about *all* the above propositions.

Furthermore, there is something special about the assumptions deterrence theorists make. In the first place, they are uniformly tendentious, and the tendency is always and simply to support the moderate or liberal American view of the cold war—that is, to make an unquestioning application of the appeasement model to the present international conflict (see note 102, Chapter V). If Communism is not innately militarily aggressive; if the arms race is technologically uncontrollable; if the N-country problem or the German problem or the Vietnam problem or the China problem or the cold war ethos in general may lead to military breakdown or domestic dissolution; if a disarmament agreement would by changing expectations about international behavior make disarmament workable; if nothing is worth the potential catastrophe of nuclear war; if moral qualms about the use of nuclear weapons cannot be overcome; if, generally, the international system as it now stands is unsatisfactory both practically and morally — then the sophisticated deterrence strategy that has come to prominence in the past few years is not really defensible when compared with disarmament and minimum deterrence strategies.

In the second place, by constantly assuming away, as we have seen, the most important questions in the field of inquiry being investigated, deterrence theorists engage in what I have elsewhere called the vice of the depoliticalization of the political: the attempt to fit essentially political questions into the strait jacket of so-called scientific analysis.[3]

The root error in all theorizing of this type, which is finally unpersuasive because it claims to demonstrate so much more than it possibly can, lies in the attempt somehow to separate the "analytical" components of a policy problem from the political and moral ones. It is necessary to insist that this cannot be done: policy proposals rest on assertions about politics, and such assertions consist primarily of complex and indissoluble political *judgments*.[4] A judgment is an expression of belief based on one's entire training and experience, and is thus inevitably both "moral" and "analytical," "technical" and "political," "subjective" and "objective." Whether "in principle" political judgments can eventually be broken down into analytic categories is an interesting but irrelevant question, in that the basic issues of "the arms debate" relate not to abstract matters of principle but to immediate practical needs.[5] All we can do at present is to recognize that there are various kinds of inseparable evaluative elements in all political judgments, and not attempt to hide this frustrating fact under the camouflage of theoretical social science. With regard to statements such as Kahn's,

> Despite a widespread belief to the contrary, objective studies
> indicate that even though the amount of human tragedy

would be greatly increased in the postwar world, the increase would not preclude normal and happy lives for the majority of survivors and their descendents.

or even Wohlstetter's calmer, ". . . at critical junctures in the 1960's we may not have the power to deter rational attack,"[6] the notion that we can distinguish between the factual and the evaluative parts of a political judgment is useless.

Thus we are led back to the statement that sophisticated deterrence theory is of only the most limited value. If one thinks that over-all questions of policy are beyond debate, then there is certainly a sense in which strategic analysis can be both "scientific" and useful. The virtue of the RAND study of overseas bases was precisely that by the nature of its commission it assumed the need for some kind of strategic Air Force role; within the bounds set by that assumption alternatives could be fairly rigorously compared. The same considerations apply generally to the kind of weapons system comparisions that Hitch and McKean have explained in their *Economics of Defense in the Nuclear Age*. And more broadly, once one accepts the need for some policy of nuclear deterrence, it certainly becomes helpful to have as policy consultants persons who can think logically about such a policy, and who understand the basically intuitive insight into the process of mutual deterrence.

But when one is dealing with the choice of fundamental policies itself, about which debate is still widespread among the interested public, deterrence theorizing becomes simply delusive. There is still much value in the rebuttal that Brodie, Kaufmann, and a few others delivered to the early Dulles version of massive retaliation[7]—but the latter is not today the most intellectually respectable alternative to mutual deterrence. And nothing of any obvious usefulness has been added to the original insights of deterrence theory. The elaborations that have been suggested since then are all based on unassessed assumptions and are therefore of no value unless one happens for one's own reasons to agree with them.[8] The refined methods of justifying these strategies, we have observed, merely take one possible outcome of a certain kind of international conflict, trick it out in a "scenario" or a set of matrices or a complicated systematic-looking argument, manipulate it if possible with numbers to make the exercise look "scientific," and then treat the result as though it represented not a vague possibility but a near certainty. The general notion of rationality, similarly though less definitively, accomplishes the same result of substituting abstract propositions about theoretically possible human behavior for concrete propositions, such as the ones I have outlined above, about the probable behavior of relevant persons.[9] And the result is essentially irresponsible strategic thinking.

The problems of deterrence are treated as problems of calculation, in which any overbalancing of probable cost by probable gain leads inevitably to action, and any overbalancing of probable gain by probable cost to inaction. It is this oversimplified view of policy-making that leads Wohlstetter to extol the "scientific method" of policy analysis, leads Glenn Snyder to conceive of a "national interest" which rises above "politics," and leads deterrence theorists generally to neglect all considerations of public opinion and its effects in presenting their proposals.[10] Thus are naturally produced such ideas as that the balance of terror is or was "delicate" and needs or needed strengthening on our side; that the astonishing ideas of "limited strategic war" or "controlled central war," conceived in a void of abstract speculation, are necessary and reasonable types of war to plan for; that complicated arms control arrangements are more likely to be the genesis of enduring agreement than uncomplicated, dramatic disarmament arrangements; and that a counterforce first strike backed up by a massive civil-defense program is less likely to lead to the end of civilization as we know it than is even the most unreasonable of disarmament schemes. No other reason but sheer assertion is offered for giving credence to any of these ideas, in the works of professional "expertise" that have been analyzed in this thesis. Virtually everywhere one looks for serious discussion, one finds airy speculations about what rational men might or might not do.*

Some of these ideas seem irrelevant to reality. Others are all too relevant, for they have helped stretch out the arms race farther and faster than might have been the case if the real world of, say, Soviet behavior had been investigated, instead of the abstract world of decision-makers who all seem to think exactly like Wohlstetter and Kahn. In the near future we may be once again encountering, with Communist China, the same kinds of problem that we have had to face in constructing a strategy for dealing with the Soviet Union; and given

---

*The abstracted rationalism of deterrence theory finds its apotheosis in Morton Kaplan's remark that "If, in the real world, it is not possible for political or emotional reasons to adopt the strategy indicated in this article [the strategy of 'limited nuclear reprisals'] the calculus employed can be used to discover whether a reasonably effective alternative exists and, if so what it is." [11] Why a calculus that has already given one worthless answer should be employed to find alternatives to that answer, Kaplan does not make clear.

the apparent inevitability of further nuclear proliferation before the arms race is brought under control (if it ever is) we shall be doing this in an even more complex and tense situation than has existed so far. The ideological rigidity with which we approach the needs of policymaking will be, it can safely be predicted, even greater than it has been in the past, because of the special relationship that the American national psyche appears to be in with Communist China. Under these circumstances, the need for control will be even more vital than it has been, and the penalties for making "self-negating prophecies" may be even greater. The abstracted, Hobbesian rationalism with which we have hitherto viewed, and added fuel to, the arms race will have only a negative contribution to make in meeting these difficulties.

It hardly needs adding, finally, that what we are talking about has nothing to do with "science." To use inappropriate techniques that permit analysis to consist wholly of the manipulation of one's own prejudices; to rest one's theorizing on an assumption that already contains in it the conclusions that one wishes to reach—this is exactly the opposite of what genuine scientists in any field actually do.*

*It is sometimes claimed on behalf of biased work that anyway science can never be "objective." Extended discussion of such a viewpoint is profitless since regardless of whether the premise is true, the implied conclusion does not follow. Even if we can't be objective, still scientists and philosophers of diverse schools have little difficulty agreeing on what constitutes the *ideal* of objectivity. Therefore we can at the very least always judge how closely a given piece of scientific work approximates the condition of being bias-free. A genuine scientist will feel no hesitancy to claim that under certain conditions hydrogen and oxygen combine to make water, for the statement that they do so is true whether we like it to be or not. But the statement that the assumption of rationality

As for Wohlstetter's claim that the people who do this kind of work are more qualified to offer policy advice than the people who sign letters from Pugwash conferences, it should be juxtaposed with his comment that "today it is hardly necessary to argue for deterrence."[12] Among deterrence theorists the case for deterrence apparently has the epistemological status of the case for electromagnetism. No doubt such true believers can find a commonly perceived framework within which to exchange their rigorous and convincing studies of each other's assumptions. For others, however, such a mode of thought hardly seems so systematic or analytic as to call for, let alone compel acceptance of, its conclusions.

II. The Political Significance of Deterrence Theory

Why, we might ask, does such an overwhelming proportion of the academic theorists of deterrence leap from a world of inappropriate or unverified theorizing into a world of national policy-making with such confidence? The most likely answer raises some disturbing questions about the future of social science in democratic society.

No doubt a large part of the explanation of this phenomenon is to be found in the desire of some persons to be influential, even at the cost of misusing their claims to professional authority. But this tells only a part—and a relatively unimportant part—of the story. What is more important and disturbing is the impression one gets that some of these writers genuinely imagine themselves

---

makes a given strategy preferable to another is true only if we *like* it to be true—and a genuine scientist will therefore never claim that such a statement is factually descriptive. Although it may in a given instance be impossible to avoid subjectivity, we can at least avoid the pretense that it is objectivity.

to be unable to make meaningful statements unless these be cast in the form of "scientific" propositions, which have either been in some sense tested, or are soon to be so.

To have such a belief leads to serious difficulties. The only way that social scientists have found for creating a social "science," is to hypothesize abstract models of behavior, which are then refined through continuous testing until "all the evidence is in" concerning the explanatory power of the final versions of the models. At the present moment, at least, it is safe to say that there are few non-trivial hypotheses in the social sciences with regard to which "all the evidence is in."[13] But while such a state of affairs is manageable in the world of academic social science, it certainly is not manageable in the world of policy-making. For in that world choices must always be made, regardless of the state of "the evidence."

Without going into the question of whether there can ever be a social "science," I think we can say without question that it is fallacious to think that scientific propositions (and what exactly they may be is still an open question) are the only epistemologically meaningful statements. That interpretation of knowledge will be true *if* one defines "epistemologically meaningful" so that it is true; but such a definition is totally arbitrary. More to the point, that definition of "meaningful" is exclusively logical, and thereby suffers from the disability that social action is not completely logical. By ordinary standards a "meaningful" statement is any statement that convinces the person to whom it is addressed that it is "true" (or useful). This is an intersubjective standard of meaning: the only standard of meaning that is not merely esoteric.

Some would-be "pure" social scientists apparently prefer to try for an objective standard of meaning on the grounds that such a standard enables analytical statements to be convincing beyond dispute if the audience can be made to understand the scientific procedure that led to their formulation. The apparent reason for this preference is the wish to avoid what seems to be the logical result of a subjective standard of meaning; namely, that all opinions are methodologically "equal." That result, it is feared, opens the way for sheer demagogy to replace reason in discussion. Again, this may be true in logic, but it does not necessarily follow that that is what will happen in fact. There is not necessarily any more danger that the non-scientist will stoop to demagoguery, or to invoking the charisma of arcane knowledge, or to misrepresentation of the evidence for a proposition, than there is that the scientist will do so. A methodological bias against the misuse of intellectual endeavor cannot take the place of a personal commitment against it. Indeed, what is suggested by Gilpin's study of scientists in government, and what should have been suggested by the material contained in this essay, is that the methodological stance of the scientist may easily become a façade behind which another *persona* of the scientist — the would-be policy-maker who hides within his psyche—manipulates his esoteric knowledge to convince the public of the scientific reputability of statements which as science are really spurious. I do not mean to suggest, either, that such a misuse of science must always—or even often—be conscious or wilful. It may simply be that in the act, repeated again and again, of assuring one's self that one is a scientist, one may gradually forget that skill through the exercise of which one learns to detect one's own departures from the standard of scientific detachment. In any event, is the public record of those who consciously cast their work in a "scientific" mold any better than the record of those whose type of mind favors speculation and poetic metaphor on the one hand, or "mere" scholarly and systematic immersion in subject matter, without "scientific" rigor, on the other? If there is any evidence for an affirmative answer to that question, it is certainly a well-kept secret.[14]

Of course, as Wohlstetter and Brodie have argued, one hardly wants to replace the analysts' efforts at scientific reasoning with the military man's supposed reliance on authority, unimpressive intuition, common sense, and assumptions that are even more arbitrary and unstated than, say Kahn's.[15] But that is not really what most serious critics propose; and thus it is not true that, as several practitioners of systems analysis have suggested, the limitations of the scientific method for studying policy problems are shared by all the serious alternative methods.[16] For the gist of the case against the methods described in this book is that, applied to politics, they demonstrate political obtuseness and moral obscurantism. And what is proposed is that, for this reason above all, such methods be replaced with that traditional scholarly or even intelligent lay analysis that does not slight fundamentals but rather begins with them: that we rely not on easily impeachable "common sense" but on the *uncommon sense* of the thoughtful student of politics.

Certainly there have been scholars and other writers willing to discuss the crucial issues in international politics. In recent years alone, the names of Louis J. Halle, Hedley Bull, Hans Morgenthau, John Strachey,

George Kennan, Walter Lippmann, David Lilienthal, D. F. Fleming, John Herz, and others come immediately to mind.[17] Many of these have made substantive proposals which are ultimately not too unlike those offered by deterrence theorists. They have done so without benefit of conflict systems designs, formal behavioral models, matrices and calculi, and theories of rationality, and without the pretention to being more scientific or rigorous than their colleagues. Their analyses have consisted of a willingness to state what they believe about the world, the evidence which leads them to believe it, and what conclusions seem to follow from such beliefs. No doubt the more systematically such an argument is put, the better an argument it is—rigorous thought is always preferable to sloppiness. But rigor is not a substitute for thought, and rigorous deterrence analysis has been empty of real thought about the major problems of national policy.

To see this distinction more clearly, we may ask what it is that the non-scientist can do when he is asked for advice on matters of policy or when he wishes to offer such advice unasked. What does he do, that is, if he wishes to guard against misusing his reputation, in the same way that the scientist tries to make his methodology guard against misusing his?

Generally, the political analyst can acknowledge that his wisdom is both limited and more or less informed by a personal moral bias; but he can still assert that he is qualified to advise by the fact of being more thoughtful and knowledgeable about the matter at hand than the average man—it is his occupation rather than merely a casual hobby to be familiar with the material under consideration. If he values standards of "scientific" work highly, or tries to do such work himself, but wants to make clear that he is not speaking with the authority of science, he may say that he speaks only as an exceptionally well-trained citizen. That is, he may acknowledge that the conclusions he is offering are less rigorously justified than he would require in his academic work—but he will still offer them.

Concretely, he may do one or more of several things. (1) He may test the commonplace assumptions of political actors by pushing them to their logical conclusions, thus showing how much more is involved in them than appears on the surface—this is something the policy-maker will usually avoid doing. (2) He may simply gather material—either empirical material or the speculations of others (or himself) whom he considers worthy —and point to it; policy-makers may very well be unfamiliar with such material. (3) He may order systematically a body of thought, which to the layman seems diffuse. (4) He may attempt systematically to clarify available alternatives, or even to point out that additional alternative formulations of a problem exist. (5) He may point to the unrecognized underlying implications of "commonsense" statements, and to the conjectural element inherent in what less thoughtful people assume to be knowledge. (One way of doing this, of course, is to expose the misstatements of so-called science.) (6) He may try *where possible* to separate the descriptive elements of knowledge on which policy-makers are relying from the (hidden) normative ones if he thinks that this has not been done properly so far.

In all these cases, what the political analyst is really doing is to point out to the policy-maker that the latter's simplified version of reality does not exhaust the possibilities. Unless he also wishes to don the mantle of politician or statesman himself, he really does little more than this most of the time. Some of the deterrence theorists whom by implication I have slighted here have certainly tried to do something like this—most notably among them Herman Kahn. But the systematic consideration of unfamiliar material, which he and others have made their special competence, has been so organized as to dovetail with the science-mongering that accompanies it. Thus it is not truly systematic; and the unfamilar material is also, as we have seen, in a very important sense unreal.

These writers, it may be, are caught on the horns of the peculiar dilemma whereon the would-be social scientist often finds himself. If his science is still in a stage in which his propositions are neither reliable nor valid by his methodological standards—and certainly social science promises to be in that stage for a long time to come[18]—then he must opt out of social action. But should he leave the field of action to those who do not have scientific scruples? Can we expect him, as a man much better trained than the average, to have the humility required to tell those policy-makers who come to him for advice that his opinions are not really worth much from the scientist's point of view? The non-scientist can say that he speaks "merely as a thoughtful and informed citizen" without meaning anything invidious by it. But the kind of would-be scientist we are considering here cannot happily make such a statement—he is the man who doubts the cognitive value of all non-scientific statements. The result, I think, is that the consultant who has not thought through this problem, or who has adopted a naïvely positivistic view about "the meaning of meaning," has no firm principle to guide him in the use of an expert knowledge, which, *as such,* is really extremely limited from a practical point of view. And thus the chance arises that this social scientist (or others who think as he does) will put a distorted version of that knowledge, and thus a distorted version of his professional reputation, at the service of whoever can command his loyalty.

In the case of deterrence strategy, the potential dangers in such a situation are great. The constant false references to a workable theory (or theories) of strategy can only have a deleterious effect on public debate. By this I mean much more than that deterrence theorists themselves are, as I have claimed, discussing the wrong propositions. In addition, they threaten to affect public discussion generally in other unfortunate ways, which can be indicated by reference to some selected examples. What is central to all of these examples is the suggestion that, instead of being at worst an alternative mode to the one I have suggested, of dealing seriously with the issues of national security, deterrence theory is beginning to *replace* it.

Thus a well-known student of international law and organization remarks that "the science of game theory has shown that an understanding of international relations may be acquired by comparing the rules of governmental conduct to those of a game."[19] Again, Kenneth Thompson, who has written widely on the subject of power politics and diplomacy, now forsakes his own tradition of scholarly investigation of political phenomena to accept unquestioningly the claims of Herman Kahn on the virtues of civil defense, with Kahn being metamorphosed into "experts in the government and the

RAND Corporation. . . ."[20] As a *reductio ad absurdum* of the uses of deterrence theory, a newspaper reporter writes a book (lauded on the dust jacket by Kahn) consisting mostly of semiofficial statements in justification of a "no-cities" nuclear strategy, in which the proposed strategy is justified entirely by reference to scenarios and war games that have been played on computers in the Pentagon; the book contains hardly a reference to the real political world that exists outside the minds of those who decide what assumptions shall be fed into the computers.[21]

Finally, and in a way most significantly, an economist, Michael D. Intriligator, has seized on the formal discussion of deterrence theory to present a paper on the supposed economic analysis of deterrence, which is not only useless but is highly misleading as well. The paper treats of all the abstract economic models I have referred to in this thesis, and some that I have not, in the most technical possible manner (so technical indeed as to be incomprehensible to the non-economist) ; but there is not one word in it that even vaguely relates to the problems of deterrence: that is, problems of international relations in the nuclear era.[22] Intriligator's paper thus not only distorts the nature of the economist's contribution to matters of policy but—and this is its broader significance —like most formal deterrence theory it has the political effect of suggesting that "deterrence" refers to an area of study rather than to a specific political proposal.[23] In fact, Intriligator seems merely to be one would-be exemplar of Bernard Brodie's remark that "RAND and other comparable institutions have played a role very much like certain great universities and research centers in the past, where some dedicated scholars and their students have opened up whole new fields of knowledge."[24]

If the pseudo-science of strategic analysis comes to be viewed generally in the light Brodie casts on it, the results can only be unfortunate. Those who discuss international politics in a more traditional—one might say a more historically conscious—[25] fashion, whether in support of, or in opposition to, current American nuclear policy, have hardly lost their voices. But certainly such persons do not have as much of the public ear as they used to have. Rather we find a public reaction suggested by the laudatory quotations about the new deterrence theorists, which I have noted earlier in Chapter II. And since, as we have seen, the overt content of deterrence theorizing is always an analysis of the *military* significance of a proposition, the growth of deterrence theory further puts immense pressure on whatever opponents remain to cast their own arguments also in as militarized a framework as possible: to prove that they too can be guardians of the national security. Thus the very content of debate, as well as its method, is changed by one of the parties to the debate.

Nor is distortion of genuine public debate the only possible consequence of the new intellectual imperialism. Considering the nature of the deterrence theorist's use of the supposed materials of social science, one can only understand those materials as having been selectively adapted to bolster an already internalized political stance. To dignify such a posture by calling it "expert," and to give those who adopt it special access to the public ear and to policy-makers for that reason, are actions that must have significant consequences.

One probable consequence lies in what appears to have become a permanent fact of modern life, in the United States at least. In a given area of knowledge "experts" command both more prestige and higher salaries, on the whole, than do "amateurs." The temptation for those who are intelligent and interested in a given field is thus to become experts in it. If becoming "expert" requires not only the possession of a technical education but also the adoption of a particular political and ethical stance, then there is trouble ahead for democratic politics. In the course of a gloss on ex-President Eisenhower's famous remarks about the threat posed by "the military-industrial complex," John Bennett has described this problem trenchantly:

> Increasingly the close connection between the scientific community and, even more broadly, the academic community with defense policy adds to the complex of power which Eisenhower mentions. . . . The link between the RAND Corporation with the air force on the one hand and with the universities on the other dramatizes what I have in mind. Herman Kahn's book, *On Thermonuclear War*, is a great intellectual achievement and deserves much attention but it was designed by agencies within the defense department [sic] to change the attitudes of the American people about nuclear war and it was published by the press of a great university. The contribution of the academic community to government, including the defense department, is in itself not subject to criticism. And we may welcome, first of all, the sophistication and intellectual ferment that it has brought government. But in the long run there is a great danger that those who are most competent to criticize the policies of government will be inhibited by their responsibility in relation to those policies. There is danger that we shall confront one vast "establishment" which includes business, the military, the civilian government, the scientific community, foundations and the universities, and that informed public debate about the great moral issues concerned with national defense will be inhibited.[26]

One can also describe the problem differently by looking at it the other way around. An elite can be defined, as Bennett defines it, by specifying those who are included in it. An elite may also be defined by specifying those who are *excluded* from it, and, further, by specifying the grounds on which they are excluded. When an "elite" consists merely of those who happen to hold political power at the present moment, and the struggle to replace them is an open one, then by the most usual definition of political democracy we may say that they are subject to replacement by its natural processes. However, when the elite is also defined by its possession of some particular expertise, then it will be relatively "open" or "closed" depending on the extent to which capability for attaining that expertise is evenly distributed throughout the different political and social groups in the society. The very worst case, I should think, is one in which so-called technical expertise is in actuality defined by one's explicit or tacit adherence to the substantive political position of those already in power. And that case is precisely the one that seems to obtain with regard to "expertise" in the field of national security policy. The intellectual imperialism of deterrence theory is not just an academic fact, but a political act. *If* game theory, systems analysis, and the naïve deterrence theory assumption of rationality are in fact the relevant techniques and assumptions for learning to think about such problems; *and* if thinking about those problems in this way is invariably associated with programmatic support of a deterrence policy, *then* a committed advocate of, say, general and complete disarmament who wishes to attain the status of a consulting "expert" is confronted with an arbitrary political obstacle.[27]

Of course, deterrence theory may not have quite the importance attributed to it here. It may be that the actual public policy function of deterrence theory is not to influence policy-makers, but rather to provide them with rationalizations for decisions already made by more conventional methods. Or it may be that the course of American policy is already too rigidly set for the sources of that policy to be of practical concern.

With regard to the first possibility, however, the argument that one's work is not really influential hardly relieves one of the intellectual obligation to do it properly; and one should not provide rationalizations unless one believes in their validity. As to the more profound question concerning American political reality, if deterrence theory really has "won" whatever debate its proponents were engaging in, it still at least stands as an object lesson about how such debates ought *not* to be conducted in the future.

For the more solidified the reputation of "experts" becomes, the more, to that extent, will opposing viewpoints be blocked from getting a hearing. The possibility of influencing governmental decision-making, through available techniques of petition and pressure, is what chiefly defines the ability of different social groups to participate effectively in the democratic political process. The false attribution of expertness to an intellectual elite, which has in effect passed a test of political acceptability, narrows rather than enlarges the channels of influence. Pseudo-science such as that of deterrence theorists thus constitutes a disservice not only to the scholarly community, but ultimately to the democratic political process as well.

Notes on the text

Notes on the text

PREFACE

1. *New York Times*, September 8, 1961, p. 25.

2. Joseph Kraft, "The War Thinkers," *Esquire*, LVIII (September, 1962), 103 (for a similar comment by a social scientist who has written extensively in the national security area, see Gene M. Lyons, "The Growth of National Security Research," *Journal of Politics*, XXV [August, 1963], 489–508) ; Max Lerner, *The Age of Overkill: A Preface to World Politics* (New York: Simon & Schuster, 1962), p. 27; and J. David Singer, "Arms Control and Beyond: a review of Thomas C. Schelling and Morton H. Halperin, *Strategy and Arms Control*; and David Frisch, *Arms Reduction: Program and Issues* [*sic*]," *Journal of Conflict Resolution*, V (September, 1961), 311.

3. For example, Jerome Spingarn, review of *On Thermonuclear War*, by Herman Kahn, *New York Times Book Review*, January 1, 1961; Glenn H. Snyder, *Deterrence and Defense: Toward a Theory of National Security* (Princeton: Princeton University Press, 1961), hereinafter cited as *Deterrence and Defense*; Morton H. Halperin, *Limited War in the Nuclear Age* (New York: John Wiley & Sons, 1963) ; the Foreword by Klaus Knorr, in Herman Kahn, *On Thermonuclear War* (Princeton: Princeton University Press, 1960), p. v (hereinafter cited as *OTW*) ; and Kraft, *loc. cit.*, quotes an extremely laudatory reference by U.S. Air Force Chief of Staff General Thomas White about Herman Kahn.

CHAPTER I

1. Kraft, *ibid.*

2. Thomas C. Schelling, *The Strategy of Conflict* (Cambridge: Harvard University Press, 1960), pp. 6 ff. (hereinafter cited as *SOC*).

3. Glenn H. Snyder, *Deterrence by Denial and Punishment* ("Princeton Center of International Studies: Research Monograph No. 1"; Princeton, N.J.: 1959).

4. See Hook's example in Chapter VI below, pp. 226–27.

5. On the novelty of the nuclear age, see Bernard Brodie, *Strategy in the Missile Age* (Princeton: Princeton University Press, 1959).

6. This point is made in Thomas C. Schelling and Morton H. Halperin, *Strategy and Arms Control* (New York: Twentieth Century Fund, 1961). See also Thomas C. Schelling, "The Role of Deterrence in Total Disarmament," *Foreign Affairs*, XL (April, 1962), 392–406.

7. See Schelling and Halperin, *op. cit.*, on the distinction between arms control and complete disarmament.

8. J. David Singer, *Deterrence, Arms Control, and Disarmament* (Columbus: Ohio State University Press, 1962) (hereinafter cited as *Deterrence*).

9. Robert A. Levine, *The Arms Debate* (Cambridge: Harvard University Press, 1963). For a more complete discussion and critique of Levine's work, see my "Method and Substance in the Arms Debate," *World Politics*, XVI (July, 1964), 642–67.

10. Kahn, *OTW*, pp. 126 ff; Robert Strausz–Hupé, William R. Kintner, and Stefan T. Possony, *A Forward Strategy for America* (New York: Harper & Row, 1961).

11. In *Thinking about the Unthinkable* (New York: Horizon Press, 1962), hereinafter cited as *TAU*, Herman Kahn describes fourteen different policy stances which he finds current in American thought (pp. 233 ff.). Some of his distinctions are significant, but I do not think that any of them really stretch the categoriza-

tion suggested here, and by Levine. It can be observed that, according to his categorization, his own position is close to Strausz-Hupé's.

12. See Albert Wohlstetter, "The Delicate Balance of Terror," *Foreign Affairs*, XXXVII (January, 1959), 211–34, for a more extended treatment of the rather complicated operational requirements for fulfilling this loosely stated mission. See also Thornton Read, *Command and Control* ("Princeton Center of International Studies: Policy Memorandum No. 24" [Princeton, N. J., 1961]); Herbert D. Benington, "Command and Control for Selective Response," in *Limited Strategic War*, ed. Klaus Knorr and Thornton Read (New York: Frederick A. Praeger, 1962); and, generally, Kahn.

13. Wohlstetter, *ibid.*; on the failure yet to achieve true invulnerability, see Kahn, *OTW*, chaps. vi, x.

14. Wohlstetter, *ibid.*

15. Robert S. McNamara, "Defense Arrangements of the North Atlantic Community," *Department of State Bulletin*, XLVII (July 9, 1962), 64–69. See also Halperin, *op. cit.*, chap. vi.

16. For a full discussion of this requirement, see Kahn, *OTW*, chaps. iv and v.

17. On the concept of "credibility," see the essays by Kaufmann in William W. Kaufmann (ed.), *Military Policy and National Security* (Princeton: Princeton University Press, 1956).

18. On tactical nuclear war, see Henry Kissinger, *Nuclear Weapons and Foreign Policy* (New York: Harper & Row, 1957).

19. This strategy is discussed at length by the various contributors to Knorr and Read, *op. cit.*

20. A concise statement of this approach is that of Malcolm W. Hoag, "On Stability in Deterrent [*sic*] Races," in Morton A. Kaplan (ed.), *The Revolution in World Politics* (New York: John Wiley & Sons, 1962), pp. 388–410.

21. It is useful here to define some terms that will come up from time to time in the ensuing discussion, namely, "finite deterrence" and "minimum deterrence." The definitions are my own; though they are not idiosyncratic, neither are they necessarily acceptable to every deterrence theorist, and thus the reader must remember that only these definitions are intended when reference is made to these terms.

Minimum deterrence, then, is defined here as a deterrent posture based simply on the possession of enough nuclear weapons to do serious damage to an "enemy" nation. The definition is neutral on the question of the security of the deterrent force; or rather, the question of security is taken to be secondary to the question of avoiding an "arms race." Thus, a decade ago a proposal of minimum deterrence was a proposal that the United States build no more nuclear weapons, or few more, than it then had. However, since then a large arsenal of relatively secure, or "invulnerable" weapons has been developed, and to propose minimum deterrence now would be to propose disarming all but a small number of the most secure weapons. (This definition, in other words, is a situational one.) Advocacy of finite deterrence, on the other hand, is based on the fear that in a crisis a nation may be tempted to make a surprise attack if it calculates that its potential opponent's forces could be knocked out or otherwise neutralized in a first strike. Therefore it is proposed that a deterrence force must be large enough to absorb an all-out counterforce first strike and still have enough weapons left over to do unacceptable damage —whatever that might be—in a countercity retaliatory strike. Again, the definition is intended to be situational: a decade ago, the proposal to buy more "invulnerable" weapons was a proposal to move from minimum to finite deterrence; today, we would probably have to do some disarming to move even to a finite deterrence posture.

This definition of finite deterrence is intended also to be neutral on the question of the stringency of the requirements for the deterrent. One could, with Wohlstetter and Kahn, insist that the requirements are very stringent indeed if one is to avoid the prospect of being blackmailed out of one's counterstrike; if, that is, one's deterrent threat is to be credible. If one adopts this approach, one worries about the reliability and accuracy of one's weapons and the state of the opponent's active air defenses, and one may thus wind up proposing a truly immense force—large enough, even, to accept a first strike and still have enough weapons left over not only to damage the attacker's society but also (or perhaps rather) to make a blunting attack on its remaining weapons so that it cannot make a counter-counterstrike. On the other hand, one might mean by finite deterrence simply that after the most damaging first strike an attacker could make one would still have a lot of dangerous weapons left over. For the first approach to finite deterrence see Hoag's article, in Kaplan, *op. cit.*; for the second approach, see Singer, *Deterrence* (although, as one observes from Singer's discussion, the "minimum" approach to finite deterrence begins to shade into a "maximum" approach to minimum deterrence). A good popular discussion of this whole subject, less sophisticated but also less dogmatic than Kahn's, is Ralph E. Lapp, *Kill and Overkill* (New York: Basic Books, 1962).

CHAPTER II

1. Wohlstetter, "Scientists, Seers, and Strategy," *Foreign Affairs*, XLI (April, 1963), 462–78; and "Analysis and Design of Conflict Systems," in Edward S. Quade, *Analysis for Military Decisions* (Chicago: Rand-McNally, 1964), pp. 103–48.

2. See Levine, *op. cit.*, for a detailed description of "the arms debate" that effectively demonstrates the ubiquitous influence of Kahn's work; as for opponents of Kahn, one of them, H. Stuart Hughes, remarked that "Kahn has written one of the great works of our time," in "The Strategy of Deterrence," *Commentary*, XXXI (February, 1961), 186.

3. See, e.g., Richard Fryklund, *100 Million Lives* (New York: Macmillan Co., 1962), a semiofficial exposition of the "credible first-strike no-cities" doctrine.

4. *OTW, passim.* The quotations about systems analysis and operations research occur on pages 119 and 331 respectively. However, Kahn has little reference to operations research in this book, at least with regard to concrete studies of nuclear war, and I therefore shall refer to systems analysis throughout my discussion. In any event, the distinction is a hard one to make, though we can say generally that operations research is a technique for the study of systems less broadly construed—in military affairs, tactical rather than strategic "systems." Cf., C. West Churchman, Russell L. Ackoff, and E. Leonard Arnoff, *Introduction to Operations Research* (New York: John Wiley & Sons, 1957), especially p. 16; Patrick M. S. Blackett, *Studies of War* (New York: Hill and Wang, 1962), Part II; and Albert Wohlstetter, "Strategy and the Natural Scientists," in Robert Gilpin and Christopher Wright (eds.), *Scientists and National Policy-Making* (New York: Columbia University Press, 1964), pp. 204–5.

From here on I shall ignore when possible Kahn's peculiar notions of capitalization, preferring, as J. David Singer put it in his review of *OTW* ("The Strategic Dilemma: Probability versus Utility," *Journal of Conflict Resolution*, V [June, 1961], 197–205), not to be Kahn's accomplice in sloganeering.

5. Quade, *op. cit.* (And see generally the journal *Operations Research* for examples of military operations' studies.)

6. "The Selection and Use of Strategic Air Bases: A Case History," *ibid.*, pp. 24–64. The original study is by Albert Wohlstetter, F. S. Hoffmann, R. J. Lutz, and H. S. Rowen, *Selection and Use of Strategic Air Bases*, RAND R–266, April, 1954.

7. Charles J. Hitch and Roland N. McKean, *The Economics of Defense in the Nuclear Age* (Cambridge: Harvard University Press, 1960). It is impossible to tell whether Hitch thinks of his contribution as being chiefly relevant to "operations research" or "systems analysis," since he uses neither of these phrases.

8. Quade, *op. cit.*, p. 24, quotes *Life* as reporting an Air Force estimate that the bases study saved the U.S. a billion dollars.

9. See the quotation from Walter Stein in Chapter vi, p. 230.

10. Quade, *op. cit.*, pp. 4, 8, 23, 105, 321. The definitions are by Quade, Quade, Hitch, Wohlstetter, and Quade, respectively.

11. Wohlstetter, in Gilpin and Wright, *op. cit.*, p. 195; and Roland McKean, *Efficiency in Government through Systems Analysis* (New York: John Wiley & Sons, 1958), p. 7. For Kahn's own essay in definition see Herman Kahn and Irwin Mann, *Techniques of Systems Analysis*, RM–1829 (Santa Monica, Calif.: The RAND Corporation, December, 1956), especially pp. 4–6; and *OTW*, pp. viii–ix.

12. *OTW*, p. v. For lengthier and more sophisticated version of the same argument, see the article by Aaron Wildavsky, "Practical Consequences of the Theoretical Study of Defense Policy," *Public Administration Review*, XXV (March, 1965), 91. And see Kahn and Mann, *op. cit.*, p. 7.

13. Santa Monica, Calif.: The RAND Corporation, July 1, 1958.

14. *OTW*, pp. 7–35, contains Kahn's various definitions for deterrence doctrine. "Multistable" simply means that one has a unique capability for dealing with each potential level of provocation or aggression; elsewhere Kahn has suggested "not incredible" in place of "credible" to illustrate the point that a nuclear strike threat can be made persuasive in some circumstances with

very little effort, because of the awesome power of nuclear weapons; cf. Knorr and Read, *op. cit.*, p. 64.

15. See John C. Polanyi, "Armaments Policies for the Sixties," *Bulletin of the Atomic Scientists*, XVII (December, 1961), 404.

16. *OTW*, p. 55.

17. Robert Paul Wolff, "The Rhetoric of Deterrence" (unpublished manuscript), p. 42 n. 1. I have relied heavily on Wolff's excellent essay.

18. Thus Kahn criticizes other theorists, such as Morgenstern, for being overly rationalistic in their assumption that a first-strike capability will never be needed—i.e., that deterrence will never fail; *OTW*, pp. 14–18.

19. Kahn, *On Escalation* (New York: Frederick A. Praeger, 1965), p. 189. The original assumption is found at *OTW*, p. 307. (*On Escalation*, hereinafter cited as *OE*).

20. *TAU*, p. 68.

21. *OTW*, p. 566. The whole discussion is at pp. 564–68.

22. *Ibid.*, p. 90.

23. *Ibid.*, p. 86.

24. *Ibid.*, pp. 74–78. The level of destruction Kahn refers to is presumably the destruction of the fifty-three largest Standard Metropolitan Areas.

25. *Ibid.*, pp. 79–80.

26. *Ibid.*, pp. 80–84.

27. *Ibid.*, p. 84.

28. *Ibid.*, pp. 84–91.

29. *Ibid.*, p. 30.

30. *Ibid.*, p. 29.

31. *Ibid.*, pp. 50–54

32. *Ibid.*, pp. 63–74. Tables 9 and 11 are at pages 57 and 61.

33. *Ibid.*, p. 59.

34. *Ibid.*, p. 50.

35. *Ibid.*, Table 25, p. 113. "Early" and "late" are synonymous with "light" and "heavy" attacks.

36. *Ibid.*, p. 114.

37. *Ibid.*, p. 98.

38. *TAU*, p. 68; the entire passage is at pp. 60–68. Kahn seems to consider the third of all these types of attack and damage (1

to 20 or 5 to 30 million, increasing by up to a factor of 5) to be the most likely to occur.

39. *OE*, p. 181. The phrase about striking second in the above paragraph is from *TAU*, p. 61.

40. *OTW*, p. 55, Table 8.

41. *Ibid.*, pp. 56 ff.

42. *Ibid.*, pp. 59–62.

43. *Ibid.*, pp. 63–66.

44. *Ibid.*, p. 62.

45. *Ibid.*, p. 59.

46. I am indebted to Wolff for this point.

47. Wolff, "The Rhetoric of Deterrence," p. 44.

48. *OTW*, p. 55, e.g. Kahn's use of "bearable" occurs at p. 54 and again at p. 62.

49. *Ibid.*, p. 84.

50. *Ibid.*, p. 307, italics in original.

51. *Ibid.*, pp. 114–15.

52. There have been projects, mostly sponsored by the Office of Civil and Defense Mobilization, that purported to study this problem. All of those with which I am familiar assume quite fanciful attempts to provide a normal happy life (including usually good wages) for the volunteers. For an analysis of these projects, see Robert A. Dentler and Phillips Cutright, *Hostage America: Human Aspects of a Nuclear Attack and a Program of Prevention* (Boston: Beacon Press, 1963), chap. ii.

53. *OTW*, p. 58. Three pages later the range of 2 to 100 changes to one of 1 to 100.

54. *Ibid.*, pp. 74–96 for the whole discussion.

55. Dentler and Cutright, *op. cit.*, p. 57.

56. *OTW*, pp. 93–94.

57. Compare, e.g., Paul Samuelson, *Economics: An Introductory Analysis* (5th ed.; New York: McGraw-Hill, 1961); Neil J. Smelser and Talcott Parsons, *Economy and Society: A Study in the Integration of Economic and Social Theory* (Glencoe, Ill.: Free Press, 1956). Indeed, one of the major current trends in empirical analysis of resource allocation and of production—input-output analysis—is impossible to conceive of except on the assumption that the economy is some kind of interrelated entity, the

parts of which must mesh to produce the level of activity that we associate with a given society.

58. Cf., W. Arthur Lewis, *The Theory of Economic Growth* (Homewood, Ill.: Richard D. Irwin, 1955) ; W. W. Rostow, *The Stages of Economic Growth* (Cambridge, England: Cambridge University Press, 1962).

59. *OTW*, p. 20.

60. In *OE* Kahn has made this concept of strategic evacuation the lynchpin of his strategic thinking, and now goes so far as to propose that no attack be made on populations without being preceded by a warning that would permit such evacuation. "I think," he writes (pp. 160–61), "that targeting civilians is not necessary, even for wars with a large countervalue element." Unfortunately one does not know how seriously to take this statement, since this is but one of many conflicting strategic postures Kahn discusses, and since he fails to indicate which of them he *really* means.

61. Wohlstetter, *Foreign Affairs*, XXXVII, 230. But in n. 9 228–29, Wohlstetter cites the RAND civil-defense study as though it is merely a report of scientific research.

62. Halperin, *op. cit.*, p. 117.

63. *OTW*, pp. 94–95.

64. Wolff, "The Rhetoric of Deterrence," p. 46.

65. *OTW*, pp. 91–92; emphasis added. Compare the paragraph quoted immediately above.

66. *Ibid.*, p. 44.

67. *Ibid.*, p. 78, and see n. 24 above.

68. Dentler and Cutright, *op. cit.*, pp. 51–52, point out that "Major sanitation facilities would have been destroyed, making all survivors vulnerable to typhus and a host of other infectious diseases. . . . Man's 'natural' enemies are, ironically, more likely to survive high radiation levels than man himself. Viruses, insect pests and bacteria will still exist in the postattack world. We will not have the highly developed human and technological means to counter their effects in human and plant diseases that we now rely on for our own survival and for continued food production." See also their discussion of medical practice and medical facilities after a nuclear war, pp. 65–70.

69. *OTW*, p. 89.

70. Cf., *OTW*, p. 61.

71. For example, see *ibid.*, p. 78. This argument is repeated several times.

72. Dentler and Cutright note: "People struggle to resolve a crisis by adjustive action. If they succeed, tension is reduced and a new balance is established. If they fail, they fail to survive. . . . A severe crisis unleashes new sources of motivation, for men require will and purpose as well as resources to survive. They must choose to act in the way they must act; they have to want what is necessary for survival. In a postattack crisis, many of the *ordinary* props that provide social motivation . . . would fail to apply to the realities of the situation . . . *Americans would require a radical transformation of social motives to survive a nuclear attack* . . . [F]or example . . . we count on competition to stimulate effort, to develop abilities and unleash innovative action. In the extreme crisis of the post-attack society, bases for regulating competition would be damaged, and scarcity would be unlike any pattern of scarcity the nation had ever faced before. . . . " (*op. cit.*, pp. 73–74, emphasis in original).

The last sentence is extremely important, for though disasters have been studied, we have few if any grounds for generalization about the impact of society-wide disasters on such a scale as might be caused by the kind of attack Kahn envisages. Two attempts have been made to relate previous disaster studies to the problem of survival in a future nuclear war: Jack Hirshleifer, "Some Thoughts on the Social Structure After a Bombing Disaster," *World Politics*, VIII (January, 1956), 206–27, and Edward A. Tiryakian, "Aftermath of a Thermonuclear Attack on the United States: Some Sociological Considerations," *Social Problems*, VI (Spring, 1959), 291–304. Unfortunately, Hirshleifer's paper is worthless, being glib and shallow, and concerned chiefly with prospects for the survival of "free enterprise," (although he does make the one valid point that after all the Black Death did not destroy Western European society). Tiryakian's essay is much more scholarly and thoughtful, and highly informative about the conclusions that can be drawn from earlier disaster studies. However, as far as one can tell even Tiryakian does not think that many of those conclusions are very relevant to the case of all-out nuclear attack, and thus the essay ends in limbo. The closest he comes to a conclusion of his own is the following: "The United States in the aftermath of a nuclear disaster may well be characterized by either of two polar forms of social organization. On the one hand, there may be a national *anomie* consisting of an aggregate of regional, community, or kinship groups, loosely if at all related to one another economically and politically, each autonomous surviving social group living more or less at the subsistence level. On the other hand, a semblance of predisaster national functional interdependence may be achieved—but only at the cost of replacing democratic controls by rigid authoritarian structures." (p. 302). Needless to say, Tiryakian does not seem to feel that endorsement of strategies that increase the likelihood of nuclear war is warranted by his conclusions; he is concerned with the question of what may happen, not what we ought to do.

73. In "Western Values and Total War: A Round-Table Discussion," *Commentary*, XXXII (October, 1961), 281.

74. Dentler and Cutright, *op. cit.*, p. 73. They add: "Continuing health and safety, too, are more than problems in social control and medical care. If standards of health and safety drop too low in any society, survival is threatened. Yet the matter is relative; a folk community equipped through generations with natural immunities and conditioned to survival in the face of low standards of health could sustain a drop in standards that would decimate a civilization based on scientific medicine. The abrupt removal of our medical technology would be relatively disastrous. This is an instance in which we are rendered vulnerable by a heritage of civilized life." This same point is made at greater length in one of the major speculative works of the postwar period, Harrison Brown's *The Challenge of Man's Future* (New York: Viking Press, 1954).

75. Dentler and Cutright, *ibid.*, p. 58.

76. For Kahn's optimism, see *OTW*, pp. 68–69, e.g. The assumption about high-altitude bursts is on p. 169.

77. *TAU*, p. 85.

78. In *OE*, Kahn writes that "the effects of multi-megaton weapons are so powerful and complex that even if they do not destroy a system by blast, they may damage it by more subtle effects or change the environment in such fashion that the system will be temporarily or permanently inoperable." (p. 187).

79. Wohlstetter, *Foreign Affairs*, XXXVII, 216, gives the example of the early claims about the costs of missiles, one of which was eventually outmoded "by a factor of over 50. . . . "

80. *OTW*, p. 71.

81. *Ibid.*, pp. 70–72.

82. *Ibid.*, pp. 145–49. Kahn defines a Doomsday Machine as a device set to destroy all human life upon being given the appropriate stimulus, such as the explosion of a certain number of nuclear weapons anywhere on the territory of the nation which has built the machine. The Doomsday-in-a-Hurry-Machine, also mentioned by Kahn, is better left undefined.

83. *Ibid.*, p. 71, e.g.

84. *Ibid.*, p. 514.

85. Hanson Baldwin, "The Treaty and Power," *New York Times*, August 15, 1963, p. 6.

86. Dentler and Cutright, *op. cit.*, p. 20.

87. *OTW*, p. 538.

88. Klaus Knorr, "NATO Defense in an Uncertain Future," in his *NATO and American Security* (Princeton: Princeton University Press, 1959), pp. 280, 284–85.

89. Robert E. Osgood, "Nuclear Arms: Uses and Limits," *New Republic*, September 10, 1962, p. 16. For an interesting explanation of some technical difficulties that helped to bring about this miscalculation, see "Goldwater on the Gap," *The New Republic*, December 21, 1963, p. 5.

90. John C. Bennett, "Moral Urgencies in the Nuclear Context," in John C. Bennett, (ed.) *Nuclear Weapons and the Conflict of Conscience* (New York: Charles Scribner's Sons, 1962), p. 98.

91. The best critical discusion are Singer, *op. cit.* and *loc. cit.* (n. 4 above) ; Polanyi, *loc. cit.*; and Amitai Etzioni, *The Hard Way to Peace* (New York: Collier Books, 1962).

92. In Gilpin and Wright, *op. cit.*, p. 208.

93. *OE*, p. 180.

94. *OTW*, p. 21; *TAU*, pp. 86–87, 99; see also *OE*, pp. 159–60.

95. *OTW*, p. 35, for example.

96. Singer's review of *OTW* discusses the book from this perspective.

97. Singer, *Deterrence*, suggests such a strategy for the short run.

98. Singer, *ibid.*; Etzioni, *op. cit.*; Arthur I. Waskow, *The Limits of Defense* (Garden City: Doubleday & Co., 1962).

99. "The Cold War and the West: A Symposium," *Partisan Review*, XXIX (Winter, 1962), 62.

100. *OTW*, pp. 345–46; For Kahn's estimate of his own proposals, see Lecture I, *passim*, especially pp. 7–35.

101. Cf., Singer, "Deterrence and Shelters," *Bulletin of the Atomic Scientists*, XVII (October, 1961), 310–14; Arthur Hadley, *The Nation's Safety and Arms Control* (New York: Viking Press, 1961), pp. 29, 101. For Kahn's own notion of "insurance," see *OTW*, p. 24.

102. In Gilpin and Wright, *op. cit.*, p. 214.

103. *OTW*, p. 5.

104. *OE*, p. 17.

105. The whole tone of Kahn's strategic discussion is infused with this viewpoint; see especially pp. 523–76, *passim.*

106. See my discussion of deterrence bias in chap. vi below.

107. See especially *TAU* for the latter.

108. On the relationship between political positions and proposed military strategies in the arms debate, see Levine, *op. cit.*

109. Arthur Herzog, *The War-Peace Establishment* (New York: Harper & Row, 1965), pp. 63–64.

110. Wohlstetter, "Scientists, Seers, and Strategy," *Foreign Affairs*, XLI, 478.

111. Examples of such application are given throughout Quade, *op. cit.*

112. "Operations Research and National Planning—A Dissent," *Operations Research Quarterly*, V (October, 1957), 718. (The dissent, it should be noted, is not from opposition to the point under discussion here, but to a different point made in the paper to which Hitch's article is a reply). See also James R. Schlesinger's "Quantitative Analysis and National Security," *World Politics*, XV (January, 1963), 295–315, for an extended presentation of the same argument. Like Hitch, Schesinger has been engaged in such work himself.

113. Wohlstetter, *loc. cit.*, (n. 110 above), 468.

114. *OE, passim.* (For example, p. 49.)

115. See the discussion of Orwell's *1984* in Irving Howe, *Politics and the Novel* (New York: Horizon Press, 1957), pp. 235–51.

CHAPTER III

1. John von Neumann and Oskar Morgenstern, *Theory of Games and Economic Behavior* (1st ed.; Princeton: Princeton University Press, 1944).

2. Albert Wohlstetter, "Sin and Games in America," in Martin Shubik (ed.), *Game Theory and Related Approaches to Social Behavior* (New York: John Wiley & Sons, 1964), 209-25 (hereinafter cited as *Game Theory*). The best presentation of the case against the critics is Donald G. Brennan's review of Anatol Rapoport's *Strategy and Conscience* (see n. 8 below), *Bulletin of the Atomic Scientists*, XXI (Dec., 1965), 25-30. This review itself is often exaggerated, however.

3. For an "outsider" discussion of deterrence, which contains many references to game theory or material drawn from it, see Richard C. Snyder, *Deterrence, Weapon Systems, and Decision-Making* ("Studies in Deterrence, No. III" [China Lake, Calif.: U. S. Naval Ordnance Test Station, 1961]). And see generally, over the last ten years, the *Journal of Conflict Resolution*. The author, in 1960, attended an *Arms Control and Limitation* conference at Princeton University at which an extremely abstract paper about tacit negotiation in experimental bargaining games was presented—but at which a question from the floor about disarmament was ruled out of order by the Chairman, Oskar Morgenstern.

4. Bernard Brodie, in Gilpin and Wright, *op. cit.*, p. 252. An earlier commentator has written, "While there are specific applications today, despite the current limitations of the theory, perhaps its greatest contribution so far has been an intangible one: the general orientation given to people who are faced with overcomplex problems, Even though these problems are probably for the indefinite future—it helps to have a framework in which to work on them. The concept of a strategy, the distinctions among players, the role of chance events, the notion of matrix representations of the payoffs, the concepts of pure and mixed strategies, and so on, give valuable orientation to persons who must think about complicated conflict situations." J. D. Williams, *The Compleat Strategyst* (New York: McGraw-Hill, 1954). p. 217. See also Hayward Alker's discussion of minimax in his *Mathematics and Politics* (New York: Macmillan Co., 1965), pp. 133-36. And Thomas Schelling, in Quade, *op. cit.*, pp. 199-216, has written an article, "Assumptions about Enemy Behavior," which is an attempt to show how a game-theoretic orientation helps the analyst build enemy behavior into his analysis.

5. Brodie, *op. cit.*: Part I. The quotation is from Gilpin and Wright, *op. cit.*, p. 252.

6. Anatol Rapoport, "Various Meaning of 'Theory'," *American Political Science Review*, LII (December, 1958), 972–88, has a stimulating discussion of the kinds of heuristic uses to which abstract theory can profitably be put, as has Karl Deutsch, in his *The Nerves of Government* (London: Free Press, 1963), chap. i. And Arthur L. Burns, in a review of Rapoport's *Strategy and Conscience*, has recently written an excellent brief account of the chief heuristic use of game theory: "The game-theoretical matrix . . . probably never provides *directly* an hypothesis about strategic or political events in the real world. . . . The use of game theory and its matrices, as some of us have come to realize, is to set a standard of explicitness and rigor in the discussion of acts that are competitive and, in a constrictive and almost obsessional sense of the term, 'rational.' In the place of hunches about the working of the balance of power, for instance, game theory provides an exact grammar, which for the most part simply exposes the arbitrariness and untestability of our hunches: we now know what it would be like to have knowledge of these matters—and we know that on the whole we cannot have it." (In "Must Strategy and Conscience be Disjoined?", *World Politics*, XVII [July, 1965], 698).

7. E. S. Quade notes that "Game theory is now being successfully applied to various tactical problems—such as radar search and prediction, the allocation of defense to targets of unequal value, the study of missile penetration aids, the scheduling of missile fire under enemy pindown, and other problems as diverse as antisubmarine warfare and inspection for arms control." (Quade, *op. cit.*, p. 245). Of course, one does not have the faintest notion what Quade means by "successfully"; but assuming he means that whoever commissioned these various studies was satisfied by the results, one is willing to take his word for it. For examples of similarly successful costing analyses that have sometimes been aided by insights derived from theories of choice generally, see Hitch and McKean, *op. cit.*, and Malcolm W. Hoag, "Some Complexities in Military Planning," *World Politics*, XI (July, 1959), 553–77.

8. See especially Rapoport's discussions of game theory, in his *Fights, Games, and Debates* (Ann Arbor: University of Michigan Press, 1960), Part II, and his *Strategy and Conscience* (New York: Harper & Row, 1964), Parts I and II; also R. Duncan Luce and Howard Raiffa, *Games and Decisions* (New York: John Wiley & Sons, 1957), which is at the same time an expository text on,

and critique of, game theory; Karl Deutsch, *op. cit.*, chap. iv; Wolff, "The Rhetoric of Deterrence"; and Richard E. Quandt, "On the Use of Game Models in Theories of International Relations," in Klaus Knorr and Sidney Verba (eds.), *The International System: Theoretical Essays* (Princeton: Princeton University Press, 1961), pp. 70–76. In this last-named volume also appear essays by Morton A. Kaplan and Arthur L. Burns, both of whom more or less renounce their earlier excursions into game-theoretic modes of explanation in international relations.

9. See Luce and Raiffa, *op. cit.*, pp. 54–55, for "the rules of the game;" pp. 62–63 for their discussion of the meaning of "maximization-of-security-level." The expected payoff of a strategic choice, it should be made clear, is the value of an outcome to one's self multiplied by the (estimated) probability of that outcome's being the one that eventuates. This estimated probability is actually not an "estimate" but is rather calculated from one's knowledge of the opponent's valuations of the various possible outcomes to him, and from one's knowledge of *his* knowledge of one's own valuations of the possible outcomes—a circumstance which in theory eliminates the ordinary form of subjectivity in probability estimates, reduces guesswork about an opponent's move to calculation of it, and gives to game theory its peculiar flavor.

One point I have neglected here is the distinction between zero-sum and non-zero-sum games. In the zero-sum game, one player wins exactly what the other loses—their interests are strictly competitive, that is, as in betting on the toss of a coin—and the total payoff of the game is zero. In the non-zero-sum game, by contrast, interests are not completely conflicting; it is thus possible for both players to achieve positive or negative payoffs, or if one "wins" and the other "loses," for the payoffs not to be reciprocal, so that the total payoff of the game is not zero. (I am in both cases speaking of two-person games, the n-person game presenting too many additional problems even to be suggested here.)

Everyone who has contributed to the discussion of game theory and deterrence agrees that international conflict is best seen as an example of the non-zero-sum (partially competitive, partially co-operative) game. However, this fact creates some difficulties in analysis, in that the theory of the non-zero-sum game is poorly developed compared with the theory of the zero-sum game; cf., Luce and Raiffa, chaps. iv-v. The difficulties indeed are apparently so great that Luce and Raiffa themselves, for instance, cannot always overcome them. Thus George Kent has pointed out to me that when Luce and Raiffa define such terms as "minimax," they do so in the context of the zero-sum game only—e.g., pp. 61 ff— and never reveal in discussing the *non*-zero-sum game what application, if any, the earlier definitions are supposed to have. This should be kept in mind during the discussion of game theory— we cannot be certain, for example, whether the "rules of the game" as defined here fully apply to the non-zero-sum game. However, since the inapplicability to international conflict of game theory, strictly conceived, seems to me to be perfectly obvious in any event, I have simply ignored these difficulties in the ensuing pages.

10. *Ibid.*, p. 55.

11. The phrase is Charles Lindblom's, borrowed from him by Verba. See Lindblom, "The Science of Muddling Through," *Public Administration Review*, XIX (Winter, 1959), 86–87. (Also see his "Policy Analysis," *American Economic Review*, Vol. XLVIII [June, 1958], and David Braybrooke and Charles Lindblom, *A Strategy of Decision* [New York: Free Press, 1963]). I have relied heavily on this article of Lindblom's, here and in chap. v when discussing the meaning of rationality in decision-making.

12. Sidney Verba, "Assumptions of Rationality and Non-Rationality in Models of the International System," in Knorr and Verba, *op. cit.*, pp. 108–13. Similar remarks have been made by Harold Garfinkel in "The Rational Properties of Scientific and Commonsense Activities," *Behavioral Science*, V (January, 1960), 72–83.

13. *Op. cit.*, p. 5, emphasis added. The authors go on to make the same kind of defense of game theory for *heuristic* purposes as do Rapoport and Deutsch (see note 6 above).

14. Oskar Morgenstern, *The Question of National Defense* (2d ed. revised; New York: Vintage Books, 1961), p. 62.

15. *Ibid.*, pp. 169, 198, 235, e.g.

16. Morgenstern, "Cold War Is Cold Poker," *New York Times Magazine*, February 5, 1961, p. 14.

17. Morgenstern, *op. cit.*, p. x.

18. Schelling, *SOC*, pp. 205–54.

19. *Ibid.*, p. 228.

20. *Ibid.*, p. 234. In his other writings on arms control and disarmament, Schelling has continually made the same point, though he has tended to be vague as to his personal feelings about the condition he describes; see, e.g., Schelling and Halperin, *op. cit.*, *passim*; Schelling, "The Role of Deterrence in Total Disarmament," *loc. cit.*; "Reciprocal Measures for Arms Stabilization," in

Donald G. Brennan (ed.), *Arms Control, Disarmament, and National Security* (New York: Braziller, 1961), pp. 167–86; and "Arms Control: Proposal For a Special Surveillance Force," *World Politics*, XIII (October, 1960), 1–18.

21. *SOC*, pp. 235 ff., Schelling and Halperin, *op. cit.*, pp. 54 ff.

22. Ellsberg, *The Crude Analysis of Strategic Choices*, RAND P–2183 (Santa Monica: The RAND Corporation, December, 1960). This paper has also been published under the same title in the *American Economic Review*, LI (May, 1961), 472–78; and in Martin Shubik, *Game Theory*, pp. 230–39. For further references to Ellsberg's paper I have cited the Shubik collection, as it is most likely to be immediately available to those with a joint interest in game theory and deterrence theory.

For some laudatory references to Ellsberg's work, see the comments by Glenn Snyder, *Deterrence and Defense*, pp. 17, 19; Schelling, *SOC*, p. 13; Thornton Read, *op. cit.*, Acknowledgments.

23. Shubik, *Game Theory*, p. 238.

24. *Ibid.*, p. 231.

25. The comment is by Shubik, *ibid.*, p. 230.

26. *Ibid.*, pp. 232, 238.

27. In Quade, *op. cit.*, p. 22.

28. That can be described within the framework of the game, of course. See Rapoport, *Fights, Games, and Debates*, chap. viii. A game can be put in what is called "extensive" or "extended" form, in which a sequence of "moves" rather than a single exchange of moves describes the game. In "normal" form, this sequence would either be collapsed into a (rather complicated) single-move game, or into many, now analytically separate single-move games, in which the results of one game would enter into the next game only in stating each side's payoff function. In addition to Rapoport, Luce and Raiffa, *op. cit.*, pp. 47–48, discuss games in extensive form.

29. On this distinction, see J. Schlesinger, *loc. cit.* (above, chap. ii, n. 112).

30. Lindblom, *Public Administration Review*, *loc. cit.* See also Harold Stein (ed.), *Public Administration and Policy Development: A Casebook* (New York: Harcourt, Brace & World, 1952), *passim*.

31. Cf., Karl Deutsch, *op. cit.*, pp. 57 ff.

32. *Op. cit.*, p. 44.

33. To see this point more clearly, one may consider the "extended game" discussed in chap. v of Luce and Raiffa, *op. cit.*, the "Prisoner's Dilemma." In their discussion they analyze a hundred-move game; in this game the player's values, and therefore their expectations of the game's payoffs, are the same before, during, and after every move, right up to the end. It is almost impossible, I think, to conceive of such a situation's happening in real life.

34. Rapoport's description, in *Fights, Games, and Debates*, pp. 234 ff., of the Othello-Desdemona game, a relatively simple one, conveys the immense complexity of this problem.

35. Luce and Raiffa have an elegant proof (*op. cit.*, chap. v) that such a disparity is possible. Offhand I should think that their complicated mathematics is not completely necessary, since to assert the contrary would seem to be to commit the fallacy of composition.

36. Burns, *World Politics*, XVII, 701.

37. Deutsch, *op. cit.*, pp. 57–59.

38. In Shubik, *Game Theory*, p. 235.

39. On "unilateral initiatives," see Charles E. Osgood, *An Alternative to War or Surrender* (Urbana: University of Illinois, 1962).

40. The phrase is Schelling's, of course: "The reciprocal fear of surprise attack."

41. In his "The Delicate Balance of Terror," *Foreign Affairs*, XXXVII, 222.

42. Here and throughout I must apologize for the aggressiveness of my language; the constant references to enemies and opponents who may very well be nonexistent at a particular moment, or in a particular instance. That one cannot discuss deterrence theory or game theory without using such language says much about the relationship between them. See my further comments on this subject, pp. 207–8.

43. See, e.g., *New York Times*, December 12, 1960, 1:6; whether the U.S.S.R.'s constantly reiterated concern with America's mobile missile force is sincere or merely propagandistic, one cannot tell.

44. *World Politics*, XI (October, 1958), 20–43. Arthur L. Burns has engaged in similarly abstract theorizing about nuclear deterrence; see his "From Balance to Deterrence: A Theoretical Analysis," *World Politics*, IX (July, 1957), 494–529.

45. Morton A. Kaplan, *The Strategy of Limited Retaliation* ("Princeton Center of International Studies: Policy Memorandum

No. 19" [Princeton, N.J., 1959]); "Problems of Coalition and Defense," in Knorr, *op. cit.*; "Limited Retaliation as a Bargaining Process," in Knorr and Read, *op. cit.*

46. "Princeton Center of International Studies: Research Monograph No. 2" (Princeton, N.J., January 12, 1959).

47. *Deterrence and Defense,* pp. 16 ff.

48. *Ibid.,* p. 269.

49. *Ibid.,* chaps. ii, iii.

50. *Ibid.,* pp. 269–72, for the whole "example."

51. For an explanation of the utility index, see Von Neumann and Morgenstern, *op. cit.,* pp. 17–29.

52. *Ibid.,* pp. 19–20.

53. Levine, *op. cit.,* pp. 35–36, makes this point, but ignores the question of the logic that is actually used by policy-makers.

54. Alfred Schultz, *Collected Papers* I: *The Problem of Social Reality* (The Hague: Martinus Nijhoff, 1962), p. 55.

CHAPTER IV

1. See, e.g., Kahn, *TAU,* p. 178; Thornton Read, *A Proposal to Neutralize Nuclear Weapons* ("Princeton Center of International Studies: Policy Memorandum No. 22" [Princeton, N.J., 1960]), p. 11; Halperin, *op. cit.,* pp. 30 ff.; G. Snyder, *Deterrence and Defense,* p. 23. J. David Singer has written that "almost no serious scholar in the field today has escaped his [Schelling's] valuable influence," reviewing Schelling and Halperin's *Strategy and Arms Control, Journal of Conflict Resolution,* V, 312 n. 4. And see the remarks by Charles A. McClelland in "The Reorientation of the Sociology of Conflict: A Review of Thomas C. Schelling, *The Strategy of Conflict*; and Kenneth E. Boulding, *Conflict and Defense: A General Theory,*" *Journal of Conflict Resolution,* VI (March, 1962), 88–95.

2. Schelling's interpretation of game theory has, in fact, been criticized by several commentators. See the reviews of *The Strategy of Conflict* by Morgenstern, *Southern Economic Journal,* XXVIII (July, 1961), 103–5; Martin Shubik, *Journal of Political Economy,*

LXIX (October, 1961), 501–3; and Morton A. Kaplan, "Strategy and International Politics," *World Politics*, XIII (July, 1961), 642–52. And see Rapoport, *Fights, Games, and Debates*, pp. 228 ff.

3. Thus Richard C. Snyder in *Essays on the Behavioral Study of Politics* (Urbana: University of Illinois Press, 1962), a collection edited by Austin Ranney, remarks that "the application of Schelling's analysis thus far has been directed to limited war, deterrence, and arms control problems." (p. 160). As to Schelling's preference for arms control, see above, chap. iii, n. 20.

4. Previously published, with the same title, in the *Journal of Conflict Resolution*, I (March, 1957), 19–36. On the use of this essay in discussion of policies for limited war, see Knorr and Read, *op. cit., passim*; and Halperin, *op. cit.*, especially chap. ii.

5. That is, non-zero-sum games. See chap. iii n. 9.

6. *SOC*, pp. 54 ff., Appendix C.

7. *Ibid.*, pp. 263–64.

8. *Ibid.*, pp. 14–16.

9. *Ibid.*, pp. v, vi.

10. *Ibid.*, p. 20.

11. See Kaplan's review, cited n. 2 above, for a sophisticated statement of that judgment.

12. Schelling's discussion may be read as an implicit answer to Henry Kissinger's argument for NATO tactical nuclear war strategy in Western Europe, in his *Nuclear Weapons and Foreign Policy*. Kissinger himself, perhaps influenced by Schelling's arguments, later retreated from this position; see his *The Necessity for Choice* (New York: Harper & Row, 1960).

13. At pp. 263–64 of *The Strategy of Conflict*, Schelling writes: "Which policy we should follow depends on whether we consider the distinction between nuclear and other weapons to be an asset that we share with the USSR, a useful distinction . . . or instead a nuisance. . . . Those who believe that atomic weapons ought to be used at the earliest convenience, or whenever military expedience demands, should nevertheless recognize the distinction that exists so that we can take action to erode the distinction during the interim."

14. By "escalation" we mean the transgression on an implicitly or explicitly established limit by one side in a military conflict.

15. Schelling, *SOC*, pp. 262–63.

16. *Ibid.*, p. 76.

17. *Ibid.*, p. 63 n. 4.

18. Shubik, "Some Reflections on the Design of Game Theoretic Models for the Study of Negotiation and Threats," *Journal of Conflict Resolution*, VII (March, 1963), 3–4; a similar point is made by Kaplan, in Knorr and Verba, *op. cit.*, p. 19. It should be said that Schelling, when he is not engaged in his policy discussions, is properly modest about the usefulness of his own approach; see, e.g., his comments at pp. 48, 54–55 and, especially, 166 of *The Strategy of Conflict*.

19. Morton Deutsch and Robert M. Krauss, "Studies in Interpersonal Bargaining," *Journal of Conflict Resolution*, VI (March, 1962), 58, 73–74.

20. The studies referred to are reported, respectively, in Alvin Scodel *et al.*, "Non-Zero-Sum Games," *Journal of Conflict Resolution*, III (June, 1959), 114–19; and Robert R. Blake and Jane S. Mouton, "Comprehension of Own and Outgroup Positions under Intergroup Competition," *Journal of Conflict Resolution*, V (September, 1961), 304–10 (on the point about intergroup competition, see also Bernard M. Bass and George Dunteman, "Biases in the Evaluation of One's Own Group, Its Allies and Opponents," *Journal of Conflict Resolution*, VII [March, 1963], 16–21). Rapoport has reported on a number of such experiments in progress, in his *Strategy and Conscience*, chap. xiv, and a recent issue of the *Journal of Conflict Resolution*, IX (March, 1965), 66–117, contains a section entitled "Gaming," which presents three reports of recent experiments of this type.

Of course these studies, if offered as evidence in support of specific policies, are subject to the same criticisms as Schelling's. Thus one of three reports mentioned immediately above, Harold H. Kelley's "Experimental Studies of Threats in Interpersonal Negotiations," is a methodological critique of the Deutsch-Krauss experiments. And Nehemiah Jordan, in "International Relations and the Psychologist," *Bulletin of the Atomic Scientists*, XIX (November, 1963), 29–32, has attacked the political assumptions that have been implicit in the more policy-oriented of these experiments. Jordan's attack, however, misses the point. All that these simulations really do—and do convincingly—is offer evidence that an author's independently derived assumptions about politics are at least not antiempirical. It is still the assumptions, whether Schelling's or Deutsch's, that we are interested in. And what we are especially interested in is the extent to which the experimenter hides the fact that whatever policy statements he makes depend primarily on his assumptions, not his experiments. For an interesting discussion of these points, see the introductory and concluding remarks by Herbert C. Kelman, in Kelman (ed.), *International Behavior: A Social-Psychological Analysis* (New York: Holt, Rinehart & Winston, 1965); this book also contains many additional examples of the kind of study we have been discussing.

21. Schelling, *SOC*, pp. 259–60.

22. Some examples of similar traditions that decayed are given by Kahn, *OE*, p. 261. Like Schelling, however, Kahn has his problems with current history; he writes: "The conventions that have come to exist have included the following major restraints. With the exception of the exemplary attack on North Vietnam in August, 1964, the United States has refrained from overt interventions within the areas militarily held by the Communist bloc at the end of World War II (and, as in China and North Vietnam, in areas that became part of the Communist bloc as a result of disorder created during World War II and left unresolved in 1945)." (pp. 261–62).

23. The different kinds of "games" are defined and discussed in Herman Kahn and Irwin Mann, *War Gaming*, RAND P–1167 (Santa Monica: The RAND Corporation, July, 1957). See, e.g., Morton A. Kaplan, Arthur L. Burns, and Richard E. Quandt, "Theoretical Analysis of the 'Balance of Power'," *Behavioral Science*, V (July, 1960), 240–52; and Thomas C. Schelling, "Experimental Games and Bargaining Theory," in Knorr and Verba, *op. cit.* (p. 65 n. 7, of the latter article contains a short bibliography of the writings on "war gaming"); The Raytheon Company, *Design For a Strategic Model*, BR–1354 A, (September, 1961); Richard A. Brody, "Some Systemic Effects of the Spread of Nuclear Weapons Technology: A Study through Simulation of a Multi-Nuclear Future," *Journal of Conflict Resolution*, VII (December, 1963), 663–753. The latter article contains an informative statement of some problems in generalization from simulation studies (at 747–48). And see Richard Snyder's discussion of various games and simulations (and his bibliographical footnote 12) in Ranney, *op. cit.*, pp. 148 ff.

24. In the most important recent work on simulation, this is made clear; see Harold Guetzkow, "A use of simulation in the study of international relations," in Guetzkow (ed.), *Simulation in Social Science: Readings* (Englewood Cliffs: Prentice-Hall, 1962), p. 83.

25. Kahn, *TAU*, p. 157.

26. Richard Snyder, in Ranney, *op. cit.*, p. 150.

27. Sidney Verba, "Simulation, Reality, and Theory in International Relations," *World Politics*, XVI (April, 1964), 502, emphasis in original. Verba adds (at 504) that " 'seriousness' can be built into a simulation by appropriate manipulation of the setting, even if the wars do not involve real deaths or the trade real exchanges of goods." His comment that "It is unfortunate . . . that further exploration of this problem has not been undertaken in simulation research" applies with special force to Schelling's work, however. On the general problem of relating experimental findings to the real world of international conflict, see also J. David Singer, "The Relevance of the Behavioral Sciences to the Study of International Relations," *Behavioral Science*, VI (October, 1961), 324–35.

28. Schelling, *SOC*, p. 201.

29. Karl Deutsch, *op. cit.*, p. 70.

30. J. Shepley, "How Dulles Averted War," *Life*, January 16, 1956, p. 70.

31. See the remarks by Karl Deutsch, *op. cit.*, p. 71.

32. This point is made by J. David Singer in his review of Schelling, *Journal of Conflict Resolution*, V, 314; compare Schelling's astonishing remark that "A weapon that can hurt only *people*, and cannot possibly damage the other side's striking force, is profoundly defensive . . . " (Schelling, *SOC*, p. 233, emphasis in original).

33. Schelling, *SOC*, pp. 122 ff.

34. *Ibid.*, pp. 120–21, emphasis added.

35. Morgenstern, *The Question of National Defense*, p. 32.

36. New York has recently repealed the provision of its Penal Code setting an automatic death penalty for those convicted of first-degree homicide (*New York Times*, April 2, 1963, p. 1).

37. Cf., Frederick Wertham, *The Show of Violence* (New York: Doubleday, 1949).

38. Sigmund Freud, "Why War?", in *Collected Papers* V (New York: Basic Books, 1959), pp. 273–87.

39. Compare with Schelling's comments about threats on pp. 150–51, below. Since the words "to illustrate" in the quoted passage refer to a previous paragraph that deals wholly with the nuclear deterrence situation, Schelling's dogmatic assurance cannot be passed off lightly.

40. Karl Deutsch, *op. cit.*, p. 69.

41. Schelling, *SOC*, pp. 10–11. Schelling's way of treating such ideas is reminiscent of an occasionally irritating technique of post-Eliot modern poetry: the knowing offhand use of the fictitious "the," as in Eliot's "The moment in the rose garden." What moment, what garden? To achieve the compression which heightens language the poet spares himself the work of establishing that suspension of disbelief upon which poetry usually rests; he acts as though the subjective world of his poem already had an objective existence of which the reader was perfectly aware. In the hands of a poet like Eliot, this device is often effective, but it is much like a sleight-of-hand trick, and therefore has much more place in poetry than in social science.

42. Chalmers W. Sherwin, "Securing Peace through Military Technology," *Bulletin of the Atomic Scientists*, XII (May, 1956), 163. Sherwin's article is a commentary on Warren Amster's summary of his own RAND paper on deterrence; see Amster, "Design for Deterrence," *Bulletin of the Atomic Scientists*, XII (May, 1956), 164–65.

43. Schelling, *SOC*, p. 7 n. 2.

44. Thomas C. Schelling, "War without Pain, and Other Models," *World Politics*, XV (April, 1963), 486–87. This article is an extended review of Kenneth Boulding's *Conflict and Defense* (New York: Harper & Row, 1962).

45. In addition to *The Strategy of Conflict* (especially chaps. iii, v. and vii), see Kaplan, *Some Problems in the Strategic Analysis of International Politics*; also, in Knorr and Read, *op. cit.*, the essays by Knorr, Kaplan, and Kahn.

46. Quoted in Herzog, *op. cit.*, p. 52.

47. Wohlstetter complains about the hostility to "the fact of hostility itself" of some critics, as quoted by Herzog, *op. cit.*, p. 68. And see his article "Sin and Games in America," in Shubik, *Game Theory*, especially pp. 220 ff.

48. Quoted by Herzog, *op. cit.*, p. 93.

49. This point is made by Rapoport in his "Critique of Strategic Thinking," an essay in Roger Fisher (ed.), *International Conflict and Behavioral Science, The Craigville Papers* (New York: Basic Books, 1964), p. 212.

50. Quoted by Herzog, *op. cit.*, p. 51.

51. That *military* sanctions are necessary in a disarmament system is assumed implicitly and occasionally stated explicitly

throughout Schelling's "The Role of Deterrence in Total Disarmament," *Foreign Affairs*, XV, 392–406.

52. The notion of co-operative rationality is particularly associated with the names of John Nash and Kenneth Arrow. For description of and comment on their work, see Luce and Raiffa, *op. cit.*, chaps. vi and xiv, and Alker, *op. cit.*, pp. 176 ff. And see also Rapoport, *Fights, Games, and Debates*, pp. 174 ff.

53. As noted by Luce and Raiffa, *op. cit.*, especially the Introduction and chap. vi.

CHAPTER V

1. For example, Felix Oppenheim, "Rational Decisions and Intrinsic Evaluations," in Carl J. Friedrich (ed.), *Nomos VII: Rational Decision* (New York: Atherton, 1964), pp. 217–20.

2. The qualification is necessary, since few deterrence theorists claim that even rational behavior can avert nuclear war in all circumstances.

3. C. W. Sherwin, *loc. cit.*, 160.

4. Wohlstetter, in Quade, *op. cit.*, p. 116.

5. *OE*, pp. xi, 220–21.

6. Brodie, *op. cit.*, p. 280.

7. Knorr, in Knorr and Read, *op. cit.*, pp. 24–25.

8. Robert Osgood, quoted in Richard Snyder, *op. cit.*, p. 33.

9. Wohlstetter, *Foreign Affairs*, XXXVII, 221.

10. Kissinger, *The Necessity for Choice*, pp. 40–41, 211.

11. W. W. Kaufmann, *op. cit.*, p. 17.

12. Burns, *World Politics*, IX, 495. Burns makes it clear that deterrence is such an "aspect of policy."

13. Schelling, *SOC*, p. 13.

14. In this regard Kahn is an exception; c.f., *OE*, p. 246. However, this new viewpoint represents a massive change of heart for Kahn, as he says himself; in *OTW* and *TAU*, he denounced such thinking.

15. I have heard this said by both Kahn and Knorr, in conversation.

16. On this point, see Levine's discussion of "maximizing mechanisms," *op. cit.*, pp. 36—40.

17. A good, concise explanation of the categories of rationality, non-rationality, and irrationality, is in Marion J. Levy, Jr., *The Structure of Society* (Princeton: Princeton University Press, 1952), pp. 242–46.

18. Schelling, *SOC*, p. 17.

19. Kahn, *TAU*, pp. 111–12.

20. See, for example, Levine, *op. cit.*, pp. 159–60.

21. *Deterrence and Defense*, p. 25.

22. Arthur L. Burns, *World Politics*, IX, *loc. cit.*, has perhaps come closest.

23. The qualification about credibility is added in deference to Kahn's argument, in Knorr and Read, *op. cit.*, that theoretically the problem of making an ultimate deterrent threat credible is not really very great.

24. Halperin, *op. cit.*, discusses the various limited-war strategies from the perspective of deterrence theory; and see his "Annotated Bibliography" on limited war, pp. 133–84.

25. The most exhaustive discussion of the etiology of escalation is of course Kahn's *On Escalation*.

26. Although Kahn never says this explicitly, it seems to be his implicit viewpoint throughout *OE*.

27. Cf., Coral Bell's excellent study, *Negotiation from Strength* (New York: Knopf, 1963).

28. Not quite no deterrence theorist, perhaps. See Schelling's remarks in his interview with Herzog (cited above, p. 152) about getting the Russians to agree to a "fairly expensive inferiority."

29. Levine, *op. cit.*, pp. 93–95.

30. Rovere, *The American Establishment and Other Reports, Opinions, and Speculations* (New York: Harcourt, Brace & World, 1962), p. 267. Rovere quotes Walter Lippmann and many other "estimable people" as also holding this view.

31. *TAU*, p. 173.

32. Charles McClelland, "Decisional Opportunity and Political Controversy," *Journal of Conflict Resolution*, VI (June, 1962), 211–12. (Emphasis added.)

33. Wolff, "The Rhetoric of Deterrence," pp. 9–10.

34. Cf., Schelling's essay in Knorr and Read, *op. cit.*, pp. 241–58; Kahn, *OE*, pp. 94–133. Again, this argument, tentative as it is, represents a considerable change of heart on Kahn's part.

35. I have earlier quoted Schelling's injunction about breaking down the nuclear–non-nuclear distinction if one wants to (chap. iv n. 13 above); for Kahn's views, see especially pp. 118–20 of *OE*.

36. *OTW*, pp. 124–30, 305–6, 428–33.

37. At *OE*, p. 145, Kahn writes: "Alternatively [to other forms of limited reprisal, that is] there could be attacks with bacteriological or chemical weapons against food or crops." On the buildup of a biochemical arsenal by the United States, see the chillingly factual (when not celebratory) article, "Toxic Weapons," by Frank J. Granzeier, *Industrial Research* (August, 1965), 68–74.

38. Clark C. Abt, "Controlling Future Arms," *Disarmament and Arms Control*, III (Spring, 1965), 19–40.

39. On arms races, see Arthur L. Burns, "A Graphical Approach to Some Problems of the Arms Race," *Journal of Conflict Resolution*, III (December, 1959), 326–42; and Samuel P. Huntington, "Arms Races: Prerequisites and Results," in Carl J. Friedrich and Seymour E. Harris (eds.), *Public Policy* (Cambridge: Harvard Graduate School of Public Administration, 1958), pp. 41–86. Huntington argues that the "qualitative" nuclear arms race may in effect become a stable substitute for war, rather than a destabilizing incentive *to* war; that is, he claims that certain kinds of arms races are "self-damping." Whether a "research and development" race must really be self-damping, however, is a topic that still needs considerably more discussion; on this point, see Hoag, in Kaplan, *The Revolution in World Politics*.

40. Quoted by Herzog, *op. cit.*, p. 23.

41. Cf., McNamara, *loc. cit.*

42. Freeman J. Dyson, "Defense Against Ballistic Missiles," *Bulletin of the Atomic Scientists*, XX (June, 1964), 12–18.

43. *OE*, p. 158.

44. A "catalytic" attack is one made covertly by a minor power on a major power (or perhaps on another minor power), in order to provoke war between the major powers, or having that result. Such a war is known as a "catalytic war." See Arthur L. Burns, *The Rationale of Catalytic War* ("Princeton Center of International Studies: Research Monograph No. 3" [Princeton, N.J.: 1959]); Donald H. Kobe, "A Theory of Catalytic War," *Journal*

of Conflict Resolution, VI (June, 1962), 125–42; Herman Kahn, "The Arms Race and Some of Its Hazards," in Brennan, *op. cit.*, pp. 89–121; Richard S. Leghorn, "The Problem of Accidental War," *Bulletin of the Atomic Scientists*, XIV (June, 1958), 205–9. Obviously the problem of "catalytic war" is associated with the more general problem of the breakdown of bipolarity and the spread of nuclear weapons—what is popularly known as the "Nth-country" problem. Although the widespread possession of nuclear weapons is generally feared, the argument can be made that it is just as likely to stabilize the deterrence system as to destabilize it, ultimately; compare Leonard Beaton and John Maddox, *The Spread of Nuclear Weapons* (New York: Frederick A. Praeger, 1962); W. C. Davidon *et al.*, *The Nth Country Problem and Arms Control* ("National Planning Association, Planning Pamphlet No. 108" [Washington, D.C.: 1960]); Fred C. Iklé, "Nth Countries and Disarmament," *Bulletin of the Atomic Scientists*, XVI (December, 1960), 391–94; R. S. Leghorn *et al.*, *1970 without Arms Control* ("National Planning Association, Planning Pamphlet No. 104" [Washington, D.C.: 1958]); Albert Wohlstetter, "Nuclear Sharing in NATO and the N+1 Country," *Foreign Affairs*, XXXIX (April, 1961), 355–87; Klaus Knorr, "Nuclear Weapons: 'Haves' and 'Have Nots'," *Foreign Affairs*, XXXVI (October, 1957), 167–78; and Kahn, *OE*, pp. 94–133. However one judges the desirability of proliferation, it is clear that so far the likely speed of proliferation has been overestimated by some of the above analysts (especially those associated with the National Planning Association). On the other hand, not much proliferation is necessary to pose whatever problems may be posed.

On "accidental war," see Etzioni, *op. cit.*, pp. 44 ff.; Kahn, *TAU*, pp. 40 ff.; John B. Phelps *et al.*, *Accidental War: Some Dangers in the 1960's* (Mershon Center for Education in National Security, Ohio State University, June, 1960); Harrison Brown and James Real, *Community of Fear* (Santa Barbara, Calif.: Center for the Study of Democratic Institutions, 1960).

45. Kahn, *OE*, pp. 132–33. On the West German attitude, see the *New York Times* story, "Bonn Sets Price for Ban on Nuclear Weapons," July 13, 1965, p. 8.

46. Schelling and Halperin, *op. cit.*, assert that arms control is the generic term for all proposals having to do with limitations on arms, and disarmament merely one species. That definition is rejected here on the grounds that it is tendentious: it implies that by definition getting rid of arms (the traditional notion of disarmament) is but one path, and a minor one at that, toward a

"warless" world. I prefer to use "arms control," therefore, to refer to proposals for keeping the peace by means of a balance of armed power, rather than its elimination.

47. See, e.g., Thornton Read's *A Proposal to Neutralize Nuclear Weapons*; Schelling, *World Politics*, XIII, *loc. cit.*; Kahn, *OTW*, pp. 238–39.

48. John Polanyi, *Bulletin of the Atomic Scientists*, XVII, 405–6, 432. Polanyi's remarks are specifically in response to the volume edited by Louis Henkin, *Arms Control, Issues for the Public* (Englewood Cliffs: Prentice-Hall, 1961), and even more specifically in response to Robert Bowie's contribution to that volume, but they are meant to apply equally to other arms control proposals.

49. Halperin, *op. cit.*, 90–91. A nuclear local-war strategy, of course, is not *ipso facto* irrational according to Halperin; cf., Schelling and Halperin, *op. cit.*, pp. 62–65.

50. Kahn and Mann, *Techniques of Systems Analysis*, p. 115.

51. Read's *Command and Control* is the best discussion of this problem.

52. I have borrowed this example from Hans J. Morgenthau, "The Four Paradoxes of Nuclear Strategy," *American Political Science Review*, LVIII (March, 1964), 27.

53. Levy, *op. cit.*, p. 242.

54. See my remarks about game theory and invulnerability, for example.

55. Gabriel Almond, *The American People and Foreign Policy* (New York: Frederick A. Praeger, 1960), chap. vii, has an exposition of the meaning of the term, "informed public," which is roughly the same as what is intended here.

56. In recent years Samuel P. Huntington has forcefully argued the proposition that policy-making in military affairs is essentially legislative in character; see his "Strategic Planning and the Policy Process," *Foreign Affairs*, XXXVIII (January, 1960), 285–99; "Interservice Competition and the Political Roles of the Armed Services," *American Political Science Review*, LV (March, 1961), 40–52; and *The Common Defense: Strategic Programs in National Politics* (New York: Columbia University Press, 1961). For first-hand reports, see, e.g., Cordell Hull, *The Memoirs of Cordell Hull* (New York: Macmillan Co., 1948), Vol. II, *passim*; Dean G. Acheson, "Thoughts about Thought in High Places," *New York Times Magazine*, October 11, 1959, pp. 20 ff.; and, in summary, Roger Hilsman, "The Foreign Policy Consensus: An Interim Research

Report," *Journal of Conflict Resolution*, III (December, 1959), 361–82. A more theoretical consideration than any of these is James Thompson and Arthur Tuden, "Strategies, Structures, and Processes of Organizational Decision," in Thompson (ed.), *Comparative Studies in Administration* (Pittsburgh: Pittsburgh University Press, 1961), pp. 195–216.

57. Arthur I. Waskow, *The Limits of Defense* (Garden City: Doubleday & Co., 1962), p. 59. See Maxwell Taylor, *The Uncertain Trumpet* (New York: Harper & Row, 1960); James M. Gavin, *War and Peace in the Space Age: A New Approach* (New York: G. P. Putnam's Sons, 1960); Robert Gilpin, *American Scientists and Nuclear Weapons Policy* (Princeton: Princeton University Press, 1962); Brodie, *op. cit.*; Glenn Snyder, *Deterrence and Defense, passim*, especially chap. v; Saville Davis, "Recent Policy-Making in the United States Government," in Brennan, *op. cit.*, pp. 951–66; Etzioni, *op. cit.* See also Thomas K. Finletter, *Foreign Policy: The Next Phase* (rev. ed.; New York: Harper & Row, 1960), and Arthur Smithies, *The Budgetary Process in the United States* (1st ed.; New York: McGraw-Hill Book Co., 1955).

58. Harold and Margaret Sprout, "Environmental Factors in the Study of International Politics," *Journal of Conflict Resolution*, I (December, 1957), 320–21.

59. Sprout and Sprout, *ibid.*, 327, and Blackett, *op. cit.*, Part I, *passim*, discuss this point.

60. Robert Gilpin, *op. cit.*

61. *Ibid.*, pp. 312–13.

62. Charles Percy Snow, *Science and Government* (Cambridge: Harvard University Press, 1961); see also Winston Churchill, *The Gathering Storm* (New York: Houghton Mifflin Co., 1948), pp. 135 ff.; Blackett, *op. cit.*, chap. viii.

63. Compare the *New York Times*, July 23, 1962, Sec. 4, 8:5, and December 24, 1962, 3:1. Also see the *New York Post*, July 15, 1963, p. 5; and *I. F. Stone's Newsletter*, Washington, D.C., throughout 1961–62.

64. Cf. Ronald Steel, *End of Alliance: America and the Future of Europe* (New York: Viking Press, 1964), and Edmond O. Stillman and William Pfaff, *The New Politics: America and the End of the Postwar World* (New York: Coward-McCann, 1961).

65. Sidney I. Ploss, "The Uncertainty of Soviet Foreign Policy," *World Politics*, XV (April, 1963), 456–58.

66. *Ibid.*, 459.

67. Cf. George F. Kennan, *Russia and the West under Lenin and Stalin* (Boston: Little, Brown & Co., 1961). With regard specifically to military strategy Raymond L. Garthoff (*Soviet Strategy in the Nuclear Age* [New York: Frederick A. Praeger, 1958], and *The Soviet Image of Future War* [Washington: Public Affairs Press, 1959]) and Herbert S. Dinerstein (*War and the Soviet Union* [New York: Frederick A. Praeger, 1959]) both document the extent to which Communist ideology interfered with what most Americans consider to be sound strategic analysis in the 1950's. However, that may have been merely a case of cultural lag, as is somewhat evidenced by a more recent Garthoff paper, "Military Power and Soviet Policy," presented to the Institute for the Study of the U.S.S.R.'s International Symposium on *The Impact of the Modern Military Revolution on Strategy and Foreign Policy* (Munich, October 22-24, 1964). Kennan's general point that Soviet leaders refuse to perceive the rest of the world except in a distorting mirror seems to me to be more important.

68. Bernard C. Cohen, "Military Policy Analysis and the Art of the Possible," *Journal of Conflict Resolution*, VI (June, 1962), 158. Cohen's article is a review of Glenn Snyder's *Deterrence and Defense*.

69. Kaufmann, *The McNamara Strategy* (New York: Harper & Row, 1964); the quotation is from Todd Gitlin, "The Linear Theory of Arms Policy," *Council for Correspondence Newsletter*, May, 1963, pp. 27-28.

70. See Green, *World Politics*, XVI, 651 ff., for a further discussion of this point.

71. The ambiguity in the concept of "national interest," which is in many respects similar to the ambiguity in the concept of "rationality," is discussed by Warner R. Schilling, "The Clarification of Ends, or, Which Interest Is the National?", *World Politics*, VIII (July, 1956), 566–78; see also Arnold Wolfers, "'National Security' as an Ambiguous Symbol," *Political Science Quarterly*, LXVII (December, 1952), 481–502.

72. In the period 1960–61 there was a flurry of thinking in high places concerning the prospects for producing a sense of "national purpose" in the United States. It resulted in the volumes *Goals for Americans*, the Report of the President's Commission on National Goals (New York: Prentice-Hall, 1960), and John K. Jessup *et al.*, *The National Purpose* (New York: Holt, Rinehart & Winston, 1960). The flurry was singularly abortive; see Philip Green, "National Purpose and New Frontiers," *Commentary*, XXXI (June, 1961), 493–500.

73. As Richard Snyder, *op. cit.*, p. 78, says, there is no "clearly identifiable, coherent set of national purposes or a stable self-image which the United States desires to project [or] a commonly understood or acepted over-view interpretation [sic] of the international environment and the major factors which shape it."

74. Glenn H. Snyder, "The Politics of National Defense: A Review of Samuel P. Huntington, *The Common Defense*," *Journal of Conflict Resolution*, VI (December, 1962), 371-72.

75. Although Cohen's comments occur in a review of Snyder's *Deterrence and Defense*, they apply inferentially to such writers as Kahn, Schelling, Kaplan, *et al.*, as well.

76. Cohen, *loc. cit.*, 155-57.

77. See n. 44 above.

78. Kaplan, *World Politics*, XI, 23; Burns, *World Politics*, IX, 495-96.

79. Compare Levine's distinction between "marginalists" and "extremists," in Levine, *op. cit.*

80. *Ibid.*, p. 281.

81. Again, I have borrowed this formulation from Lindblom's writings on policy-making.

82. Karl Deutsch, "Mass Communications and the Loss of Freedom in National Decision-Making: A Possible Research Approach to Interstate Conflict," *Journal of Conflict Resolution*, I (June, 1957), 200.

83. Donald N. Michael, "Psychopathology of Nuclear War," *Bulletin of the Atomic Scientists*, XVIII (May, 1962), 28-29.

84. For a mordant view of these attitudes and their effect on American policy-making in the postwar years, see Almond, *op. cit.*, pp. xii ff.

85. See the *New York Times*, March 27 and 28, 1964, for the speech and the Republican response.

86. James Roosevelt, (ed.), *The Liberal Papers* (New York: Doubleday & Co., 1962); for the Republican response, see the *New York Times*, March 26, 1962, p. 18.

87. See Philip Green, "Alternatives to Overkill: Dream and Reality," *Bulletin of the Atomic Scientists*, XIX (November, 1963), 25.

88. David Riesman, quoted by Herzog, *op. cit.*, p. 170. See also Michael Maccoby, "The Foundations of the Grand Design," *Council for Correspondence Newsletter*, February 1963, pp. 1-7. Dis-

cussion of American ideological rigidities has become rather popular of late; cf. Fullbright's *Old Myths and New Realities* (New York: Random House, 1964); and George F. Kennan's *On Dealing with the Communist World* (New York: Harper & Row, 1964). Two less popular but sometimes excellent discussions are C. Wright Mills, *The Power Elite* (New York: Oxford Book Co., 1959), chaps. xiii and xiv, and Sidney Lens, *The Futile Crusade: Anti-Communism as American Credo* (Chicago: Quadrangle, 1964).

89. Kennedy has recently been quoted as estimating, after having decided on a blockade, that the risk of nuclear war was one-third to one-half; see "Kennedy: Part Four," by Theodore C. Sorenson, *Look*, September 21, 1965, p. 57.

90. Charles E. Osgood, "Suggestions for Winning the Real War with Communism," *Journal of Conflict Resolution*, III (December, 1959), 295–325.

91. Chester C. Ward, "New Myths and Old Realities of Nuclear War," *Orbis*, VIII (Summer, 1964), 255–91.

92. Thomas Milburn, "What Constitutes Effective Deterrence?", *Journal of Conflict Resolution*, III (June, 1959), 139–40

93. Kenneth E. Boulding, "Organization and Conflict," *Journal of Conflict Resolution*, I (June, 1957), 122–34; "National Images and International Systems," *ibid.*, III (June, 1959), 120–31.

94. Raymond A. Bauer, "Problems of Perception and Relations between the United States and the Soviet Union," *Journal of Conflict Resolution*, V (June, 1961), 223–29.

95. Ole R. Holsti, "The Belief System and National Images: A Case Study," *Journal of Conflict Resolution*, VI (September, 1962), 250–51. More recently almost a whole issue of this *Journal*, VIII (December, 1964), 329–491, has been devoted to a research report, "Social Values and Foreign Policy Attitudes of Soviet and American Elites," by Robert C. Angell, Vera S. Dunham, and J. David Singer, which extends and generalizes earlier inquiries such as Holsti's. Although stated more cautiously, Angell *et al.'s* findings are similar to those of Bauer and Holsti. (Of course biased images exist on both sides; the recent study makes this clearer, perhaps, than did Holsti's; see my remarks about Communist ideological blinkers above.)

96. Osgood, *op. cit.*

97. Cf. chap. iv, n. 20 above.

98. Soviet decision-making is also sometimes interpreted as a locus of conflict between "hards" and "softs," the implication of

such analyses being that continuation of the cold war helps the former have their way; see, e.g., Kennan's *On Dealing with the Communist World* (and I recall seeing a letter to the *New York Times* by Alexander Dallin, which made this point in relation to the bombing of North Vietnam).

99. Richard C. Snyder, H. W. Bruck, and Burton M. Sapin, *Decision-Making as an Approach to the Study of International Politics* (Princeton: Princeton University Press, 1954).

100. Lindblom, *Public Adminstration Review*, XIX, *loc. cit.*

101. During the summer of 1965, for instance, a host of articles appeared in the *New York Times* analyzing the Vietnam and Dominican crises from this viewpoint. See, e.g., Tom Wicker, "Washington: The Bay of Pigs and Vietnam," July 23, 1965, p. 26.

102. Robert C. North, "Decision-Making in Crises: An Introduction," *Journal of Conflict Resolution*, VI (September, 1962), 198–99. "Richardson processes" are named for Lewis Fry Richardson; for a discussion of his work on arms races, see Rapoport, *Fights, Games, and Debates*, Part I, and Boulding, *op. cit.*, chaps. vii, xii–xiv. Wildavsky, *loc. cit.*, refers to this view of international conflict as the "spiral model," and contrasts it to the "appeasement model," which sees the outbreak of war as a failure of rational calculation rather than as the inevitable result of a historical process which is out of control. Wildavsky points out that World War I is often interpreted as an example of the "spiral model," and World War II as an example of the "appeasement model," and suggests that we need to decide which model best describes our present situation. In chap. vii below I have suggested some important questions about the cold war, which ought to be further discussed; one of the purposes of such a discussion would be to help resolve this question.

103. *OTW*, p. 368.

104. Cf., Herbert McCloskey's thoughtful review of the decision-making approach, "Concerning Strategies for a Science of International Politics," *World Politics*, VIII (January, 1956), 281–95.

105. See, for example, Glenn Snyder, *Deterrence and Defense*, p. 243; Wohlstetter, *Foreign Affairs*, XXXVII, *loc. cit.*, *passim*. "The Delicate Balance of Terror" is replete with this particular locution: one could multiply such examples endlessly.

106. Cf. Glenn Snyder, *ibid.*, pp. 231–38.

107. Roberta Wohlstetter, *Pearl Harbor: Warning and Decision* (Stanford: Stanford University Press, 1962), pp. vi–x.

108. On World War I, Kahn, *OTW*, chap. viii (quoting an article from the *Observer* by A. J. P. Taylor at p. 358), G. Lowes Dickinson, *International Anarchy* (New York, 1926), Sidney B. Fay, *The Origins of the World War* (New York: Macmillan Co., 1931), Dinna A. Zinnes, Robert C. North, and Howard E. Koch, Jr., "Capability, Threat and the Outbreak of War," in James N. Rosenau (ed.), *International Politics and Foreign Policy: A Reader in Research and Theory* (New York: Free Press, 1961), pp. 469–83, and Ole R. Holsti, "The 1914 Case," *American Political Science Review*, LIX (June, 1965), 365–78; on World War II, Roberta Wohlstetter, *op. cit.*, Herbert Feis, *The Road to Pearl Harbor* (Princeton: Princeton University Press, 1950), and, for some specific examples, Kahn, *OTW*, pp. 375–87, and Sprout and Sprout, *loc. cit.*, 327; on the Korean War, Allen Whiting, *China Crosses the Yalu* (New York: Macmillan Co., 1960), and Morton Halperin, *op. cit.*, chap iii.

109. E.g., Sidney Hook, Commentary, XXXII, 278. (See chap. ii n. 73 above).

110. On saturation bombing, Blackett, *op. cit.*, pp. 223 ff., and George Quester, "Bargaining and Bombing during World War II in Europe," *World Politics*, XV (April, 1963), 417–37; on the atomic bomb, Robert C. Batchelder, *The Irreversible Decision, 1939–1950* (Boston: Houghton-Mifflin Co., 1962), Michael Amrine, *The Great Decision* (New York: G. P. Putnam's Sons, 1959), and Robert Jungk, *Brighter than a Thousand Suns* (New York: Harcourt, Brace & World, 1958).

111. Quester, *op. cit.*, p. 437.

112. See Klaus Knorr, *Foreign Affairs*, XXXVI, *loc. cit.*; Charles McClelland, "The Acute International Crisis," in Knorr and Verba, *op. cit.*

113. Hedley Bull, *The Control of the Arms Race* (New York: Frederick A. Praeger, 1961), pp. 48–49.

CHAPTER VI

1. Kahn has said that "the right wing has an enemy, I have an opponent and the peace movement has a misguided friend." Quoted in Herzog, *op. cit.*, p. 81.

2. See, e.g., Oppenheim, in Friedrich, *op. cit.*

3. See above, pp. 94–95.

4. Rapoport, *Fights, Games, and Debates,* pp. 174 ff., has an excellent discussion of this point.

5. Karl Mannheim, *Man and Society in an Age of Reconstruction* (New York: Harcourt, Brace & World, 1940), pp. 49–75.

6. Levy, *op. cit.,* p. 242.

7. Examples of "rational illogic" (or illogical rationality) may be found in Mannheim, *op. cit.,* in the pages referred to. The insistence of mankind on using up the resources of Earth as quickly as possible, in order to maximize self-interest, is one such example.

8. In "Method and Substance in the Arms Debate," *World Politics,* Vol. XVI, I have developed this argument at greater length.

9. The term is Levine's; see Levine, *op. cit.,* and chap. i above.

10. Robert A. Levine, "Open Letter from a Military Intellectual to a Sophisticated Liberal Leader," *Bulletin of the Atomic Scientists,* XX (September, 1964), 24–27.

11. Bernard Brodie, Book Reviews, *Survival,* VII (August, 1965), 208. Kahn has said, answering objections similar to my own, that he favors a "morality of consequences" rather than a "morality of acts" (quoted by Herzog, *op. cit.,* p. 84). The distinction is not a helpful one, however, in that everyone except possibly the most absolute pacifists—and even perhaps they—favors a "morality of conquences." That is, nuclear bombing, or war generally, or killing generally, are objected to because of the consequences, not because of some supposed "evil essence" in the act. Thus what we must be most interested in is what kinds of consequences deterrence theory is willing to bring about, under what circumstances. Brodie's remark suggests that the answer is *any* consequences if the ends of strategy are achieved. The ensuing discussion in this chapter attempts to explicate some of those consequences, and reveal what those ends are.

12. In Knorr and Read, *op. cit.,* p. 253.

13. *Ibid.,* p. 60.

14. *Ibid.,* pp. 44, 52; also see *OE,* p. 144.

15. Deterrence theorists sometimes seem to suggest that the "utility" of human life is linear. One wonders if the difference between 28,654,833 deaths and 28,654,832 deaths is really as morally significant as the difference between one death and none, or if saving a few lives in a war which has taken millions is a very great contribution.

16. In fairness, it should be noted that there is widespread disagreement among those who call themselves pacifists as to whether the prohibition against killing should be taken as "absolutely absolute"—see n. 11 above.

17. The comment is by Professor Sidney Hook, one of America's most distinguished ethical philosophers; see Levine, *op. cit.*, who identifies Hook as a prominent "middle marginalist."

18. *Commentary*, XXXII, 300.

19. Hook, *loc. cit.*, 277–304, *passim*.

20. "The Case for Making 'Just War' Possible," in Bennett, *op. cit.*, p. 149. And see also Walter Stein (ed.), *Morals and Missiles: Catholic Essays on the Problem of War Today* (London: James Clarke, 1959).

21. Knorr's comment is in *OTW*, Foreword, p. v; the comment about Kahn as a moralist, or moralizer, is from James R. Newman's review of *OTW*, *Scientific American*, March 1961, p. 197.

22. *Commentary, loc. cit.*, 278, 285–86, 299.

23. Cf., Brodie, *Strategy in the Missile Age, passim*.

24. Dyson, *Bulletin of the Atomic Scientists, loc. cit.*, 12–18.

25. "Moral Urgencies in the Nuclear Context," in Bennett, *op. cit.*, p. 109. I think it was not Muste but A. J. Toynbee, though of course such epigrams are always hard to track down to their true sources.

26. *The Christian Conscience and Weapons of Mass Destruction*, The Dun Report of a Special Commission appointed by the Federal Council of the Churches of Christ in America, 1950, pp. 10–11 (cited by Ramsey in Bennett, *ibid.*, p. 152).

27. E.g., *OTW*, p. 157.

28. Stein, *op. cit.*, pp. 25–27.

29. This point has been made well by Paul Ramsey, in the following passage from Bennett, *op. cit.*, pp. 150–55: "How can the 'facts' of warfare between modern industrial and metropolitan societies prove that there are now no non-combatants when this conclusion depends in every respect upon whether we have in our heads such notions as the moral significance of the degrees of proximity or remoteness of cooperation in unjust aggression. . . . ?

"The traditional distinction between combatant and non-combatant, it is asserted, today is 'far less clear' than in the past. Evident here is no conception of the fact that, in the moral choice between direct and indirect killing of civilians, or between counter-forces and indiscriminate counter-retaliatory warfare, this distinction *does not need to be clear.* We do not need to know *who* or *where* the non-combatants are. . . . We have only to know that there are non-combatants . . . in order to know the basic moral difference between limited and total war. . . . At stake also in this discrimination is not only the defense of civilization against total war, but against totalitarianism as well. In stating so blandly that practically no one 'stands outside' the war effort and no one is 'innocent' and there is no one who may not be directly killed for some good cause, have we not in principle included practically everyone, to the whole extent of his being, within the direction of the common life toward political goals?" See also Dwight McDonald's "The Responsiblilty of Peoples," in *Politics,* II (March, 1945), 82–92 (reprinted in his *Memoirs of a Revolutionist* [New York: Farrar, Straus & Cudahy, 1957], pp. 33–72), an attack on the saturation bombing of Nazi Germany, which is, I think, the best general statement on this subject to have been made in modern times.

30. *Commentary, loc. cit.,* 299.

31. On the Christian doctrine of "Just War," see Paul Ramsey, *War and the Christian Conscience: How Shall Modern War Be Justly Conducted?* (Durham, N. C.: Duke University Press, 1961); Robert W. Tucker, *The Just War: A Study in Contemporary American Doctrine* (Baltimore: Johns Hopkins Press, 1960); Morton A. Kaplan and Nicholas Katzenbach, *The Political Foundations of International Law* (New York: John Wiley & Sons, 1961), pp. 201–10; G. W. Anscombe, "War and Murder," in W. Stein, *op. cit.,* pp. 45–62.

32. E.g., the American Revolutionary War, the Seven Years War, the Crimean War. See generally John U. Nef, *War and Human Progress* (Cambridge: Harvard University Press, 1950).

33. W. Stein, *op. cit.,* p. 30.

34. Quoted in Herzog, *op. cit.,* pp. 112–13.

35. Thomas E. Murray, *Nuclear Policy for War and Peace* (New York: World Book Co., 1960).

36. McNamara, *loc. cit.,* p. 67.

37. Halperin, *op. cit.,* p. 101.

38. See Rapoport's remarks in Fisher, *op. cit.,* p. 212.

39. *OE,* pp. 169–70.

40. *TAU,* p. 68.

41. *OE*, p. 69. The quotation is from Marshal V. D. Sokolovsky's *Military Strategy* (2d ed.; Moscow, 1963).

42. Morgenthau, *American Political Science Review*, LVIII, 29, gives the examples of Phoenix, Arizona, and Cheyenne, Wyoming.

43. Knorr and Read, *op. cit.*, p. 44; see also *OE*, p. 145.

44. See the Bibliographical Note below for proponents of minimum deterrence and low-level finite deterrence strategies.

45. As I noted earlier, Kahn, who is necessarily an exception to every generalization since he takes all sides of every question, has retreated from his earlier scornful remarks about deterrence-as-façade. (*OE*, pp. 245–46). But in the rest of that book he discusses force postures that are considerably more than façades. I think that he is intellectually interested in every possibility, like a Talmudic scholar.

46. *OTW*, p. 185. See also Schelling, *SOC*, p. 6.

47. Quoted by John Herz in Bennett, *op. cit.*, p. 34.

48. Ramsey, in *ibid.*, pp. 163–64.

49. Despite the many references to this so-called ancient principle by writers such as Schelling, it never occurs to any of them to ask just what kind of people were chosen as hostages by medieval chieftains, etc. Not, I would speculate, a random sampling of the women and children of their demesnes. For a *voluntary* hostage-exchange program that attetmpts to make deterrence more traditional in this sense, see Morton Deutsch's "Reducing the Reciprocal Fear of Surprise Attack," in Quincy Wright, William M. Evan, and Morton Deutsch (eds.), *Preventing World War III: Some Proposals* (New York: Simon & Schuster, 1962), pp. 83–86. See also Leo Szilard's satire (or is it?), "The Mined Cities," *Bulletin of the Atomic Scientists*, XVII (December, 1961), 407–12.

50. Cf. Ramsey's statement, in Bennett, *op. cit.*, pp. 166–67. "The fact is that contemporary weapons analysts are not simply using pure reason, in the form of technical reason wholly stripped of moral *scientia*, in producing their designs for invulnerable weapons systems and arms control. They are using pure reason interfused with moral themes and judgments furnished them by characteristics of the American ethos. They are persuaded by this that . . . when force is used . . . there then supervenes a state of war to which no norms or limits apply. . . . Contemporary proposals for arms control based on the total deterrent represent the final product of this ethos."

51. Bennett, *op. cit.*, pp. 109–10.

52. Levine, *The Arms Debate*, pp. 33–36; on moral choice, see my comments in *World Politics*, XVI, 652–54. I suppose that one could refuse to choose among one's conflicting values by using some kind of lottery principle to make the choice or by tossing a coin. But then one has to agree to accept the result, and that in itself is a choice.

53. This is also the conclusion reached by Levine, *The Arms Debate*, pp. 207–8.

54. *OTW*, p. 566.

55. Levine, *Bulletin of the Atomic Scientists*, XX, 24–25.

56. Levine, *The Arms Debate*, p. 200.

57. In Robert C. Tucker *et al.*, *Proposal for No-First Use of Nuclear Weapons: Pros and Cons* (Princeton: Center for International Studies, 1963).

58. See *OE*, p. 120.

59. Quoted in Herzog, *op. cit.*, p. 118.

60. Compare Halperin's remarks, in Halperin, *op. cit.*, pp. 90–91. See also Morgenstern, *op. cit.*, pp. 300–301, and Kaufmann, *Military Policy and National Security*, p. 1.

61. Kissinger, *Nuclear Weapons and Foreign Policy*, pp. 52–54.

62. *In Strategy and Conscience*, p. 184.

63. Cf. George F. Kennan, *Russia, the Atom, and the West* (New York: Harper & Row, 1958); Fred Warner Neal, *U.S. Foreign Policy and the Soviet Union* (Santa Barbara, Calif.: Center for the Study of Democratic Institutions, 1961).

64. See, e.g., Kissinger, *The Necessity of Choice*, pp. 16–17; similar remarks were made by Harold Brown, "Arms Control and Military Security," address to the Princeton University Conference on Arms Control and Limitation, October 20, 1960. On this point see Schelling and Halperin, *op. cit.*, p. 54.

65. Singer, *Journal of Conflict Resolution*, V, 201–2.

66. Kissinger, *The Necessity of Choice*, p. 238; G. Snyder, *Deterrence and Defense*, Part II, *passim*.

67. Schelling, *SOC*, p. 64.

68. In Knorr and Read, *op. cit.*, pp. 145 ff.

69. Snyder, *Deterrence and Defense*, p. 198.

70. Snyder, *ibid.*, p. 79; Kahn, *OTW*, pp. 211–15; Wohlstetter, *Foreign Affairs*, XXXVII, 229. Cf. Harold Swayze on "Manicheanism at the Foreign Policy Research Institute: A Review of Robert

Strausz-Hupé, William R. Kintner, James E. Dougherty, and Alvin J. Cottrell, *Protracted Conflict*; and Robert Strausz-Hupé, William R. Kintner, and Stefan Possony, *A Forward Strategy for America," Journal of Conflict Resolution*, VI (June, 1962), 169–74.

71. Glenn Snyder, *Deterrence and Defense*, p. 259.

72. For similar comments, see Halperin, *op. cit.*, pp. 90–91; Thornton Read, *A Proposal to Neutralize Nuclear Weapons*, p. 5; and Donald G. Brennan, "Setting and Goals of Arms Control," in Henkin, *op. cit.*, p. 32.

73. An interesting example of this tendency is that, according to Hanson Baldwin in "Pentagon's 'New' Policy," *New York Times*, February 27, 1965, Secretary McNamara seems to have renounced the "no-cities" strategy, because of changing political and technological considerations.

74. Cf., the remarks of Richard A. Falk, *Law, Morality, and War in the Contemporary World* ("Princeton Studies in World Politics Number 5" [New York: Frederick A. Praeger, 1963]), chap. iii.

75. Barry Goldwater, *The Conscience of a Conservative* (New York: Hillman, 1960), pp. 126–27.

76. *Journal of Conflict Resolution*, VI, 372. The quotation from Huntington may be found at p. 441 of *The Common Defense*.

77. Cf., Levine, *The Arms Debate*, p. 59, on the exclusion of "antiwar" and "anti-Communist systemists" from the upper echelons of the Kennedy administration.

78. This is not necessarily an invidious comment; a professional consultant may rightly feel that he is responsible to the representatives of "the will" of the American people, as interpreted by them. He is, then, not eliminating ethical choice in Hook's sense (see p. 220 above) but consciously adopting the values of his clientele, as part of his sense of professional responsibility. The objection, to repeat, is not to his doing this, but to the pretense that one is merely engaging in a "rational" decision process.

79. See Levine, *Bulletin of the Atomic Scientists*, XX, *loc. cit.*; Wohlstetter, as quoted by Herzog, *op. cit.*, p. 68; Bernard Brodie, "Morals and Strategy," *Worldview*, VII (September, 1964), 4–8.

80. Levine, *The Arms Debate*, pp. 165 ff. But see his contradictory statement on page 168.

81. For a more extended discussion of this point, see my "Method and Substance in the Arms Debate," *World Politics*, XVI, 652–60.

82. See Levine, *The Arms Debate*, pp. 245 ff., for a representative sampling of statements of this position, and see note 61 above.

83. Morgenthau, in *Commentary*, *loc. cit.*, *passim*; Falk, *op. cit.*, *passim*; Halle, "Peace in Our Time?", *New Republic*, December 28, 1963, pp. 16–19. On close reading, it turns out that Falk avoids any direct reference to the problem of all-out nuclear war but explicitly justifies only various kinds of less-than-all-out war. Still, the direction of his argument is to justify, if only very half-heartedly, at least the *threat* of all-out nuclear war as a preservative of international order.

84. In Falk's case, the position is also a legalistic one (Falk, *op. cit.*, *passim*, especially chap. iv).

85. *OTW*, p. 574.

86. Levine, *The Arms Debate*, p. 212.

87. On the essential normativeness of the idea of rational action, see Rapoport, *Fights, Games, and Debates*, pp. 174 ff., and his *Strategy and Conscience*; John R. Seeley, "Social Science? Some Probative Problems," in Maurice Stein and Arthur Vidich (eds.), *Sociology on Trial* (Englewood Cliffs: Prentice-Hall, 1963), pp. 55 ff., and in the same volume Alvin Gouldner's essay, "Anti-Minotaur: The Myth of a Value-Free Sociology," *passim*.

CHAPTER VII

1. See note 45, chap. v above.

2. Cf. John W. Spanier and Joseph L. Nogee, *The Politics of Disarmament* (New York: Frederick A. Praeger, 1962); Richard J. Barnet, *Who Wants Disarmament?* (Boston: Beacon Press, 1960); and *The Soviet Stand on Disarmament* (New York: Crosscurrents Press, 1962).

3. *World Politics*, XVI, 664.

4. One need only note the instructive fact that somehow the values and analyses, so-called, of the writers Levine discusses in *The Arms Debate*, always seem to wind up leading in the same direction. With the possible exception of H. Stuart Hughes, who might thereby qualify if medals were given for intellectual de-

tachment, none of them has values that lead him to ignore his analyses, or analytical views that cast doubt on the relevance of his values. I do not mean to be cynical; the point is that these writers have not developed their "values" and "analyses" separately and then looked at the result to see in what direction it "logically" leads them: rather they have made complex political judgments, which can only be broken down into analytical and evaluative components after the fact, if at all.

5. On the question of the possibility of a "genuine" social science, see the Bibliographical Note below.

6. *Foreign Affairs*, XXXVII, 217.

7. On the various contributions to deterrence theory, see my Bibliographical Note below; for Dulles' version, see John Foster Dulles, "Policy for Security and Peace," *Foreign Affairs*, XXXII (April, 1954), 353–64.

8. Kahn's work, however, at least has the virtue of logical exhaustiveness.

9. The practical effect of this substitution, as Hedley Bull notes in the same passage from which I have quoted on pp. 210–11 above, is to assume that all relevant decision-makers in the major nuclear powers have the minds of "university professor(s) of unusual intellectual subtlety. . . ." (Bull, *op. cit.*, p. 48.)

10. An exception is the contribution by Abt and Pool in Knorr and Read, *op. cit.* However, their discussion of the possible relationships between public opinion and limited nuclear war is so antidemocratic in tone that one must assume it to be satirical.

11. Kaplan, *World Politics*, XI, 43.

12. In Quade, *op. cit.*, p. 127.

13. By "all" I mean here only that amount of evidence, whatever it may be, that the convention of those interested in the further theoretical development in the field at hand habitually requires. To see how tentative is the realm of hypothesis within which political science still moves, one need only consult the various essays, in addition to Richard Snyder's, in Ranney, *op. cit.*

14. Cf., Gilpin, *op. cit.*, and Wohlstetter's polemic against natural scientists in Gilpin and Wright, *op. cit.*; see also C. P. Snow, *op. cit.*

15. For example, in Shubik, *Game Theory*, p. 220; Quade, *op. cit.*, p. 105; and see also Brodie's remarks in Gilpin and Wright, *op. cit.*, pp. 241–43. It seems clear that Wohlstetter would extend

his indictment of military men to natural scientists as well—in fact, he might even prefer the intellectual mode of the former to that of the latter, where policy-making is concerned.

16. For example, see the remarks by Quade, Hitch, and Wohlstetter, in Quade, *op. cit.*, pp. 23, 135, and 328.

17. In addition to the article of Halle's cited in chap. vi n. 84 above; see also his "The Wrangle over Strategy," *New Republic*, January 18, 1964, pp. 19–21, and his *Dream and Reality: Aspects of American Foreign Policy* (1st ed.; New York: Harper & Row, 1959). Kennan's most recent writings are *Russia, the Atom, and the West* (New York: Harper & Row, 1958), and *On Dealing with the Communist World.* Other particularly interesting discussions of East-West relations in the context of nuclear strategy are Hedley Bull, *op. cit.*; John Strachey, *On the Prevention of War* (New York: St. Martin's, 1963); David Lilienthal, *Change, Hope, and the Bomb* (Princeton: Princeton University Press, 1963); and Walter Lippmann, *The Communist World and Ours* (Boston: Little, Brown & Co., 1959), and *The Coming Tests with Russia* (Boston: Little, Brown & Co., 1961). A precondition to any discussion of nuclear strategy is, as I have suggested throughout, a thorough discussion of the cold war. The literature on this subject is voluminous, and I shall mention only a few books that raise the critical issues with particular incisiveness: Denna Frank Fleming, *The Cold War and Its Origins, 1917–1960* (2 vols.; Garden City: Doubleday & Co., 1961); Edmund O. Stillman and William Pfaff, *op. cit.*; Coral Bell, *op. cit.*; Hugh Seton-Watson, *Neither War nor Peace* (rev. ed.; New York: Frederick A. Praeger, 1962); John Lukacs, *A History of the Cold War* (Garden City: Doubleday & Co., 1962); and Robert G. Wesson, *The American Problem: The Cold War in Perspective* (New York: Abelard-Schuman, 1963). The relevancy of what Wildavsky calls the "appeasement model" (see above, chap. v. n. 102) to the cold war is discussed by John H. Herz, "The Relevancy and Irrelevancy of Appeasement," *Social Research*, XXXI (Autumn, 1964), 296–320; and see his *International Politics in the Atomic Age* (New York: Columbia University Press, 1959).

The ideas about the Soviet Union of those social scientists (especially psychologists) who think that, in Kahn's phrase, we have a "misguided friend," are summed up in Rapoport's *Strategy and Conscience*, Part III.

18. For a persuasive argument that even some of the natural sciences are not yet in a stage where it is possible to justify their

central propositions with anything approaching true rigor, see Gertrude Himmelfarb, "The Scientific Imagination," *New York Review of Books*, December 12, 1963, pp. 5–8.

19. Roger Fisher, quoted by Francis D. Wormuth, "The Politics of Bedlam," *Bulletin of the Atomic Scientists*, XIX (December, 1963), 29. Wormuth's article is a particularly telling indictment of the ahistorical nature of most deterrence theory.

20. Kenneth Thompson, "Ethical Aspects of the Nuclear Dilemma," in Bennett, *op. cit.*, pp. 82–84; cf. Thompson, *Political Realism and the Crisis of World Politics* (Princeton: Princeton University Press, 1960).

21. Fryklund, *op. cit.* Kahn finds it possible to praise this third-hand report of "war games" which, for all the reader can tell, were never played, and about which not even the vaguest information is given regarding the assumptions on which they and the policies extrapolated from them were based.

22. Michael D. Intriligator, "Economic Models and Deterrence," a paper read before the annual meeting of the American Political Science Association, New York City, September 6, 1963.

23. At the A.P.S.A. meetings at which Intriligator's paper was presented, several panel groups met under the rubric "The Transformations of Deterrence." These groups discussed topics that normally would be considered to fall in the area of "foreign policy," etc.

24. Brodie, in Gilpin and Wright, *op. cit.*, p. 244. It is only fair to point out that Brodie is occasionally more modest than this: cf. p. 253.

25. Herman Kahn, as usual anticipating all possible objections to his work, has written (*TAU*, pp. 33–34): "Nor should . . . technical treatments of thermonuclear war be considered unacceptable unless they include extensive accounts of such related problems as foreign policy, limited war, arms control, or the moral and theological problems of war and peace . . . the importance of related topics hardly diminishes the need for specialized studies on thermonuclear war—in itself a subject too vast to be completely grasped." If one accepted the basic premise that these studies are "technical," Kahn's statement would be more defensible than it is. But in any event, the specific assertion about the vastness of the subject-matter is much too modest, considering that the man who made it moves freely into almost any field of expertise he pleases when it will advance his discussion. And of course, considerably

vaster subjects have been managed before, even by single individuals—Thucydides, Gibbon, and Toynbee come immediately to mind. No doubt they were not "scientists"—but the claim that we must be "scientific" in order to have anything worthwhile to say is exactly what needs to be most sharply questioned. Three particularly trenchant comments on this subject, which forcefully put the argument that no important policy question is in the last analysis technical, and that "technical" deterrence expertise is, therefore, pseudo-expertise, are Hans Morgenthau, "Modern Science and Political Power," *Columbia Law Review*, LXIV (December, 1964), 1386–1409; David Lilienthal, "A Skeptical Look at 'Scientific Experts'," *New York Times Magazine*, September 29, 1963, pp. 23 ff.; and David W. Tarr, "Military Technology and the Policy Process," *Western Political Quarterly*, XVIII (March, 1965), 135–48.

26. Bennett, *op. cit.*, pp. 111–12.

27. An apparent exception to this generalization is J. David Singer's work, especially *Deterrence, Arms Control, and Disarmament*. But see the comments in my review, *Dissent*, X (Autumn, 1963), 392–95.

Bibliographic note

THE ANALYSIS in this study has been based on two different types of material: first, original documents in the development of deterrence theory; second, those substantive and methodological works that have influenced the author's intellectual viewpoint. Both parts of this bibliographical note, but especially that part dealing with intellectual background, are only meant to be suggestive, not exhaustive. More complete bibliographical listing of specific subjects related to deterrence theory may be found in footnotes in the appropriate chapters.

I. Deterrence and Its Critics

The literature of nuclear deterrence continues to come forth in an apparently endless stream. Most of it is repetitive, and much of it is trivial. Probably the basic document in the development of deterrence theory was the (classified) RAND study of overseas SAC bases, ALBERT WOHLSTETTER et al., *Selection and Use of Strategic Air Bases* (RAND Report R-266; Santa Monica, Calif.: The RAND Corporation, April, 1954); in this study the all-important, first-strike–second-strike distinction apparently first entered the discourse of civilian strategists in a sophisticated form. A description of this study is contained in Chapter III of E. S. QUADE (ed.), *Analysis for Military Decisions* (Chicago: Rand-McNally, 1964). The beginnings of general public discussion of deterrence theory may be located in three books, of which the first—and for purposes of theory-building most important—was WILLIAM W. KAUFMANN's *Military Power and National Security* (Princeton: Princeton University Press, 1956). This book is still the best introduction to the mode of reasoning of deterrence theorists. For a more complete picture of the place of deterrence theory in international relations generally and the cold war in particular, one should consult HENRY KISSINGER's *Nuclear Weapons and Foreign Policy* (New York: Harper & Row, 1957), and RAYMOND ARON's *On War* (London: Secker & Warburg, 1958).

In the first years after the publication of Kaufmann's book many articles and book reviews dealing with the nature of nuclear deterrence appeared in such journals as *World Politics, Bulletin of the Atomic Scientists*, and *Journal of Conflict Resolution*. Since 1962 or 1963, however, original contributions to deterrence theory have virtually vanished from the pages of the first two of those journals. The most instructive of these articles and reviews are WARREN AMSTER's "Design for Deterrence" and C. W. SHERWIN's commentary on it, "Securing Peace through Military Technology," *Bulletin of the Atomic Scientists*, XII (May, 1956), 159–65; MORTON A. KAPLAN's "The Calculus of Nuclear Deterrence," *World Politics*, XI (October, 1958), 20–43; and ARTHUR L. BURNS's "Disarmament or the Balance of Terror," *World Politics*, XII (October, 1959), 326–42. During this period of initial interest in deterrence theory, several military journals, such as *U.S. Naval Institute Proceedings, Air Force, Army*, and *Royal Canadian Air Force Journal* also presented numerous discussions of deterrence.

At the same time, various themes developed in the Kaufmann book became the subject of extensive subliteratures in such areas as (1) limited war; (2) limited nuclear retaliation; (3) "invulnerability"; and (4) arms control. All reflect dissatisfaction among academic strategists with John Foster Dulles' notorious doctrine of "massive retaliation." Some of the most important works on each of these subjects are:

1. Limited War

OSGOOD, ROBERT E., *Limited War: The Challenge to American Strategy* (Chicago: University of Chicago Press, 1957).

SCHELLING, THOMAS C., "Bargaining, Communication and Limited War," *Journal of Conflict Resolution*, I (March, 1957), 19–36.

————. *Nuclear Weapons and Limited War* (RAND Paper P-1620; Santa Monica, Calif.: The RAND Corporation, February 20, 1959). Both of the articles by Schelling also appeared in his collection, *The Strategy of Conflict* (Cambridge: Harvard University Press, 1960); his work, of course, makes more use of "advanced" techniques of social science than does any other writing in this area.

KING, JAMES E. JR., "Collective Defense: The Military Commitment," in ARNOLD WOLFERS (ed.), *Alliance Policy in the Cold War* (Baltimore: Johns Hopkins Press, 1959), pp. 103–45.

KISSINGER, HENRY, *Nuclear Weapons and Foreign Policy*, especially Chaps. vi–viii, and *The Necessity for Choice* (New York: Harper & Row, 1960), especially Chap. iii. On the subject of tactical nuclear limited war, discussion of which is associated chiefly with Kissinger, see W. W. KAUFMANN's review, "The Crisis in Military Affairs," *World Politics*, X (July 1958), 579–603. Kissinger himself appears to have accepted most of Kaufmann's criticisms in writing the later book.

KNORR, KLAUS (ed.), *NATO and American Security* (Princeton: Princeton University Press, 1959); especially the contributions by Knorr, Malcolm W. Hoag, A. L. Burns, and Denis Healey.

HALPERIN, MORTON H., *Limited War in the Nuclear Age* (New York: John Wiley & Sons, 1963). This book, which attempts to summarize and clarify the entire discussion of limited war strategy, also contains a complete, annotated bibliography, not only of limited war, but of nuclear strategy in general.

2. Limited Nuclear Retaliation

KAPLAN, MORTON A., *The Strategy of Limited Retaliation* ("Princeton Center of International Studies Policy Memorandum No. 19" [Princeton, N.J., 1959]).

KNORR, KLAUS, and READ THORNTON (eds.), *Limited Strategic War* (New York: Frederick A. Praeger, 1962).

The reader who has waded through the often informative literature on limited war may be surprised to discover that treatment of the more critical issue of limited nuclear retaliation is not only sparse but completely speculative in its lack of solid information. Although most academic strategists appear to have endorsed the notion of limited nuclear retaliation, reasons are adduced in the preceding text for regarding items in this category as symptomatic of the state of nuclear deterrence theory rather than as a contribution to it.

3. Invulnerability

The most striking development of Kaufmann's discussion of the requirements of nuclear deterrence is OSKAR MORGENSTERN's *The Question of National Defense* (New York: Random House, 1959). However, though Morgenstern's discussion of the "Oceanic Force" was convincing to many people, it actually deals with a rather narrow range of considerations. A broader gauge and more systematic work is BERNARD BRODIE's *Strategy in the Missile Age* (Princeton: Princeton University

Press, 1960). Indeed, Brodie's is the most useful, single contribution to the literature of deterrence—and this without recourse eo the pseudo-science that has been that literature's all-too-customary hallmark. For an appreciation and critique of Brodie, see JAMES E. KING, JR.'s review of Brodie, "Airpower in the Missile Gap," *World Politics*, XII (July, 1960), 628–39.

4. Arms Control

By far the most sophisticated and challenging discussion of arms control is in HEDLEY BULL's *The Control of the Arms Race* (New York: Frederick A. Praeger, 1961). Bull's book is, at the same time, not so programmatic as much of the American literature, and not so marred by the rationalistic approach of the latter. For both these reasons it does not by itself suffice as an introduction to arms control, and to the relationship between arms control theory and deterrence theory. Instead, readers are referred to DONALD G. BRENNAN (ed.), *Arms Control, Disarmament, and National Security* (New York: Braziller, 1961); LOUIS HENKIN, *Arms Control: Issues for the Public* (Englewood Cliffs; Prentice-Hall, 1961); DAVID H. FRISCH, *Arms Reduction: Program and Issues* (New York: Twentieth-Century Fund, 1961); and, SCHELLING and HALPERIN's *Strategy and Arms Control* (New York: Twentieth-Century Fund, 1961). Several of Schelling's articles, such as "Surprise Attack and Disarmament" (in both his *The Strategy of Conflict* and KNORR's *NATO and American Security*); "Arms Control: Proposal for a Special Surveillance Force," *World Politics*, XIII (October, 1960), 1–18; "Reciprocal Measures for Arms Stabilization," in the volume edited by Brennan; and "The Role of Deterrence in Total Disarmament," *Foreign Affairs*, XL (April, 1962), 392–406, are also of major interest because of Schelling's importance as a theorist. As is the case with limited war, his is the most theoretically sophisticated treatment of the subject matter. Two other thoughtful, concrete proposals involving a no-first-strike pledge, THORNTON READ's *A Proposal to Neutralize Nuclear Weapons* ("Princeton Center of International Studies Policy Memorandum No. 22" [Princeton, N. J., 1960]), and MORTON H. HALPERIN's *A Proposal for a Ban on the Use of Nuclear Weapons* ("Institute for Defense Analyses Special Studies Group Memorandum No. 4" [Washington, D. C., October 6, 1961]), have had less publicity than they deserve. Of late "arms control" has tended to become a rather rarefied and technical subject, thus following the trend in deterrence theory generally. For examples of this development, see the pages of the *Journal of Arms Control*, particularly J. DAVID SINGER (ed.), "Weapons Management in World Politics: Proceedings of the International Arms Control Symposium," *Journal of Arms Control*, I (October, 1963). (Published also as the *Journal of Conflict Resolution*, VII [September, 1963].)

Although there is, of course, some relationship between proposals for arms control and those for disarmament, the latter looks, not toward ways of stabilizing the arms race, but toward ways of gradually eliminating national nuclear arsenals, and should, therefore, be considered qualitatively different. A recent collection of essays on problems of disarmament, RICHARD A. FALK and RICHARD I. BARNET (eds.), *Security in Disarmament* (Princeton: Princeton University Press, 1965), and also CHARLES E. OSGOOD's *An Alternative to War or Surrender* (Urbana, Ill.: University of Illinois, 1962), will serve to reveal those differences both of tone and of purpose which separate the discussion of disarmament from that of arms control.

The reader will be impressed by the fact that few of the works cited attempt to deal with the problem of what to do "if deterrence fails." (Some material on limited nuclear retaliation provides a partial exception to this generalization.) One can easily discern that most authors do not advocate surrender or "crash" unilateral disarmament in the event of crisis, and one can also see that they are not so sanguine as to deny that a crisis will never come. What one cannot derive from most of their publications, however, are unequivocal statements of what uses they foresee, *in extremis*, for strategic nuclear weapons.

The problem was described most vividly by ALBERT WOHLSTETTER in his famous and influential "The Delicate Balance of Terror," *Foreign Affairs*, XXXVII (January, 1959), 211–34. Indeed, one can regard Wohlstetter's article as the opening volley in a battle seeking to reclaim for strategic thought some scope for retaliation which, in countering Dulles, it seemed to many to have banished altogether. GLENN SNYDER's *Deterrence and Defense: Toward a Theory of National Security* (Princeton: Princeton University Press, 1961), and Herman Kahn's *On Thermonuclear War* (Princeton: Princeton University Press, 1960) represent major applications of Wohlstetter's approach. Compared with Kahn's, Snyder's book is thin in substance and insight. But it is the only one that attempts to integrate into a consistent theory of deterrence military *and* political perspectives on the United States overseas policy (KISSINGER'S *The Necessity for Choice* deals with foreign policy also, but has little to say about the complexities of deterrence theory).

On Thermonuclear War is certainly the most profound and significant contribution to the literature of deterrence. Its value would have been greatly enhanced had Kahn been able to distinguish between sense and nonsense in presenting all possible ramifications of the development, possession, deployment, and use of nuclear weapons. What Kahn does provide, beyond cavil, is exhaustiveness; and as an argumentative encyclopedia of the imaginary realm of nuclear war, the book is matchless. For example, he is the real father of the "no-cities" strategy, though Chap. vi of Halperin's *Limited War in the Nuclear Age* offers the most lucid exposition of it. Kahn's later books, *Thinking about the Unthinkable* (New York: Horizon Press, Inc., 1962), and *On Escalation: Metaphor and Scenarios* (New York: Frederick A. Praeger, 1965), are perhaps more lucid and better organized, but convey no impression of ratiocination. Instead they emerge as the products of a puzzle addict, or a professional hair-splitter enjoying his avocation. *On Escalation* holds more interest for the changes it reveals in the thinking of its author—the most original contributor to the creation of deterrence theory.

Two recent works attempt to bring deterrence theory and the study of world politics up to date and closer together, and to separate wheat from chaff in the former: RAYMOND ARON's *The Great Debate: Theories of Nuclear Strategy*, trans. by ERNEST PAWEL (New York: Doubleday & Co., 1965), and JOHN STRACHEY's *On the Prevention of War* (New York: St. Martin's Press, 1963). Each is the *magnum opus* of an author who is knowledgeable about international affairs, accepts the necessity for an over-all policy of nuclear deterrence in the West, and is carefully discriminating about the value of the various possible components of such a policy. LOUIS J. HALLE seeks the same integration in "Peace in Our Time?", *New Republic* (December 28, 1963), pp. 16–19; and "The Wrangle over Strategy," *ibid.* (January 18, 1964), pp. 19–21.

Critical literature is almost as extensive as that on deterrence and resembles it in repetitiveness and triviality. Fortunately, there are some exceptions which, taken together, comprise a powerful assault on the notion that either a nuclear arms race or a "stabilized" nuclear world can produce anything but disaster in the long run. Most of the authors cited below view nuclear disarmament in some form as the goal we should seek, but their prescriptions differ as to how it should be reached. None are unilateralists, and their short-run prescriptions describe a finite or, more often, minimum deterrence. (HOAG's "On Stability in Deterrent [*sic*] Races," in MORTON A. KAPLAN (ed.), *The Revolution in World Politics* [New York: John Wiley & Sons, 1962], pp. 388–410, and Hoag's article cited above may also be read as an exposition of and argument for such a deterrence strategy.)

The *Journal of Conflict Resolution* is generally the best source for critiques of deterrence theory, particularly those based on experimental work in social psychology. A fascinating attempt to begin the construction of a general theory of conflict based on that literature among others, is KENNETH E. BOULDING's *Conflict and Defense* (New York: Harper & Row, 1962). Among short articles of special interest are J. DAVID SINGER's review of *On Thermonuclear War*, "The Strategic Dilemma: Probability versus Utility," *Journal of Conflict Resolution*, XXXV (June, 1961), 197–205; JOHN C. POLANYI's critique of Kahn and of the doctrine of arms control in "Armaments Policies for the Sixties," *Bulletin of the Atomic Scientists*, XVII (December, 1961), 403 ff.; MICHAEL BROWER's analysis of the "no-cities" strategy in "Controlled Thermonuclear War," *New Republic* (July 30, 1962), pp. 9–15; P. M. S. BLACKETT's "Critique of Some Contemporary Defense Thinking," *Encounter*, XVI (April, 1961), 9–17: HANS MORGENTHAU's "The Four Paradoxes of Nuclear Strategy," *American Political Science Review*, LVIII (March, 1964), 23–35. Excellent full-length books include AMITAI ETZIONI's *The Hard Way to Peace* (New York: Collier, 1962); ROBERT A. DENTLER and PHILLIPS CUTRIGHT's *Hostage America: Human Aspects of a Nuclear Attack and a Program of Prevention* (Boston: Beacon Press, 1963), which is in large part an attack on proposals for massive civil-defense programs in the U.S.,; RALPH LAPP's *Kill and Overkill* (New York: Basic Books, 1962), and J. DAVID SINGER's *Deterrence, Arms Control, and Disarmament* (Ohio State University Press, 1962).

Singer's treatment of deterrence theory is especially interesting, in that he uses in part the rationalistic, calculating method of deterrence theorists to stand their own theory on its head and reveal its self-contradiction. Unfortunately his method is also used to demolish every reasonable alternative to deterrence, and to produce a thoroughly unreasonable alternative of his own (that the U.S. and U.S.S.R. should jointly surrender portions of their nuclear forces to an international force until the point is reached where the latter is stronger than either of them taken separately).

In addition to critical discussions of deterrence strategy, there are many works that call its *morality* into question. The best of these is a collection of essays which strikingly combines the types of inquiry conducted by British analytic philosophy and Roman Catholic ethical discourse: WALTER STEIN (ed.), *Morals and Missiles: Catholic Essays on the Problem of War Today* (London: James Clarke, 1959). The idea of "just war" and the problem of reconciling that idea with a strategy of nuclear deterrence are discussed in ROBERT W. TUCKER's *The Just War: A Study in Contemporary American Doctrine* (Baltimore: The Johns Hopkins Press, 1960); PAUL RAMSEY's *War and the Christian Conscience: How Shall Modern War Be Justly Conducted?* (Durham, N.C.: Duke University Press, 1961); and THOMAS E. MURRAY's *Nuclear Policy for War and Peace* (New York: World Book Co., 1960). A good short statement is contained in MORTON A. KAPLAN and NICHOLAS DE B. KATZENBACH, *The Political Foundations of International Law* (New York: John Wiley & Sons, 1961), chap. viii.

Of the aforecited authors, the Protestant Ramsey and the Catholic Murray directly attack the idea of counter-people warfare. Murray's presentation, though less sophisticated and complex, is the more lucid, since the reader has difficulty in finding any logical connection between what Ramsey says about ethics and what he proposes for strategy.

RICHARD A. FALK's *Law, Morality and War in the Contemporary World* ("Princeton Studies in World Politics Number 5" [New York: Frederick A. Praeger, 1963]) combines an ethical consideration of world politics with a legalistic one, though he adopts an equivocal position toward deterrence theory. Unlike the Stein collection, several collections of essays and one symposium present both sides of the ethical argument. The symposium,

"Western Values and Total War: A Round-Table Discussion," *Commentary*, XXXII (October, 1961), 277–304, is only moderately successful. In JOHN C. BENNETT (ed.), *Nuclear Weapons and the Conflict of Conscience* (New York: Charles Scribner's Sons, 1962), one should particularly note the contributions by Bennett himself (antinuclear deterrence) and by Kenneth Thompson (pro). Other collections are WILLIAM CLANCY (ed.), *The Moral Dilemma of Nuclear Weapons*, essays from *Worldview, A Journal of Religion and International Affairs* (New York: Church Peace Union, 1961), and WILLIAM J. NAGLE (ed.), *Morality and Modern Warfare* (New York: Helicon, 1960). *Worldview* is the best journal to follow for statements on this subject. Rare exceptions to the silence of deterrence theorists on their ethical positions are ROBERT LEVINE's "Open Letter from a Military Intellectual to a Sophisticated Liberal Leader," *Bulletin of the Atomic Scientists*, XX (September, 1964), 24–27; and BERNARD BRODIE, "Morals and Strategy," *Worldview*, VII (September, 1964), 4–8.

Finally, a handful of thoughtful works attempt to review all the competing viewpoints in what one of them has called "the arms debate." Three of these are superior: AARON WILDAVSKY's short review-article, "Practical Consequences of the Theoretical Study of Defense Policy," *Public Administration Review*, XXV (March, 1965), 90–103; and two books: ROBERT A. LEVINE's *The Arms Debate* (Cambridge: Harvard University Press, 1963), and ARTHUR HERZOG's *The War-Peace Establishment* (New York: Harper & Row, 1965). Anecdotal to a point, Herzog's book is always as fair and complete as journalism can be, whereas Levine's supposedly more rigorously analytical social science turns out to be the same version manifested in deterrence theory itself, thus leading him to prejudge some of his conclusions. I have elaborated on this criticism in my "Method and Substance in the Arms Debate," *World Politics*, XVI (July, 1964), 642–67.

II. Some Notes on Intellectual Background

The author's intellectual perspectives should be helpful in assessing the arguments presented in this book on international politics and the methodology or the philosophy of science.

My view of international politics has been chiefly formed from recognition of a paradox: the vague concept called "national interest" is indispensable for thinking about international relations but is wholly inadequate to that task. Any recent text in international relations should provide a satisfactory bibliography for investigating all the ramifications of this paradox. My own particular engagement (and often private quarrel), however, has been with the work of REINHOLD NIEBUHR and HANS MORGENTHAU, as represented in their *Moral Man and Immoral Society* (New York: Charles Scribner's Sons, 1932), and *In Defense of the National Interest* (New York: Alfred Knopf, 1951), respectively. Of all books in this area I find most congenial KENNETH WALTZ's critical exegesis *Man, the State, and War* (New York: Columbia University Press, 1959); and JOHN HERZ's *International Politics in the Atomic Age* (New York: Columbia University Press, 1959). In addition, two works on American foreign policy that are completely antithetical both in tone and content nonetheless present theses that must be grappled with: GABRIEL ALMOND's *The American People and Foreign Policy* (rev. ed.; New York: Frederick A. Praeger, 1960), and C. WRIGHT MILLS's *The Causes of World War III* (New York: Simon & Schuster, 1958). Finally, the evaluation of ethical criticisms of deterrence theory is influenced more than anything else by DWIGHT McDONALD's "The Responsibility of Peoples," *Politics*, II (March, 1945), 82–92 (reprinted in his *Memoirs of a Revolutionist* [New York: Farrar, Straus & Cudahy, 1957]).

Concerning methodology, a few words should first be said about game theory and systems analysis, reference to which by deterrence theorists is the source of many of the critical arguments advanced in the text above.

The uses in deterrence studies of game theory and such related analytical techniques, as simulation, are most evident in Schelling's *The Strategy of Conflict*, Snyder's *Deterrence and Defense*, Kaplan's "The Calculus of Deterrence" (*World Politics*, IX), and DANIEL ELLSBERG's "The Crude Analysis of Strategic Choices," in MARTIN SHUBIK (ed.), *Game Theory and Related Approaches to Social Behavior* (New York: John Wiley & Sons, 1964) pp. 230–39; Kahn's *On Thermonuclear War* is, of course, the most obvious exemplar of systems analysis in action. See also HERMAN KAHN *et al.*, *A Report on a Study of Non-Military Defense* ("RAND Report R-322-RC" [Santa Monica, Calif.: The RAND Corporation, July 1, 1958]). Though actually a series of essays, Quade's *The Analysis of Military Systems* is somewhat like a basic text on this subject and contains some brief treatments of game theory as one technique available to practitioners of systems analysis. Also helpful for an understanding of systems analysis is HERMAN KAHN and IRWIN MANN, *Techniques of Systems Analysis* ("RAND Research Memorandum RM-1829" [Santa Monica, Calif.: The RAND Corporation, December, 1956]), and, for an earlier and contrasting version of systems studies, P. M. S. BLACKETT's *Studies of War* (New York: Hill & Wang, 1962), Part II.

The basic—and pioneer—work on game theory is JOHN VON NEUMANN and OSKAR MORGENSTERN, *Theory of Games and Economic Behavior* (1st ed.; Princeton: Princeton University Press, 1944). A good introduction is JOHN D. WILLIAMS' *The Compleat Strategyst* (New York: McGraw-Hill Book Co., 1954), but MARTIN SHUBIK's introductory essay in the reader edited by him, *Game Theory and Related Approaches to Social Behavior* (New York: John Wiley & Sons, 1964) pp. 1–77, is much more up-to-date and probably more useful to the social scientist. The most helpful recent text that places game theory in the context of welfare economics and decision theory generally is ROBERT DUNCAN LUCE and HOWARD RAIFFA, *Games and Decisions* (New York: John Wiley & Sons, 1957). However, GEORGE KENT of the Mershon Center for Education in National Security, Ohio State University, has pointed out many of the ambiguities in all these discussions of game theory, and Chaps. iv and v above have been greatly influenced by my talks with him. His own paper, "Decision Rules in Formal Games," to be published by the Mershon Center for Education in National Security, attempts to clarify some of these ambiguities. My critical understanding has also been advanced by the excellent work of ANATOL RAPOPORT, whose *Fights Games, and Debates* (Ann Arbor: Michigan University Press, 1960), and *The Strategy of Conscience* (New York: Harper & Row, 1964), are the best available popularizations of that subject. The latter book also contributed to my comprehension of the ethical problems involved in the justification of nuclear deterrence as national policy, and should be read for this as well as for its methodological critiques. (For an overstated but often fair criticism of this book, see DONALD G. BRENNAN'S review, *Bulletin of the Atomic Scientists*, XXI [Dec., 1965], 25–30.) Two helpful articles dealing more generally with the relationship of ethics to game theory are ROBERT P. WOLFF, "Reflections on Game Theory and the Nature of Value," *Ethics*, LXXII (April, 1962), 171–79, and R. HOPKINS, "Game Theory and Generalization in Ethics," *Review of Politics*, XXVII (October, 1965), 491–99. In addition, the collection edited by KLAUS KNORR and SIDNEY VERBA, *The International System: Theoretical Essays* (Princeton: Princeton University Press, 1961), has several excellent discussions of methodological problems in the game-theoretical approach to international relations, of which the most substantial are those by Kaplan, A. L. Burns, Richard Quandt, J. David Singer, and Verba. Verba has also written the most lucid critical discussion of simulation and its uses—a discussion particularly applicable to some of Schelling's work—in his "Simulation, Reality, and Theory in International Relations," *World Politics*, XVI (April, 1964), 490–520.

As for problems of methodology in the social sciences generally, one who belongs to no particular "school" can only list those works that most influenced him, made him think, or merely seeped into his consciousness. (A fairly extensive bibliography may be found in ABRAHAM KAPLAN's *The Conduct of Inquiry* [San Francisco: Chandler, 1964]).

On the question of knowledge concerning social events and human behavior: JOHN DEWEY's *Logic, The Theory of Inquiry* (New York: Henry Holt, 1938) and *Reconstruction in Philosophy* (Boston: Beacon Press, 1948); ERNEST NAGEL, *The Structure of Science* (New York: Harcourt, Brace & World, 1961); JOHN G. KEMENY, *A Philosopher Looks at Science* (Princeton: D. Van Nostrand, 1959); STEPHEN E. TOULMIN, *Philosophy of Science* (New York: Harper & Row, 1960); ALFRED SCHUTZ, *Collected Papers I, The Problem of Social Reality* (The Hague: Martinus Nijhoff, 1962); and KENNETH E. BOULDING, *The Image: Knowledge in Life and Society* (Ann Arbor: Michigan University Press, 1956).

On theory construction and verification in the social sciences specifically: ANATOL RAPOPORT, "Various Meanings of 'Theory,'" *American Political Science Review*, LII (December, 1958), 972–88; DANIEL LERNER (ed.), *Evidence and Inference* (Glencoe, Ill.: Free Press, 1959); LLEWELLYN GROSS (ed.), *Symposium in Sociological Theory* (New York: Harper & Row, 1959), especially Parts I, IV, VI, and VII; KARL DEUTSCH, *The Nerves of Government* (London: Free Press, 1963); CARL G. HEMPEL, "Fundamentals of Concept Formation in Empirical Science," *International Encyclopedia of United Science*, II (Chicago, 1952); and for some helpful attempts at categorization and typologization, MARION J. LEVY, JR., *The Structure of Society* (Princeton: Princeton University Press, 1952).

On the place of values in social science: KARL MANN-HEIM, *Ideology and Utopia* (New York: Harcourt, Brace & World, 1936), and *Man and Society in an Age of Reconstruction* (New York: Harcourt, Brace & World, 1940), especially pp. 49–75; GUNNAR MYRDAL, "Methodological Note on Facts and Valuations in Social Science," in his *An American Dilemma* (New York: Harper & Row, 1944), pp. 1027–64; ALFRED NORTH WHITEHEAD, *Modes of Thought* (New York: Macmillan, 1938); and MAX WEBER, *The Methodology of the Social Sciences*, trans. and ed. by E. A. SHILS and H. A. FINCH (Glencoe, Ill.: Free Press, 1949).

Finally, my own viewpoint on the social function of the social scientist has been shaped by ROBERT S. LYND, *Knowledge for What?* (Princeton: Princeton University Press, 1939), and is expressed by several of the contributors to MAURICE STEIN and ARTHUR VIDICH (eds.), *Sociology on Trial* (Englewood Cliffs, N. J.: Prentice-Hall, 1963).

Index